Praise for *Redesigning Nonprofits*

"The coauthors bring long experience across philanthropy, nonprofit leadership, governance and movement building—experience that allows them to see both the sectors' aspirations and structural contradictions that repeatedly undermine them. Drawing on conversations with practitioners across the field, they offer something rarer than a diagnosis: a prescription for structural redesign."

—Sara Hudson
Interim CEO and Editor-in-Chief, Nonprofit Quarterly

"*Redesigning Nonprofits* reminds us that generosity is not simply about money—it is about putting our deepest values into action. This book calls each of us to strengthen the organizations and communities that make a more just, compassionate, and thriving democracy possible."

—Lynne Twist
author of *The Soul of Money* and
co-founder of the Pachamama Alliance

"*Redesigning Nonprofits* is a breath of fresh air for the social sector. It dares leaders of nonprofits to think bigger, act bolder, and embrace their role as catalysts for democratic renewal. I walked away inspired, informed, and ready to lead differently."

—Ellen Boneparth
Founder and President, Light My Fire

"This book underscores something urgent: we're in the middle of the largest intergenerational transfer of wealth in history, and we need real programs to help donors move resources from private bank accounts into the work of building a more just, healthy, and equitable society. Many of us are already engaged in that effort—and we welcome this call to action."

—Michael Gast
Founder, Organize the Rich, Strategist with Solidaire Network,
coauthor, *Free the People to Free the Money to Free the People*

"In this time of government curtailment of social programs and the emergence of AI in our workaday world, Nonprofits will be the critical key to preserving our humanity. Nonprofits must continue to provide support, social justice, compassion, human touch, and even employment that is rapidly diminishing in our lives. This book takes a critical look at how to sustain and support the important work of NGOs as we move into the age of AI. Whether we tax AI companies or elect a government that renews our commitment to all Americans, we need NGOs to help us get there."

—Joanne Grady Huskey
Founder, iLIVE2LEAD Young Women's Leadership Summit

"*Redesigning Nonprofits* arrives at a crucial moment for civil society. This book recognizes what many of us in the nonprofit world know deeply: nonprofits are not peripheral to democracy; they are its living connective tissue, translating care into action, values into service, and concern into collective change. The coauthors offer both an honest diagnosis of the sector's outdated operating systems and a hopeful, practical call to redesign leadership, funding, collaboration, technology, and civic purpose for the realities of our time. This is an important and timely contribution for all who believe the nonprofit sector must be strengthened to meet today's intertwined crises and help shape a more just, peaceful, and resilient future."

—David Wick
President, Pathways to Peace

"*Redesigning Nonprofits* is a powerful call to action for anyone who believes civil society can and must do better. It offers a bold vision of what is possible when purpose-driven organizations embrace their power to innovate, collaborate, and lead. It reframes nonprofits not as passive service providers but as bold democratic actors capable of reshaping communities. This book left me energized and newly convinced that transformation is not only possible—it's already underway."

—Tezikiah Gabriel
Founder of Gabriel Associates

"Healthy nonprofits and a healthy democracy depend on people willing to step up—not only with their dollars but with their time, talent and voices. *Redesigning Nonprofits* reminds us that volunteering is a powerful form of civic action and that each of us has something meaningful to contribute. When more of us get involved, our nonprofits, communities and democracy grow stronger."

—Gary Lucks
author, *We Are the Power and You Are Not Alone*

"*Redesigning Nonprofits* is a masterclass in reimagining what nonprofits can achieve when they embrace courage, creativity, and community power. Every chapter offers both inspiration and practical insight, making it essential reading for leaders who want to strengthen democracy from the ground up. It's the rare book that challenges assumptions while fueling hope."

—Geri Critchley
Nonprofit founder and advisor

"At a time when our nation longs for greater connection and trust, *Redesigning Nonprofits* reminds us that healthy, diverse nonprofits and foundation boards, staff and volunteers are essential to building stronger communities. This book is both practical and inspiring."

—China Galland
author of "*Love Cemetery*," four other books, co-producer of "Resurrecting Love: The Cemetery That Can Heal a Nation"

"*Redesigning Nonprofits* makes the case that nonprofit leaders and funders have to reinvent the sector from the ground up: new approaches to funding, leadership, and collaboration, and a human-centered approach to AI instead of bolting it onto broken systems. With authoritarianism on the rise and old structures buckling under today's demands, outdated playbooks and incremental fixes won't cut it. Drawing on history and more than 40 interviews with nonprofit leaders and innovators, the book argues for rebuilding together."

—Beth Kanter
author and trainer, Human-Centered AI Adoption for Nonprofits

"*Redesigning Nonprofits* challenges all of us to reimagine how philanthropy and nonprofits can and are serving democracy. Grounded in decades of experience and filled with practical tools and ideas for action and policy changes needed, this book is a listening practice and inspiration to focus. It's an insightful guide for anyone who believes that philanthropy, government and business should be more accountable, more courageous and responsive to communities that need our care and we seek to serve or should be serving for a better country and world."

—Aaron Dorfman
President and CEO, The National Committee for Responsive Philanthropy

"This book does what the best thinking always does: it makes the familiar suddenly strange and then shows you a better way forward. After reading it, nonprofit leaders will reframe the way they introduce themselves. We have accepted a name that defines us by absence and then wondered why the world underestimates us. This book refuses that bargain and makes the clearest, most energizing case for why this sector needs to reimagine not just what we do, but what we believe we are capable of. It blends visionary thinking with grounded strategies, courage with creativity, and urgency with hope. A pioneering read for everyone committed to making a difference."

—Anjum Malik
founder and E.D. of Global Impact Initiative

"It's time for everyone to join a team and be part of networks grounded in love, community, organizing and movement building including donors, activists, financial and philanthropic advisors. Redesigning Nonprofits is an important invitation to help us get there."

—Rajasvini Bhansali
President and Executive Director, Solidaire Network

"Women's giving circles worldwide demonstrate the sense of urgency women, girls and families feel. *Redesigning Nonprofits* uplifts giving circles and new models that make change happen while weaving tighter caring communities. We accept their call to action."

—Sondra Shaw-Hardy
co-founder, Women's Philanthropy Institute, author, *Creating a Women's Giving Circle* and three other books on women's philanthropy

"What's good about our nonprofit and foundation sector? Plenty, but there is also much that needs change and new leadership. Let's join this essential dialogue to grow greater giving and aligned investing. This combination of thoughtful reflection and a wide range of tools, charts, and resources in *Redesigning Nonprofits* offers a pragmatic combination to help us make more change happen."

—Dr. Jason Franklin
Founder & Principal, Ktisis Capital

Redesigning Nonprofits

Redesigning Nonprofits

CATALYSTS FOR A STRONGER DEMOCRACY

TRACY GARY • KIMBERLY WEICHEL
SHANNON KOLLASCH

Tools, Strategies & Insight for Social Change

WILEY

Published by John Wiley & Sons, Inc., Hoboken, New Jersey.

For general information on our other products and services or for technical support, please contact our Customer Care Department within the United States at (800) 762-2974, outside the United States at (317) 572-3993 or fax (317) 572-4002.

Wiley also publishes its books in a variety of electronic formats. Some content that appears in print may not be available in electronic formats. For more information about Wiley products, visit our web site at www.wiley.com.

Library of Congress Cataloging-in-Publication Data:

Names: Gary, Tracy, 1951- author | Weichel, Kimberly author | Kollasch, Shannon author
Title: Redesigning nonprofits : Catalysts for a Stronger Democracy / Tracy Gary, Kimberly Weichel, and Shannon Kollasch.
Description: Hoboken, New Jersey : Wiley, [2027] | Includes index.
Identifiers: LCCN 2026030983 (print) | LCCN 2026030984 (ebook) | ISBN 9781394419579 cloth | ISBN 9781394419593 adobe pdf | ISBN 9781394419586 epub
Subjects: LCSH: Nonprofit organizations | Organizational change
Classification: LCC HD2769.15 .G37 2027 (print) | LCC HD2769.15 (ebook)
LC record available at https://lccn.loc.gov/2026030983
LC ebook record available at https://lccn.loc.gov/2026030984

Cover Design: Wiley
Cover Images: Stafeeva/Adobe Stock, Ajahar/Adobe Stock, Badman/Adobe Stock

Printed and bound by CPI Group (UK) Ltd, Croydon, CR0 4YY

C9781394419579_230926

To everyone who labors to strengthen nonprofits and advance systemic change. Thank you for your tireless efforts: may your work move democracy closer to its full promise, and may we unleash more resources and solutions together.

Contents

Foreword

By Sara Hudson, PhD

On March 25, 1911, 146 garment workers—most of them young immigrant women—died in the Triangle Shirtwaist Factory fire. Why? Because owners locked the doors from the outside to prevent workers from taking unauthorized breaks. No law required otherwise. No government agency was coming to help. What happened instead: the women who survived, the organizers who had been working alongside them, and their civic networks turned grief into the International Ladies' Garment Workers' Union, into fire safety codes, into workers' compensation, into the 40-hour workweek.

For 381 days across 1955 and 1956, the Black residents of Montgomery, Alabama, refused to ride the city's buses. What made the boycott hold—through threats, through bombings, through economic pressure designed explicitly to break it—was not inspiration alone. It was infrastructure. Networks of Black churches coordinating carpools. Women's civic clubs organizing communications. The Montgomery Improvement Association managing logistics, funds, and morale for more than a year. Long before institutional philanthropy found its way to this work, a community built the civic architecture democracy required.

Let's share one more. In June 1969, New York City police raided the Stonewall Inn, a bar in Greenwich Village where gay men, drag queens, and transgender women—many of them people of color with nowhere else to be themselves—gathered. The patrons fought back. What followed was not only resistance but organization: the Gay Liberation Front, the Gay Activists Alliance, the first Gay Pride marches, and within years, the National Gay Task Force and Lambda Legal. There was no government protection coming.

No institution had sanctioned their existence. So they built the institutions they needed—and then, through those institutions, transformed what the law could recognize.

That is how American democracy has always worked. Not from the top down, but from the organized middle out—through voluntary associations, mutual aid networks, advocacy organizations, and civic institutions that have done the work that governments would not and markets could not.

In 2026, many marked "America 250." Civil society is not adjacent to this story. It is the story.

And yet what we call today "the nonprofit sector," which has built this country's democratic life, has never been built in return. The United States did not design the nonprofit sector as if it matters. That failure has shaped the sector, the institutions within it, and the people asked to sustain both.

Nearly two million nonprofit organizations employ one in ten private-sector workers. They hold communities together and have organized every major democratic advance before government was willing to ratify it—but they have been funded like charity, governed like afterthoughts, and staffed on the premise that moral purpose is its own compensation.

Nonprofit workers across generations are offered a bargain: moral worth in lieu of structural investment. Your passion is your compensation. Your sacrifice is your virtue.

The people who have and continue to accept that bargain are disproportionately women, disproportionately people of color, and disproportionately those who have witnessed firsthand that the formal economy was not built for them, and found in mission-driven work a different kind of belonging.

Public narratives call this sacrifice. It is extraction.

Today, the sector built on this exchange now carries the compounding debt of every deferred investment, every underfunded infrastructure, every leader burned through and discarded, every organization that could not survive the gap between what it was asked to do and what it was given to do it with.

I have spent 25 years inside this sector—as a post-Katrina responder, a nonprofit leader, a federal civil servant, a philanthropy officer, and now as editor-in-chief and interim CEO of *Nonprofit Quarterly*—watching this debt accumulate.

And I have watched workers, leaders, organizers, and activists in this sector absorb that debt with extraordinary creativity, extraordinary commitment, and a tolerance for conditions that no other field of comparable democratic importance would accept.

That tolerance has been the sector's greatest strength and its most dangerous vulnerability. Because every time the sector found a way to survive, it gave funders, government, and the public permission not to change the conditions.

Today, as *Redesigning Nonprofits* is published, we are in a moment when that permission has expired.

■ ■ ■

Three forces are converging in 2026 in a way they never have before, and their convergence is not coincidental. It is a crucible.

The first force is the largest intergenerational wealth transfer in American history—$124 trillion in motion, most of it without any infrastructure for civic responsibility or architecture for connecting inherited wealth to the communities that need it most.

The second is an authoritarian backlash against civil society that is not incidental but strategic. Authoritarian movements do not damage civil society as collateral damage. They target it deliberately, because they understand what Tocqueville understood: that voluntary civic association is democracy's immune system.

A fragmented sector cannot coordinate defense. A financially precarious sector can be silenced through funding threats. An exhausted sector makes worse strategic decisions.

The attacks on DEI programs, on immigrant organizations, on voting rights infrastructure, on nonprofit funding—these are not separate policy decisions. They are a coordinated effort to disable the sector before the sector can respond.

The third is the collapse of the twentieth-century model itself. The architecture that built this sector—stable government funding, predictable civic participation, leadership concentrated in a single heroic executive, organizations siloed by issue rather than connected by purpose—was designed for a world that is genuinely gone.

Organizations running that model are not failing because they lack commitment or talent. They are failing because the design no longer fits the world it was built for.

Crucibles do one of two things. They forge something new, or they consume what's inside.

Redesigning Nonprofits is the argument for forging.

Tracy Gary, Kimberly Weichel, and Shannon Kollasch bring long experience across philanthropy, nonprofit leadership, governance, and movement building—experience that allows them to see both the sector's aspirations and the structural contradictions that repeatedly undermine them. Drawing on conversations with practitioners across the field, they offer something rarer than a diagnosis: a prescription for structural redesign.

Redesigning Nonprofits traces that prescription through five interconnected shifts: how wealth transfers across generations, how technology reshapes community, how collaboration replaces competition, how funding moves from charity to power, and how leadership evolves from the heroic to the shared.

Beneath those shifts sits the thesis that holds the redesign together: organizational design is democratic design.

Chapter by chapter, the book argues that the way an organization is built either advances or undermines the democratic values it claims to hold. When the Global Fund for Women placed grassroots activists from the Global South—including grant recipients—on its board as decision-makers, it was not practicing progressive governance. It was practicing democracy.

When trust-based philanthropy places funding decisions closest to the communities most affected, it is not merely efficient. It is enacting a democratic principle: proximity to the problem produces wiser judgment about the solution.

Who holds power inside a nonprofit. How knowledge moves through it. Whether the people doing the work can actually last. These are not administrative questions. They are questions about whether democratic civil society can function under pressure, across generations, and when everything else is pulling it apart.

The new design this book proposes is not the old one made more efficient. It shares power instead of concentrating it, treats knowledge as a collective resource rather than a personal one, and builds organizations where leaders can actually last.

Not because they're tougher.

Because the structure stops requiring them to be.

What makes this book important is not that it insists the sector must change. Many people already know that. It is that the authors take seriously the harder question of how.

And answering that question requires confronting two deficits the sector has long learned to normalize: one of knowledge, one of narrative.

The **knowledge deficit** is where the sector's vulnerability runs deepest and where its democratic consequences are least honestly named. Medicine has peer-reviewed journals and outcome databases. Law has case law and shared precedent. Finance has disclosure standards and regulated data. The nonprofit sector has newsletters—and the accumulated wisdom of individual leaders who will eventually leave and take everything they've learned with them.

I think about this often: somewhere right now, a new executive director is calling her predecessor—who left for burnout, who is three states away—asking how the board chair prefers to communicate, what the relationship with the lead funder actually is, whether the program that looks good on paper actually works. The predecessor tries to remember.

That conversation, happening thousands of times a year across this country, is what passes for the sector's knowledge infrastructure.

In a democratic emergency, this is not inefficiency. It is a compounding vulnerability. And it is too often funder-created.

Traditional philanthropy has historically preferred to fund proprietary knowledge products branded to its own institutional strategy. The sector pays the price in every mistake repeated, every solution lost, every leader who had to figure out alone what someone else already knew.

The second deficit is narrative. Most Americans see, connect to, and support individual nonprofits. They do not recognize the nonprofit sector—the $1.5 trillion annual contribution to the gross domestic product (GDP), the 12.8 million jobs, the irreplaceable function of holding democratic space when institutions fail. They do not see what is actually being lost when this sector is exhausted and fragmented into two million organizations each fighting its own battles.

Until the pro-democracy nonprofit sector tells its own story as a sector—not as a collection of individual appeals but as the democratic infrastructure it actually is—it will remain the most consequential thing in American civic life that most Americans cannot name.

In the year the nation turns 250, that is no longer a communications gap. It is a democratic one.

Those two deficits are what brought me to *Nonprofit Quarterly*—not to cover the sector from a comfortable distance but to help build what it has always deserved. Right now, that work feels less like journalism and more like a civic obligation.

Read this book as what it is: not a call to resilience but a call to redesign. Resilience says: survive what's happening to you. Redesign says: build something that does not require heroism to sustain.

The sector on the other side of this crucible is one where leaders can stay, organizations can plan, communities can trust, and the coalition that democracy requires can actually hold. That is not an ambitious dream. It is a design problem. And this book is part of solving it.

Sara Hudson, PhD
Interim CEO and Editor-in-Chief, Nonprofit Quarterly

Introduction

When our government stalls and economic markets fail us, *who steps in* to defend the public good? *Who shows up* when society's most urgent problems are left unsolved?

These are the questions that brought our team together and shaped many enlightening conversations we've had with leaders across civil society. For over 250 years, the answer to the questions has been the same. From volunteer fire brigades of colonial Philadelphia to AIDS hotlines of the 1980s to "No Kings" marches in 2025 and 2026, Americans have organized themselves into social benefit coalitions to do what neither government nor business would.

We've spent decades working across the nonprofit sector as staff, executive directors, founders, donors, consultants, volunteers, and board members. What united us to write this book is a shared belief that nonprofits are crucial to the society we live in. They give voice to the voiceless, advance social justice, hold government and business accountable, and provide essential services that allow communities to function. We are excited by the impact this sector makes and believe that corporate and government worlds can learn valuable lessons from it.

We are not alone in that conviction. When we surveyed roughly 30 nonprofit professionals across the United States about what they treasure most in their work, their answers clustered around three things: the sector's support of community and equity, the people and purpose that animate it, and a genuine willingness to collaborate. These are the sector's living strengths.

Nonprofits are the sector that moves America forward. They are the heartbeat of the nation, the connective tissue of our democracy that has worked for hundreds of years for the well-being of our communities. Strong civic participation is a hallmark of our democracy. The nonprofit sector is a key partner in providing basic services, registering voters, protecting the right to vote, educating policymakers and advocating for policy changes that strengthen the sector and the communities and causes nonprofits serve.

As Kim Klein, author and lecturer at UC Berkeley, puts it, the government's job is to "set the floor below which no one can fall and the ceiling above which no one can rise." The for-profit sector's job is to deliver products to answer our many wants and needs. The nonprofit sector's job is everything in between: the moral voice, the early warning system, the bridge that turns individual concern into collective action. This sentiment is echoed by Kavita Ramdas, former CEO of the Global Fund for Women, who has said, "Nonprofits are the life and blood of democracy. . .We were created to keep democracy alive and breathing." We believe that government and business can learn from nonprofits about purpose, mission, and accountability.

And yet now, nonprofits are under strain. Demand is surging. Funding pipelines are uncertain. The world is moving faster every day, and many of the structures nonprofits rely on were designed for an economy and civic culture that no longer exist. Meanwhile, nonprofit leaders and those who work in the sector are facing high levels of burnout. Funders are trying to "get it right" but are increasingly feeling pressure from all sides. The work is harder than it should be, and the impact smaller than it could be. We've heard this from nonprofit leaders again and again, and we've felt it in our own work.

This matters now more than ever. The nation marked its 250th year shadowed by a wave of authoritarianism that threatens the civic infrastructure social impact organizations have spent centuries strengthening. Nonprofits cannot meet this moment with twentieth-century operating systems.

This book is our call to action that the nonprofit sector must be consciously redesigned to meet this moment. We must reimagine our fundamentals: how the sector is funded, how it is governed, how leadership is shared, and how organizations work together. Drawing on our research, survey, and interviews with more than 40 leaders across the field, we offer both a diagnosis and a hopeful path forward for the people doing this work.

The Sector That Supports Democracy

In the early 1980s, thousands of people across America were falling ill and dying of the same disease, yet nobody wanted to talk about it.

The CDC first reported unusual infections among young men in 1981. But when they heard about this, the federal government looked the other way. Other institutions followed suit: hospitals turned away patients, and newspapers buried the story. By 1984, AIDS had affected more than 7,700 people and killed more than 3,500. Researchers from the CDC had fully identified its cause and transmission pathways.[1] Yet the government and media clung to stigma, treating this deadly force as something unmentionable. What was happening in American communities was seen not as a public health emergency but as a scarlet letter of morality: God's punishment for being gay. Those who were sick were trapped in an inescapable atmosphere of hate, fear, and isolation.

Nobody was coming to help. So the community had to band together and help themselves.

In 1982, community members in Los Angeles founded AIDS Project Los Angeles out of what they had: a closet in a community center and a phone line. For thousands of people newly diagnosed with a terrifying disease they couldn't talk openly about, that hotline was the only reliable source of information. By 1992, APLA had assisted more than 11,500 people, evolving into a provider of medical care, counseling, and advocacy at a moment when almost no institution was willing to serve people with HIV. It offered services—but more than that, it offered a shoulder for the sick to rest on and legitimacy to the issue itself. By treating patients as people who deserved care rather than shame, APLA helped shift the conversation slowly and stubbornly from moral panic toward public health.[2]

The APLA wasn't the only organization fighting this battle. In fact, as the AIDS support community developed, organizations realized they had the power to advocate on a broader stage in New York and every major city over time. ACT UP, the AIDS Coalition to Unleash Power, was founded in New York in 1987 by people who had run out of patience with Washington. Many of its members were living with AIDS. They protested vocally, and when they weren't on the streets, they studied. They learned about drug approval pathways and federal regulatory structures around medical treatments. They found where the power and authority sat to influence drug timelines, and they went there.

On October 11, 1988, more than 1,000 ACT UP activists shut down the FDA headquarters, crowding doors and walkways. Protesters presented clear and precise demands to fast-track life-saving drugs and increase their accessibility—demands that revealed their thorough research of FDA's processes. The pressure worked: accelerated drug approval pathways, broader access to clinical trials, a roughly 20% reduction in the price of AZT, the first approved HIV treatment, and, eventually, federal anti-discrimination protections under the Americans with Disabilities Act of 1990. *The Atlantic* later called this one of the most effective demonstrations of the AIDS era.[3]

The AIDS movement, from its humble closet-hotline beginnings, had rewritten how the federal government regulated medicine, defined disability, and treated the people affected by the crisis. While AIDS remains a large issue in America and across the globe, the AIDS movement—with several visionary nonprofits at its helm—has transformed the disease from an unmentionable affliction to one with actionable paths to recovery.

What APLA and ACT UP did in the 1980s was extraordinary—and they are just two nonprofits in a long history of organizations stepping up when no one else will. Their story answers those pivotal questions from earlier: When our government stalls and economic markets fail us, *who steps in* to defend the public good? *Who shows up* when society's most urgent problems are left unsolved?

Before we move toward advocating for redesign, we start with understanding our sector's strengths and the history of how we came to be.

History of Nonprofits

Americans have been involved in collective action since our nation's earliest days. Even back when the United States was starting to feel the rumblings of independence in the late 1700s, organized service flourished. Americans came together to protect and serve each other, together meeting community needs. The drive to improve our communities often came from an entrenched desire to safeguard our freedom from rulers. As early as 1763, Benjamin Franklin organized an all-volunteer Union Fire brigade in Philadelphia, recognizing that no private enterprise or government at the time could adequately respond to the threat of fire in his growing city. He was contributing to a culture of collective responsibility, where citizens organized themselves to protect the public good.

In 1835, visiting French historian Alexis de Tocqueville remarked with amazement on how actively Americans volunteered. "Americans of all ages, all conditions, and all dispositions constantly form associations. . .of a thousand different kinds."[4] Tocqueville understood that these associations were not peripheral to democracy—they were its engine. He called it "the genius of American democracy": that these associations transformed individual power into collective power.

At this point in history, the term *nonprofit* had not yet been imagined. Yet citizens of the young United States consistently came together to meet communal needs through service. This impulse to self-organize outside of institutions or businesses became a defining feature of American civic life. Over time, that instinct grew stronger, and eventually Congress wrote it into the tax code. But the rules were written by a privileged few, and the way they wrote them shaped the sector profoundly.

The foundation for the contemporary nonprofit sector took shape in the late 1800s through the early 1900s, as the United States entered the Progressive Era. This period was marked by rapid industrialization, unprecedented wealth creation, and deep economic inequality. While many Americans prospered, power and resources became increasingly concentrated among industrialists, creating exploitative working conditions that markets wouldn't correct and governments didn't immediately regulate. In response, social movements surged. New organizations formed to confront child labor, unsafe working conditions, public health, and exclusion. These efforts helped drive reforms in these areas. Policy changed, and through the work of activists, Americans began to believe that society could be organized more justly.

This was also the moment when nonprofits and philanthropic structures were formalized. Andrew Carnegie's 1889 essay "The Gospel of Wealth" argued that the wealthy had a moral obligation to give back to society, encouraging large-scale charitable giving. In 1894, the federal government established what would later evolve into the 501(c)(3) tax-exempt designation through the Tariff Act.

Thus, the social benefit sector was created at the same historical moment that wealth concentration was climbing sharply. This timing didn't come without its consequences. It baked into the sector's foundation a set of design choices that privileged elite donors' influence and control—dynamics that favor those with resources over those closest to the problems nonprofits seek to solve. The sector we work in today still carries those choices, and any serious redesign has to reckon with them.

The public benefit sector expanded dramatically again during the 1960s, fueled by federal investment through President Johnson's War on Poverty. Government funding flowed into nonprofit communities at an unprecedented scale. This infusion of resources and paid government jobs for public service professionalized the sector and dramatically expanded its reach. But it came at a cost. Nonprofit survival became more closely tied to government contracts and the priorities of whoever held political power. The sector gained scale and lost some of its independence.

Nonprofits nevertheless played a central role as social justice movements gained traction in the 1960s and 1970s. As the nation confronted its entrenched inequities, nonprofits were on the front lines and building bridges across differences. Organizations like the Encampment for Citizenship brought together diverse youth, to learn about self-governance, history, social justice, and self-expression through the arts. During the civil rights movement, groups such as the Southern Christian Leadership Conference and the Student Nonviolent Coordinating Committee rose with diverse approaches to activism, employing direct action rather than relying solely on legislation. In the LGBTQ rights movement, the 1969 Stonewall uprising catalyzed the formation of the Gay Liberation Front. In each case, nonprofits provided infrastructure such as meeting spaces and communication lines that enabled marginalized communities to demand their rights.

The 1980s marked another turning point for the sector. During the Reagan administration, federal support for social programs declined sharply, dropping by roughly 25% in real terms in the early part of the decade and not returning to 1980 levels until the late 1990s. One might have expected this retrenchment to weaken the public benefit sector. Instead, it triggered an unexpected surge in nonprofit growth. Much of this growth came from organizations "marketizing", or learning to sell services—replacing lost government grants with new fees and reimbursements for service. This era reshaped the sector into a more entrepreneurial, decentralized force, and in the process moved it another step away from the communities it served.

In more recent history, the nonprofit sector has continued to be the first to respond effectively during crises. After the September 11, 2001, attacks, social benefit service providers mobilized immediately to provide medical care, housing, counseling, and legal assistance to victims and their families—long before federal systems were fully operational. The same was true in the aftermath of Hurricane Katrina in 2005. Before the government even arrived, nonprofits and mutual aid networks stepped in to deliver food, shelter, and medical services—particularly to underserved low-income communities and communities of color. Nonprofits didn't shy away from being embedded in communities, and they were able to act without waiting for permission. They have done the same for more recent devastation across the country and globe due to the climate crisis.

Across eras, social benefit organizations have served as first responders to the crises and injustices of society. They have mobilized faster than governments, adapted more equitably than corporations, and maintained public trust. From fire brigades to civil rights campaigns, nonprofit organizations have repeatedly expanded the boundaries of what Americans believe is possible.

The nonprofit sector is shaped as much by who it served as who funded it. Elite-donor influence was built into our founding architecture, and government dependency was layered on top in the twentieth century. These structural inheritances explain why the sector strains under today's pressures—and why redesign has to address not just what nonprofits do but how they were built to do it.

The Current Moment: What We Are Up Against

The sector that emerged from this history carries enormous significance in American life. Nearly 2 million nonprofits operate across the United States today, employing roughly 12.8 million people—about 1 in 10 private-sector workers. Dr. Lester Salamon, in *The Resilient Sector*, identifies five core functions these organizations perform for society: providing essential services, advocating for policy change, giving voice to shared values, building community, and serving as guardians of the traditions and beliefs that hold groups together across generations. Healthcare, education, the arts, faith communities, civic life—much of what gives American society its texture—runs through this sector.

Nonprofits represent around 8% of the nation's workforce and 5–5.5% of GDP, as shown in Figure I.1. This figure does not include the impact of volunteers: more than 75 million volunteers contribute nearly 5 billion hours annually to America's nonprofit and faith sectors. If paid at market value, this volunteer labor would equal more than $167 billion annually.[5,6]

Nonprofits also span a wide variety of industry sectors and issue areas, with healthcare contributing to the highest share of employment, followed by education and social assistance, as detailed in Figure I.2.

It is worth noticing that in much of the world this work is the government's job. Iceland, Switzerland, and other European countries fund broad public services through higher taxation; nongovernmental organizations (NGOs) there play supplementary roles—innovation, advocacy, niche services—rather than carrying the weight of essential services. America made a different choice, and a sector arose to do what neither government

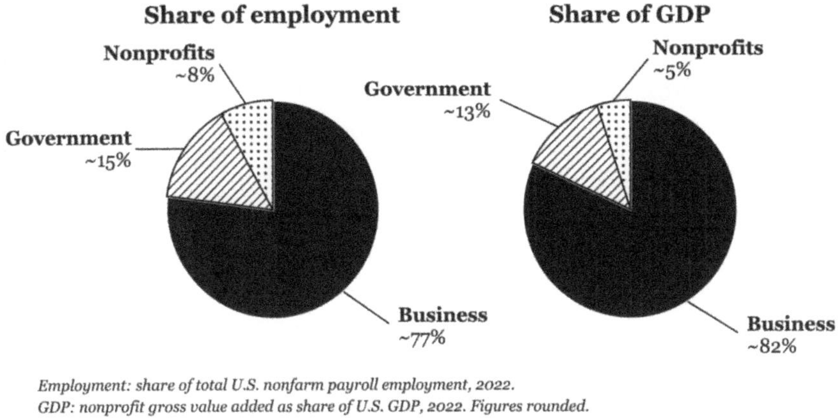

Figure I.1 Share of U.S. employment and GDP by sector, 2022[7,8,9]

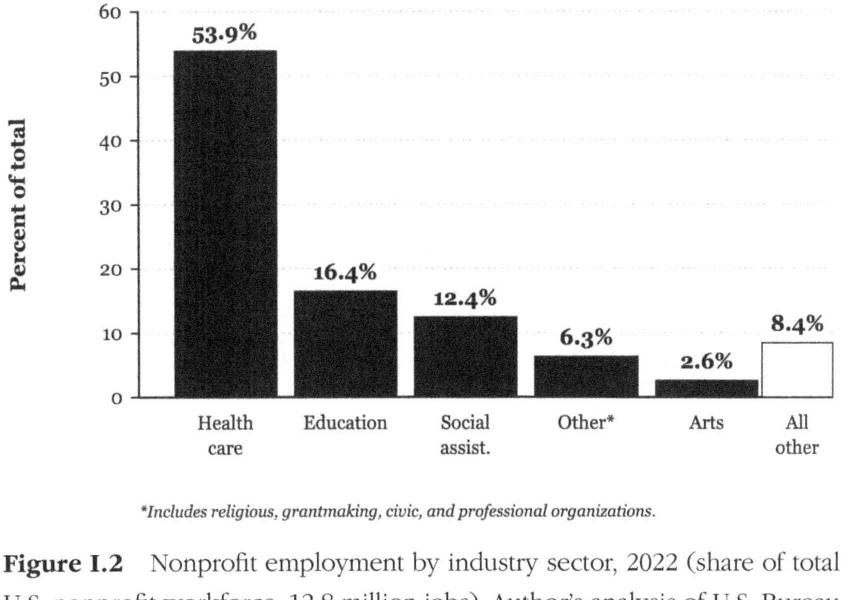

Figure I.2 Nonprofit employment by industry sector, 2022 (share of total U.S. nonprofit workforce, 12.8 million jobs). Author's analysis of U.S. Bureau of Labor Statistics, Quarterly Census of Employment and Wages, 2022 Nonprofit Research Data (released 2024). Health Care and Social Assistance Disaggregated Using Shares Derived from BLS Current Population Survey data, 2003–2022[10,11]

nor markets would. That choice has produced an extraordinary ecosystem: more than a million organizations, built largely from the ground up, addressing needs as varied as the communities that created them. It has also left the burden of public service on a sector that operates with thin reserves and contested legitimacy.

And right now, that sector is stalled.

In a recent survey, more than half of nonprofits (53%) reported struggling with adequate staffing and turnover, while more than 40% are finding it difficult to secure funding.[12] The pipeline into nonprofits is also narrowing: many young leaders carry student debt that makes mission-driven salaries difficult to choose. Volunteerism, once the backbone of civic participation, is thinning. The average volunteer commitment has fallen from 96.5 hours per year in 2017 to 70 hours in 2023, and the median from 40 hours to 24 hours.[13] Volunteers still care; they just have less time to give. At the same time, the sector has access to an enormous untapped resource: roughly 47 million U.S. retirees, many of whom want to contribute but need orientation, training, and meaningful tasks to support nonprofit missions effectively rather than redirect them. These trends weaken nonprofits' ability to build the durable relationships that have historically fueled social change.

Meanwhile, the problems public benefit organizations exist to address have grown larger and more interconnected. Economic inequality is accelerating. Political polarization has surged to levels that generate hostility and violence. Loneliness has reached epidemic proportions, fueling a widespread mental health crisis. Climate change is driving displacement and food insecurity at a growing scale. Across the political spectrum, roughly 70% of Americans now believe the system is rigged to benefit those in power at the expense of everyone else—a level of disillusionment that itself imperils democratic legitimacy.[14] These are not discrete problems for individual organizations to tackle one at a time—they are system-level challenges that demand coordinated, systemic responses.

Layered on top of these challenges is the rapid acceleration of AI and digital platforms, which are reshaping how information flows, how labor is organized, and how communities form. Technology moves quickly;

integrating it with ethics and intentionality takes time. That gap creates both real opportunity and significant risk—a tension we explore in depth in Chapter 4.

The political environment is making the work harder, not easier. As the U.S. government has defunded essential public services, nonprofits are increasingly expected to fill the gaps—even as the ground gives way beneath them. One in three nonprofits saw federal funding lost, frozen, or delayed in the first half of 2025 alone, and more than half hold three months or less of cash on hand. At the same time, a global backlash against civil society is closing democratic space in country after country. Varieties of Democracy Institute data show that 74% of the world's population now lives under autocratic rule, a level of backsliding that returns the average world citizen to 1978 levels of democratic freedom—erasing nearly the entire third wave of democratization.

In the United States, that backlash has taken the form of intensified attacks on diversity, equity, and inclusion programs and on the rights of women, immigrants, and LGBTQ communities—pressures felt acutely in a sector that is majority women and that has long served as infrastructure for the communities now most under threat. After the 2025 administration came to power, many nonprofits found themselves facing an impossible choice: continue values-based programs and risk defunding or scale them back and lose the trust of the communities they serve.

This is why the strain feels different than it has before. The sector is being asked to absorb more demand, with less funding, in a more hostile environment, while solving twenty-first-century problems with twentieth-century operating systems.

But the deeper problem is structural. As Sara Hudson, editor of *Nonprofit Quarterly*, observed in her foreword, the nonprofit sector has never built shared infrastructure, unlike in the fields of medicine, law, or finance. Workers identify with individual organizations rather than with the sector as a whole. There is no professional body that defends the sector's interests, no agreed-upon credentialing, no coordinated voice. Each organization fights its own battles, applies for its own grants, and triages its own crises.

The sector that built so much of American civic life has never been built to defend itself.

This explains why so many nonprofit leaders feel forced into incrementalism in an era that calls for structural change. It is not for lack of talent or vision. It is that the sector's foundational blueprint—designed in the Progressive Era when wealth was concentrated, layered with government dependency in the twentieth century, and never given shared infrastructure of its own—no longer matches the scale of its ambitions. As Aaron Dorfman, CEO of the National Council of Philanthropy, has argued, the legitimacy of the sector itself is at risk if organizations cannot take principled stands and clearly demonstrate their impact on American lives.

This sense of strain is not just our diagnosis. It is a consensus across the field. In our survey, every single respondent agreed that the sector needs revisioning or redesign. When asked where that redesign is most urgently needed, they pointed to the same places this book examines: funding and revenue models (55% said this area needed redesign), collaboration and partnership (39%), and leadership and governance (33%). The people doing the work already know the operating system is failing them. What they have lacked is a shared blueprint for what comes next.

And yet there is reason for hope. Beth Kanter, nonprofit strategist, observes the same pressures and sees an opening: "One boat is not going to survive the storm. But all of them together will." The crisis is real. So is the possibility of meeting it differently: together, rather than alone.

The Book: *Redesigning Nonprofits*

Our journey to writing this book began with a shared urgency and hope. After publishing her last book in 2021, Kim, a seasoned nonprofit peacebuilder, felt a calling to use her voice to empower the nonprofit sector at a time when civic institutions felt increasingly fragile. She was concerned that many nonprofits were not adapting to the trends that impacted them, to their detriment.

Kim turned to Tracy, a philanthropic powerhouse who had built and funded dozens of nonprofits. Their early conversations quickly gained momentum as the political climate intensified, and they knew the time to speak out was now. But Kim and Tracy wanted a more intergenerational perspective, so they joined efforts with Shannon, a rising nonprofit strategist with experience in both the nonprofit and Fortune 500 worlds, who brought fresh insight.

Together, we envisioned not just a book but a larger movement: a living initiative, fueled by workshops, briefings, media interviews, public dialogue, a community of advisors, and a reimagined future for the sector.

This book is for people who believe in the nonprofit sector—and who feel, in their daily work, that something has to change. It's for executive directors, fundraisers, and board members carrying organizations through chronic strain. Donors and funders trying to give more thoughtfully. Staff, consultants, volunteers, and community organizers who know the work matters and suspect the systems supporting it no longer do. Government, business, and policy leaders who look to partner with the public benefit sector. If you care about improving and uplifting the sector, this book is for you.

The sector spans the full political spectrum, from humanitarian and environmental causes to faith-based and community-rooted organizations across left and right. While the sector spans schools and universities, hospitals, food banks, churches, and global humanitarian organizations, this book is especially written with small to midsize U.S. nonprofits in mind—those with budgets under $750,000, which represent roughly 80% of the sector. These are the organizations most often expected to do the most with the least, and the ones whose redesign will most shape what the sector becomes.

You will notice that we sometimes call this work the *nonprofit sector*, sometimes the *public or social benefit sector* and sometimes the *social impact sector*. As Peter Hero, former president of the Silicon Valley Community Foundation, has observed, the term *nonprofit* itself communicates "a sort of fuzzy volunteer-driven unmanaged circus of good intentions"—language that does nothing to convey the professionalism, vigor, and skill of the people doing this work. We use these terms interchangeably as an invitation: to consider what we should call a sector that has carried so much of American civic life, and what a more accurate name might unlock.

This book is built on the voices of the people doing the work. Drawing on more than 40 interviews with executive directors, CEOs, board chairs, donors, funders, financial and legacy advisors, consultants, coaches, and community partners—and more than 30 written surveys with a circle of nonprofit leaders—we offer both a diagnosis of what is broken and a path forward built on what is already working. The chapters weave practical guidance with case studies of innovative models: trust-based philanthropy, flow funding, distributed leadership, participatory grantmaking, nonprofit/for-profit partnerships, multiyear operating support, and legacy giving. We show the redesign happening in practice, by people who refused to wait.

This book is also part of a larger initiative. We invite you to visit www.redesigningnonprofits.org, where you'll find resources, examples, and ways to join an ongoing national conversation about the future of the sector.

Overview of the Book

The book unfolds in several parts. The first two chapters establish the foundation—the mindsets and frameworks that make redesign possible. Chapters 3 through 7 explore five major forces transforming the sector and offer concrete redesign moves for navigating each one. The final chapter zooms out to the sector as a whole, proposing transformational ideas that will require coordination across organizations, philanthropy, and policy.

1. ***Why Redesign the Social Benefit Sector?***

   This chapter lays the foundation for the book. It argues that the strain so many nonprofit leaders feel today is not a failure of leadership or commitment, but the result of an operating system built for a different era. Drawing on data, lived experience, and real-world examples, the chapter shows how rising social demand and outdated structures have collided—producing chronic burnout and financial instability, and diminishing impact.

2. ***Debunking Myths to Spark Imagination of the Sector***

   This chapter tackles a core barrier: the stories we've been taught to believe about what public benefit organizations are "supposed" to be. The sector's most punishing norms—scarcity and self-sacrifice—are myths that equate virtue with deprivation. In a moment when old systems are fraying, the chapter reframes crisis as an opening for imagination. Imagination is both a survival tool and a democratic practice, helping nonprofits govern themselves differently. Leaning into imagination is not about abandoning rigor or evidence; rather, it is about expanding the range of possibilities that evidence is marshaled to serve. As we reimagine not only how nonprofits function more effectively in a changed world but also how the sector can transform, drawing on imagination will be key as we begin building the next chapter.

We then delve into five macro themes, where we present concrete examples and solutions:

3. ***Impacting the Great Transfer of Leadership and Wealth***

   As Baby Boomers and Gen X age, trillions of dollars will be passed to Millennials and Gen Z, reshaping not only the economy but also who holds power. Successful transfers—of both money and values—require careful planning: establishing trusts, mentoring future leaders, and aligning family goals with business and philanthropy. Without this preparation, families risk conflict and mismanagement. Community organizations and major institutions also face a risk: if they do not meaningfully engage the next generation, they may lose long-standing generational support. Younger generations bring their own perspectives on giving and leadership while navigating real economic pressures. This raises important questions such as "How can we nurture the next generation of givers, and how can we create spaces to thoughtfully discuss giving, stewardship, and responsibility?"

4. ***Harnessing the Shift Online and Growth of AI***

   This chapter examines how the migration of daily life to digital spaces has fundamentally changed how people connect and participate—and what that means for nonprofits whose lifeblood is community. It explores how online platforms have expanded access while simultaneously weakening depth of engagement, contributing to declining volunteer and donor cultivation. The chapter also confronts the rise of generative AI, asking how social benefit organizations can use technology while keeping our humanity at the center.

5. ***Expanding Collaboration, Diversity, Partnerships, and Mergers***

   Collaboration, diversity, partnerships, and mergers are powerful strategies that drive innovation, deepen community trust, and amplify impact. A diverse team brings a wide range of perspectives, lived experiences, and cultural insights—helping organizations better understand and serve the communities they aim to uplift. Collaboration and partnership, both internally and with external partners, foster shared learning and resource pooling. It enables nonprofits to tackle complex challenges more effectively and build coalitions that reflect the voices of those most affected. Foundations are beginning to encourage more collaborative proposals. Mergers can create value by combining resources, reducing costs, and expanding outreach, but their success depends on a good fit, solid planning together, funding, and integration.

6. ***Reshaping the Funding and Fundraising Worlds***

   This chapter examines how the public benefit funding landscape is rapidly changing before our eyes. Traditional revenue streams such as government grants and large foundation funding are becoming less predictable, pushing organizations to diversify their strategies. New approaches like digital fundraising, corporate partnerships, and earned-income models are gaining traction as nonprofits seek greater sustainability and flexibility. At the same time, the roles of boards, donors, foundations, and donor-advised funds are evolving and require re-evaluation and training. Emerging movements such as Trust-Based Philanthropy and Flow Funding encourage multiyear operating support, stronger partnerships with community leaders, and greater trust in those closest to the work. Restructuring the funding world and innovative fundraising are both necessities. A few communities of donors, advisors, and foundation leaders are engaging in new ways to proceed, and we present ideas and examples of visionary changemaking.

7. ***Emerging Models of Organizational Leadership***

   Here, we examine how to redesign nonprofits "inside the walls." How do decisions get made? Who holds power? How is collaboration structured? The chapter introduces a set of alternative models of distributed leadership that challenge the default assumptions of hierarchy. It then zooms out to show how internal redesign connects to ecosystem redesign: hubs, networks, fiscal sponsors, and coordinating entities that reduce duplication and make collaboration the default rather than the exception.

Finally, we explore truly transformational ideas that can shape the sector as a whole:

8. ***A Call to Action: Transforming the Sector***

   Transforming the sector will require a multifaceted approach, engaging people at all levels. In this chapter we explore many suggestions: reforming legal and tax systems, establishing a national office tasked with supporting the sector, setting up a National Advisory Board of corporate CEOs and social impact leaders to work together, encouraging more media coverage highlighting what the sector has accomplished, and other suggestions. We hope this will create a national dialogue that can result in uplifting the sector.

Conclusion

The 250th year of the American experiment is not a moment for incrementalism. The sector that built so much of this country's civic life is now being asked to defend democracy itself—and it cannot do that with the operating systems of a different era. But it can do it with a redesign rooted in respect for what this sector has always been: the connective tissue that turns individual concern into collective action, and the proof that when systems fail, people still organize, and when people organize, society changes.

This book is one part of a larger effort. We recognize the efforts of #WetheCivic, building a national conversation about the future of social benefit organizations and the people who sustain them. At www.redesigningnonprofits.org, you'll find frameworks, examples, and resources to use in your own work—and ways to join the organizing underway.

The work ahead is large. We believe it is possible. Let's begin.

Chapter 1

Why "Redesign" the Social Benefit Sector?

"Vision without action is merely a dream. Action without vision is merely passing time. But vision with action can change the world."

—Nelson Mandela

Imagine the executive director of a nonprofit providing after-school education on a regular Tuesday morning. A grant report is due Friday. A text comes in from her program director—one of their teachers just gave notice. The board chair wants a "quick call ASAP" about the latest audit. A parent left a voicemail asking why hours were cut. And the accountant just confirmed that the state contract payment has been delayed again; if it doesn't arrive by the 15th, they'll need to pull from reserves to make payroll.

She closes her office door, takes a breath, and thinks about the child whose parents come home late from work and now has nowhere to go after school. *I didn't get into this work to manage a constant cash flow crisis. But here I am, again.*

If this story feels like an exaggeration, many of us can attest that it isn't. Stories like this are everywhere in our sector. And though it can feel like everything rests on the leader's shoulders, this failure isn't hers—it is the fault of our underlying structures.

Now picture a different Tuesday, 17 years ago, in 2008. The financial system was collapsing, and the Global Fund for Women, like nearly every nonprofit in the country, was staring at a budget that no longer added up. They could have taken the conventional route: cut the lowest-paid staff first.

They were the easiest line items to eliminate, and every professional advisor in the sector would have called it the responsible move. Many for-profit corporations were doing exactly that.

Kavita Ramdas, the fund's president, refused. She and her senior team forfeited their retirement contributions for two years instead so that no one at the bottom of the org chart would lose their job. The CFO worked out the numbers. The board—half of whom were grassroots activists from the Global South—backed the call without hesitation. When the economy recovered, the organization was intact: its young staff were still in place, and its relationships with grantee partners had deepened rather than fractured.

What made this decision possible wasn't heroism, though Ramdas's actions were self-sacrificing. What enabled it was an intentionally designed structure. A traditionally composed board of wealthy American donors would have recommended the layoffs. A mission framed around benefactors-and-beneficiaries, rather than collective power-building, would have shielded leadership from the hit. The fund could act on its values in 2008 because, years earlier, it had chosen conscious redesigns: creating a grassroots board and treating every donor equally (the Global Fund didn't give gold stars for the size of a gift). A key operating principle had been instilled by Ramdas's predecessor: *how* we do our work is as important as what we do.

This is what redesign looks like before it is needed. And it is within reach of any organization willing to question the defaults we've inherited.

The pressures on today's leaders are even stronger than the ones Ramdas navigated. The sector still runs on assumptions built for the twentieth century, while the twenty-first has rewritten nearly every external condition—financial, political, technological, generational. This chapter examines those conditions, asks why the sector has been slow to adapt even when adaptation is overdue, and turns to what redesign means in practice.

This chapter moves forward in three parts. First, we examine the forces reshaping the ground beneath us—financial, political, technological, generational. Second, we uncover the reasons the sector has been slow to adapt. Finally, we discuss what redesign means in practice: the evolutionary mindset that leaders in nonprofits and funding can bring to our work now.

The Four Forces Reshaping the Nonprofit Landscape

The nonprofit sector has weathered hard periods before. What makes this one different is that four pressures are landing at the same time. Any one of them would strain an organization; together they multiply the effect.

Need Is Surging, Yet Resources Remain Stagnant

The mismatch between global need and nonprofits' resources is most visible in the financial pressures nonprofits face. Across the past decade, social impact leaders have consistently reported rising demand for their services. In the Nonprofit Finance Fund's State of the Sector surveys, 86% of leaders reported increased demand in 2018, 71% in 2022, and 80% in 2025—a sustained upward pressure that has persisted through vastly different economic conditions.[1] Additionally, costs such as rent, insurance, and wages have risen dramatically, growing by 27.4% per employee between 2017 and 2022.[2] However, funding streams have not kept pace. The Center for Effective Philanthropy's 2023 report shows that fundraising challenges and staff burnout are top organizational concerns, creating a cycle of exhaustion and turnover.[3] This has been exacerbated by recent dramatic government cutbacks in essential services and foreign aid.

The Political Landscape Is Volatile

Government contracts are no longer a reliable financial backbone for many organizations. Instead, these contracts are increasingly delayed, cancelled, or underfunded—and many of them are also an administrative burden. The Urban Institute's national survey of nonprofit-government contracting found that 45% of nonprofits reported late government payments, and 44%

reported problems from governments changing the terms of signed agreements—most often by increasing reporting requirements or cutting payments.[4]

Nonprofits have adapted quickly to recent challenging policy changes. Organizations across the country have launched mutual aid networks as crises arise, building peer-support models and finding ways to stretch their dollars. But this improvisation has become our permanent operating mode. This is not a sustainable model for solving society's hardest problems.

Technology Has Transformed How We Socialize and Work Together

The advent of AI is a technological transformation reshaping virtually every industry. Yet nonprofits have been slower to adopt artificial intelligence and automation at an organizational level. According to Salesforce's 2023 Nonprofit Trends Report, only 17% of nonprofits described their automation usage as being at a "high maturity" level, and nearly 90% lacked any policy addressing AI.[5] Yet many nonprofit employees and volunteers already use AI daily to draft communications and summarize documents. While we see high adoption on the individual level, there is a gap in organizational alignment. (See Chapter 4 for more information on AI.)

Public use of social platforms has also shifted dramatically. Social media has conditioned audiences to expect real-time responsiveness across multiple platforms. While nonprofits must keep up by creating an engaging social media presence and responding in real-time, we are also still expected to produce annual reports and paper communications to stay engaged with an often-older donor base. In other words, we're expected to do it all.

The Rising Generation Thinks Differently About Work

The social benefit sector was built around long-term volunteer commitments, office hours, and long evening shifts. The next generation will rewrite that rulebook.

The generation now entering the workforce cares deeply about equity, climate, mental health, and community. But they are also unwilling to accept the terms the sector has traditionally offered—unpaid internships, chronic understaffing, the quiet expectation that passion should compensate for a living wage. Deloitte's 2025 global survey reports that one of the top career goals for Gen Z and Millennials is work-life balance, behind achieving financial independence and above job stability and security, becoming a field expert, learning and development, and impacting society.[6]

This can often lead to an outcry that "Gen Z are entitled!" But in actuality, Gen Z is leading a positive evolution that can benefit everyone. Organizations that meet these expectations will have access to extraordinary talent. Those that don't will lose it to the public or private sector.

The Result: Our System Is Under Strain Because Its Assumptions and Structures Are Outdated

We are asking organizations to tackle large societal challenges with a majority-volunteer workforce and to do so in a volatile, unprecedented political landscape. Policymakers, for their part, have not meaningfully engaged the sector as these conditions have shifted.

Our model hasn't failed; the context has changed. Unless we redesign to reflect the realities of this century, nonprofits will keep running the current day's marathon in century-old shoes.

Why Are Social Benefit Organizations Stuck with Outdated Design?

Why does the sector hold onto designs that no longer serve it? The answer has less to do with the organizations than with the conditions they operate in. Adaptation in business and adaptation in the nonprofit sector answer to different pressures—and we can learn from these differences.

Credit Suisse estimated in 2017 that the average age of an S&P 500 company had fallen from nearly 60 years in the 1950s to under 20 today—a collapse attributed largely to technological disruption.[7] The for-profit world runs on Darwinian pressure: when new technologies upend business as usual, firms re-envision their strategy, retrain their workforces, and shift resources accordingly. Those that don't die.

Nonprofits face our own life-or-death churn, but ours is different in nature. Survival depends less on technological adaptation and more on whether we can sustain funder relationships and keep donors convinced our work still matters. This system rewards continuity over evolution, asking leaders to spend their energy accordingly.

We are constrained by this design, lacking the incentives and conditions to adapt to a rapidly changing environment. Six structural features explain why.

Misaligned, Narrow, and Short-Term Incentives

Restricted dollars and the "low overhead" myth push organizations to treat infrastructure and strategic development as waste. According to the Center for Effective Philanthropy, only 20% of U.S. funding for nonprofits is unrestricted.[8] For nonprofits taking this funding, that means 80% of their direction is determined by an entity outside the organization.

The public benefit funding landscape is complex, competitive, and often inequitable. Funders' priorities shift frequently, so nonprofits have to adapt just as quickly. Many grants are restricted or short term, and most are cumbersome to apply for. This doesn't just cause inefficiency—it reinforces disparities between well-resourced and under-resourced organizations. Nonprofits serving marginalized communities face compounded pressures: higher demand, fewer resources, and less access to wealthy funder circles.

Social impact organizations are trapped in short time horizons. Most grants last one year; success is measured quarterly; and renewal (if renewal is a possibility—often, grants are just given for one year) depends on demonstrating immediate outputs rather than systemic outcomes. Yet often projects require a longer timeline to achieve the results needed. This "short-termism" discourages innovation and long-term planning and doesn't do justice to either the project, those served by it, or the organization that runs it. Our interviewees consistently named long-term planning as one of the hardest things to protect—the work that keeps an organization tethered to its North Star is the work that volatility crowds out first.

The 2025 Nonprofit Finance Fund State of the Nonprofit Sector Survey found that more than half of the 2,200 nonprofit leaders they surveyed (52%) reported having three months or less of cash on hand and cited multiyear funding as critical, as "multiyear funding allows organizations to spend less time fundraising and more time delivering services to communities."[9] Constant fundraising cycles pull leadership attention away from mission and toward survival. Additionally, much of public benefit funding is restricted to a particular project or program. Without unrestricted funds, nonprofits can't invest in infrastructure, staff, R&D, or innovation. Restricted funding leaves little room for adaptation or resilience. According to the Nonprofit Finance Fund's State of the Nonprofit Sector Survey, 75% of nonprofit leaders said raising unrestricted dollars was a challenge, and nearly half (46%) said it was a major one.[10] Grants that target just one area of program impact may limit organizations' ability to construct a cohesive program strategy.

To retain innovative, long-term thinking, nonprofits need multiyear support that instills trust in grantees. A growing set of funders is beginning to demonstrate this—from MacKenzie Scott's $26 billion in unrestricted gifts to the trust-based philanthropy movement's practice of multiyear, general operating support. We return to these models, and to the broader question of how to release the roughly $1.4 trillion in charitable capital currently warehoused in foundations and donor-advised funds, in Chapter 6.

Investment in Leadership and Talent Is Stuck in Scarcity Mode

There is a chronic underinvestment problem in our sector. Bridgespan's 2006 report, The Nonprofit Sector's Leadership Deficit, warned that insufficient funding for salaries, professional development, and succession planning would create leadership vacuums across the sector. Nearly a decade later, their 2015 follow-up confirmed the prediction: organizations were filling senior roles, but a revolving door of turnover had replaced the anticipated shortage—a "leadership development deficit" driven by the same underinvestment the original report flagged.[11,12]

Burnout has become endemic to our sector. And the burden is not equally distributed. The Building Movement Project's Race to Lead research—spanning surveys of more than 13,000 social impact workers across 2016, 2019, and 2022—reveals structural inequity layered on top of scarcity: leaders of color face unequal access to mentorship, sponsorship, and well-resourced roles. Their 2022 report, "Trading Glass Ceilings for Glass Cliffs," found that fewer than a quarter of white executives planning transitions were actively mentoring staff of color, compared with nearly half of executives of color doing so.[13]

Nonprofit staff face low pay, high emotional exposure, and limited support. Many organizations can't offer competitive wages or benefits, making recruitment and retention difficult—even though the services they provide are often essential.

The problem is structural on two fronts: there are far fewer funders than the sector's demand requires, and those that do exist often restrict the very spending—competitive salaries, leadership development, succession planning—that sustainable organizations depend on.[14] Staffing and operations are not auxiliary to the work: they are the work. Sustainable impact requires investing in competitive pay, professional development, data systems, and leadership succession. We explore emerging leadership models in Chapter 7 and take up the intergenerational leadership transition and what it requires of the sector in Chapter 5.

Pulled Between Different Stakeholders

Social benefit organizations are pulled in multiple directions: serving constituents or beneficiaries, satisfying donors and sponsors, pleasing boards, supporting staff, complying with regulators and government agencies, and signaling legitimacy to the public. This multi-audience dynamic creates a misalignment between those most affected by a nonprofit's work (its constituents) and those who hold power over its funding and governance.

Each stakeholder group has distinct priorities:

- Constituents want dignity, responsiveness, and programs that meet real needs.
- Donors and sponsors expect measurable outcomes, financial transparency, and evidence of impact.
- Boards are tasked with governance, strategic oversight, fundraising, and safeguarding mission integrity.
- Regulators demand compliance with tax laws, reporting requirements, and ethical standards.
- The public looks for trustworthiness, credibility, and visible community benefit.

Balancing these expectations requires intentional strategy. When funders dictate priorities, nonprofits become reactive—and the donor's lack of trust stifles the experimentation that growth depends on.

Unlike corporations with the singular goal of profitability, social impact organizations face multiple stakeholders with different definitions of success: impact metrics, community benefit, financial sustainability, and branding. We take up the collaborative approaches that help organizations navigate these competing stakeholder demands in Chapter 5.

Governance Is Built for Compliance, Not Adaptation

Most nonprofit boards are designed to be stable and avoid risk. Governance norms emphasize fiduciary oversight, fundraising, and compliance—necessary functions but insufficient for organizations that need bold strategy. BoardSource's 2021 "Leading with Intent" report found that boards consistently underperform in the areas where today's context demands the most strength: strategic thinking, effective community relationships, and diversity among board members themselves.[15]

Many boards are small, volunteer-led, and composed of members selected for their donor networks rather than their strategic expertise or lived experience with the communities the organization serves. The result is a widening gap between what organizations need from their boards and what boards are equipped to provide. Too many boards remain locked in a compliance posture—reviewing financials and approving minutes while the strategic questions go unasked.

A growing set of organizations is beginning to demonstrate an alternative—community-centered boards where grant recipients and constituents hold voting authority, leaner "minimum viable" boards paired with advisory circles that match expertise to the moment, and compensated board structures that open governance to those historically excluded from it. We examine these models in depth in Chapter 7, alongside the leadership structures that governance reform makes possible, such as co-directorships and distributed authority.

Missions Are Often Framed as Charity vs. Community Power-Building

Many nonprofits still operate through a service delivery frame: we provide, others receive. This model is rooted in centuries of charitable tradition. But today's systemic crises demand something fundamentally different: co-creation and strategies that build community power rather than dependency.

Philanthropy often reinforces the older model. Funders reward service outputs—meals served, clients housed, students tutored—over the harder-to-measure work of structural change: shifting policy, building coalitions, redistributing decision-making power to the communities most affected. Research from Echoing Green and Bridgespan has documented the resulting disparity: organizations led by people of color—often the ones closest to community-driven solutions—receive significantly less unrestricted funding and face higher burdens of proof than their white-led counterparts.[16] Grassroots organizations aimed at shifting systems are the least resourced to do so.

This is a design flaw in how the sector defines impact. When success is measured by volume of services delivered, nonprofits are incentivized to maintain the problems they exist to solve. Moving from charity to power-building requires not only different programming but different metrics and different relationships—with funders, with boards, and, most importantly, with the communities at the center of the work. We examine the trust-based, participatory, and equity-rooted funding models making this shift possible in Chapter 6.

Innovation and Technology Treated as a Discretionary Expense

In government and business, investing in technology is seen as strategic. In the public benefit sector, it is seen as discretionary—a line item to minimize rather than a capability to build.

This underinvestment carries a compounding cost. Organizations that fall behind technologically also fall behind in their capacity to measure impact, tell their story, and respond to emerging needs. The technology gap widens the distance between what nonprofits could accomplish and what their infrastructure allows.

Some leaders are beginning to close this gap. World Pulse founder Jensine Larsen, for instance, argues that nonprofits should commit a "digital dividend" of at least 5% of their budgets to technology infrastructure—a benchmark we return to in Chapter 4, alongside frameworks for AI governance and the redesign of digital community. Closing this gap requires funders and boards to treat technology as the foundation modern mission delivery depends on.

The Result: A System That Maintains Itself Instead of Evolving

Taken together, these conditions form a reinforcing cycle:

- Restricted funding discourages investment.
- Governance rewards caution over adaptation.
- Leadership systems produce burnout and inequity.
- Missions are framed transactionally instead of systemically.
- Tech underinvestment slows responsiveness even further.

Nonprofits can break this cycle—but not by working harder within the current model. The sector is constrained by an operating architecture designed for stability in an era that demands agility. Until we redesign that architecture, we remain trapped in incrementalism while the problems we exist to solve grow exponentially.

Grassroots organizations are already positioned to lead the redesign. They are closer to their communities, and less encumbered by legacy structures. But structural barriers are only half of the diagnosis. Inside the sector, decades of operating within these conditions have produced something subtler and harder to dislodge: a set of inherited beliefs that keep organizations small even when their missions call for more. Chapter 2 takes up those beliefs.

What Do We Mean by "Redesign"?

As we worked through what social impact leaders need to meet this moment, we returned to one word: *redesign*. It became the question we asked every leader we interviewed: How can nonprofits thrive by redesigning how we approach this work?

Redesign cannot be captured by a slogan or a rebrand, and it is not merely an instruction to work harder. It is the intentional reshaping of nonprofit structures, incentives, models, and relationships so that organizations can thrive in the conditions of the twenty-first century—and so that the sector can continue its role in strengthening democracy. Redesign is systems-level rethinking: how nonprofits are funded, how they are governed, and how they are connected to the communities they serve.

Design Principles for Effective Redesign

Five "design principles" guide this work. They are not prescriptions—they are a way of approaching growth that leaders from all types of organizations can undertake. The core question they revolve around is simple: What impact are we actually creating, and is there a better way to do this work?

Some of what follows in this book will be immediately usable. Other strategies will require conditions you don't yet have. The design principles are meant to give you a place to stand: a mindset that makes more choices visible, and helps you weigh the ones that matter most.

Aim Ambitiously (Because Our Problems Demand It)

Nonprofits are the independent sector, solving problems that markets and governments ignore. They are economic engines, contributing $1.5 trillion to U.S. GDP.[17] But too often, nonprofits scale their ambitions to their yearly budget rather than to the size of the problem.

Ann Mei Chang, CEO of Candid, urges organizations to set "big, audacious goals" that match societal needs in her book *Lean Impact*. She argues that goals that merely "reduce hunger" or "improve health" are as vague as telling Google to "make more money." Goals should be concrete, measurable, and aimed at change that moves the needle relative to the need.

And she warns against starting from scarcity: goals should reflect long-term aspiration (10 years or more), not by the limited dollars available today. If accomplishing our goals feels like emptying the ocean with a spoon, then our goals are likely too small to address the problem.[18]

Since its founding in 2006, the organization Charity: Water has chased one ambitious goal: ending the global water crisis. This framing is audacious: not "reduce thirst" or "improve access" but "end the crisis." The organization scaled its goal to the size of the problem (696 million people without basic drinking water) and then built backward: 209,200 water projects, serving more than 21 million people to date. The ambition shaped the operating model, not the reverse.[19,20]

Use Good Strategy to Move Through the Current

Redesign is also about enacting smart strategy. Richard Rumelt, in *Good Strategy, Bad Strategy*, boils "good strategy" down into three core components:

Diagnosis: Honestly naming the challenge.
Example: "We are serving 3,000 families, but 20,000 need us, and our current delivery model can't scale to that many people."

Guiding Policy: A clear directional approach.
Example: "We will shift to a hub-and-spoke delivery model to multiply reach."

Coherent Actions: Targeted steps that reinforce one another.
Example: "Expand partner sites; share delivery services; collaborate on intake and impact data."

"Bad strategy," Rumelt notes, often shows up as follows:

- **Avoiding the challenge:** Broadcasting "we help the needy" without first understanding their needs and your organizational gaps
- **Confusing goals with strategy:** Setting a target to "distribute 10,000 meals" without understanding how that will sustainably lessen a hunger crisis
- **Lack of cohesion:** Prioritizing too many different directions, such as simultaneously solving homelessness, delivering education, creating cultural programming
- **Incoherent actions:** Organizing an arts program when our mission is tailored around finding a cure for cancer
- **Ignoring trade-offs:** Ten unrelated initiatives to please 10 funders

One nonprofit that has employed "good strategy" is Habitat for Humanity Egypt (HFHE). HFHE's national director, Yousry Makar, started with a diagnosis of his organization: while his chapter had capital and housing expertise, it lacked the local knowledge and trust needed to actually reduce homelessness in Egypt's communities.

The guiding policy responded to his diagnosis: rather than build that knowledge in-house, partner with local NGOs already tackling related issues—economic development, education, healthcare. "We have an Egyptian proverb that I use," Makar explains, "that 'the basket that has two handles should be carried by two people.'" Coherent actions reinforced the shift. HFHE worked through community organizations already addressing poverty, tailored housing programs to the needs these partners identified, and supported partners until they became self-sufficient rather than dependent on the national office. The result: whereas a typical Habitat for Humanity country program builds around 200 houses a year, HFHE built roughly 1,000 annually—more than 8,000 houses in eight years.[21]

Treat Infrastructure—and the People Who Run It—as Mission-Critical

The nonprofit sector narrative has long valorized operating "lean." But the truth is: you cannot deliver well if you don't invest well. Infrastructure is more than "overhead"—it is the scaffolding that makes the work possible.

Three investments in particular deserve to be protected:

- ***Reserves*** are your mission's insurance. An organization with three months of cash on hand is always one delayed payment away from crisis; an organization with 12 can absorb a shock without dismantling what it has built. Find bridge loan sources before you need them through your bank, donors, or existing funders.
- ***Staff well-being*** translates to your program's quality. This is the investment nonprofit leaders are most often asked to defer, and it is the one that compounds fastest when deferred. Research on the four-day workweek across 245 organizations and more than 8,700 employees found that when workers had real time to rest, burnout and turnover dropped while productivity held steady or improved—effects that persisted a full year later, driven by better sleep, less fatigue, and a stronger sense of work ability.[22,23] Stressed staff make worse decisions. Rested staff stay, think clearly, and deliver work that compounds. Care for your team is not a reward for performance. It is a condition of it.
- ***Technology*** gives you reach, access, and scale. The right systems let a small team serve more people, track outcomes, and respond to needs without the staff burning out in the process.

A 2014 random-assignment evaluation published in *Nonprofit and Voluntary Sector Quarterly* found that capacity-building grants measurably improved public benefit leadership, programs, revenue, and community engagement.[24] The Nonprofit Finance Fund and Center for Effective Philanthropy document that when capacity funding is absent, burnout, vacancies, and instability persist.

Some nonprofits are flipping the script. Rockwood Leadership Institute moved to a four-day, 32-hour workweek with no reduction in pay—and in the years since, has tripled its budget and expanded the number of people it serves annually, all while holding staff size steady. Investment in staff well-being fueled their growth.[25]

Shift from "Doing For" to "Doing With and By" Communities

Redesign calls on nonprofits to leave behind the old charity mindset and embrace models where communities have voice, agency, and ownership. This is the principle where grassroots organizations are already leading. Grassroots organizations are closer to community and less encumbered by legacy structures, and they have been practicing this work long before big-name foundations codified names for it.

Participatory grantmaking models and community advisory councils have demonstrated stronger trust, higher program uptake, and more durable outcomes because they are shaped by lived experience rather than distant assumptions. Brooklyn Org (formerly Brooklyn Community Foundation) transitioned all its strategic grantmaking, more than $4 million annually, to a fully participatory model in 2021.[26]

Nonprofits are tasked with community building with their constituents *and* their funders. As Tezikiah Gabriel, E.D. of Pathways to Peace, puts it, "I find many NGOs don't realize that the most important successful funding factor is to develop great relationships with your funders. It's easy to ask funders to bend some rules when they know you, trust you, and are advocates for your work." Funders who see themselves as partners in the mission behave differently than funders who see themselves as judges of it.

This shift also means moving beyond the lone heroic executive director. This model is unsustainable and increasingly repels younger leaders. Shared leadership models—co-directorships, lattice structures, staff councils—are emerging in response, particularly among younger and BIPOC (Black, Indigenous, and People of Color) leaders who reject the burnout model their predecessors inherited.[27,28] Leadership, like community, can be distributed rather than concentrated. Both shifts move in the same direction: toward organizations where power, voice, and responsibility are shared. (See Chapter 7 for a range of shared leadership models.)

Build Strategically Within Constraints, and Challenge Them When Needed

Redesign is not all-or-nothing. The temptation is to treat every constraint as fixed and capitulate, or to treat the whole system as illegitimate and fight it everywhere at once. Capitulating changes nothing and fighting every battle burns leaders out before they can create sustainable change. Most constraints in the nonprofit sector are conventions, not rules: grant restrictions can be negotiated, bylaws rewritten, reporting requirements streamlined. The work is knowing which to accept, which to negotiate, and which to challenge in the open.

JobsFirstNYC, a workforce intermediary, received a $4 million unrestricted gift from MacKenzie Scott in 2023, the largest in their history. They were struck not just by the amount but by the absence of restrictions. Rather than treat unrestricted funding as a once-in-a-lifetime windfall, they began advocating publicly for trust-based philanthropy as a sector norm, arguing it's time to move beyond charity optics and into a mindset of philanthropic equity. They worked within the constraint (most of their funding is still restricted) while actively reshaping the constraint itself.[29]

Conclusion: A Redesign to Meet Today's Moment

Across history, social benefit organizations have sparked national reckonings, reshaped policy, and built movements that changed the course of American life. They have set ambitious goals, aligning them with community power and coherent strategy. Today's challenges are every bit as urgent as those that confronted civil rights leaders or HIV/AIDS activists, and the sector remains as capable of meeting them. But its operating system has to evolve to match the moment.

Duane Elgin, author and social visionary, puts it plainly: "The nonprofit world of the past is gone. Organizations built for stability must now become organisms built for agility. It is imperative to be light on our feet, resilient in spirit, and courageous in vision as we move into these turbulent times of great transition. This is not a moment for incremental adjustment—it is a threshold crossing that demands fundamental reimagination of purpose, strategy, and collaboration."

That reimagination is already visible in the organizations throughout this chapter: the Global Fund protecting its lowest-paid staff before the crisis hit, Rockwood tripling its budget on a four-day week, Brooklyn Org handing grantmaking authority to its community, JobsFirstNYC turning one unrestricted gift into a case for changing the rules. Each of these organizations questioned one of our sector's defaults. Now the rest of us—funders, boards, sector leaders, policymakers—have to build the conditions that let more of it take root. Nonprofits have repeatedly shown that when they act boldly, the country moves with them. The conditions are what's missing now—and conditions are something we can build.

Chapter 2

Debunking Myths to Spark Imagination of the Sector

Extraordinary people visualize not what is possible or probable, but rather what is impossible. And by visualizing the impossible, they begin to see it as possible.

—Chérie Carter-Scott

Chapter 1 traced the external conditions and structural incentives that have left the sector running a modern marathon in century-old shoes. This chapter takes up what those conditions have produced inside the sector—the inherited beliefs, internalized assumptions, and operating myths that hold organizations small even when their missions call for more.

Jackie Barger, E.D. of the Children's Smile Center, sums up the nonprofit conundrum, "We are led to think that nonprofits should be poor, needy, and starving. But I don't want my local hospital cutting corners to save money."

It's a simple observation, yet it captures something that decades of nonprofit "professionalization" have failed to resolve. We've built a sector that serves the public good but punishes itself for operating like it matters. Somewhere along the way, the social benefit sector confused austerity with virtue and leaders began to suspect our own ambitions.

The myths this chapter explores are the institutional expression of a deeper scarcity imagination reinforced across society. We ask two questions: What would it take for the sector to *imagine itself differently*? And *who is responsible* for the conditions that make that imagination so hard?

The second question matters because the myths that follow are often described as if nonprofits invented them. It's easier to say that the sector's scarcity imagination is our own failure rather than the predictable conclusion of a system that rewards it. The truth is that responsibility is shared. Social benefit leaders internalize scarcity, but only because our boards enforce it. Donors and broader societal expectations demand it. Watchdogs codify it. And philanthropy—through restricted grants, short cycles, overhead caps, and risk transfer—builds the scaffolding that holds all of it in place.

A Moment of Crisis Is a Moment for Imagination

We are writing this at a moment when democracy itself feels fragile, federal funding for social services is being cut, and long-standing institutions are under strain. Being in a moment of change can often feel like a breakdown. As systems go through deep revisions and institutions fail us, the future feels suddenly precarious.

But history suggests something else: crises are also periods of creativity. When familiar models no longer work and the contours of what comes next are blurry, societies can erupt into acts of collective imagination. We hospice the old ways and midwife the new.

The social good sector has flourished in these imaginative leaps. Labor organizers throughout history thought beyond just bargaining over wages—they imagined a world where workers held power instead of the systems that confined them. Civil rights activists did not demand incremental reforms; they articulated a multiracial democracy that did not yet exist. When Martin Luther King Jr. said in 1964, "I have a dream," he ignited the collective imagination of millions. Movements like these have always been driven by moral courage and the audacity to envision alternatives.

Today, we are again in one of those threshold moments. The scaffolding of social change we're used to—stable structures of funding, predictable politics, and clear boundaries between business, state, and civil sectors—is less reliable. But many public benefit organizations still operate within inherited assumptions about where power lies.

Ruha Benjamin, a scholar of race and technology, tells us how imagination is a necessity to enact change. In *Imagination: A Manifesto*, she shows how imagination is a critical tool for social justice rather than impractical fantasy. She calls for leaders to "imagine and craft the worlds you cannot live without, just as you dismantle the ones you cannot live within."[1] Treating imagination as a political resource, she shows how dominant systems often hide their biases by presenting themselves as natural or inevitable. To imagine otherwise is a form of power: it reveals the assumptions embedded in our institutions and opens space for more just alternatives.[2] Benjamin's argument echoes feminist scholar Riane Eisler's older diagnosis of modern institutions as organized around domination—control, hierarchy, scarcity—rather than partnership, care, and mutuality. In that frame, nonprofit "myths" about austerity look less like best practices and more like artifacts of a worldview that devalues investment in people.[3]

Imagination has long been a survival tool for movements building futures they were excluded from. Generations of Black organizers, thinkers, and writers worked without the assumption that the American Dream was built for them—and so they imagined and built on their own terms, in mutual aid networks, freedom schools, cooperative economies, and artistic works. Octavia Butler's Parable of the Sower is one of that tradition's sharpest expressions. Dropped into an unstable world, Butler's characters survive by improvising new social arrangements and ethics. Imagination, in Butler's reading, is a discipline: a way of figuring out how life might persist when the old structures have nothing left to offer.[4]

Central to this imaginative power is hope for a better way forward. Ann Mei Chang's "big, audacious goals," mentioned in the previous chapter, are themselves expressions of hope: they presume a better future is possible. David Callahan, founder and editor-in-chief of *Inside Philanthropy*, notes: "[Philanthropy] operates from a place of hope. While some donors give with unsavory motives—to seek status, launder their reputations, or advance their bottom line—these are outliers. Most major givers and foundations are driven by a genuine desire to make things better, and by the belief that they can—that their money and time will have a positive impact."

Imagination is a survival tool and a democratic practice. It shapes the operational decisions nonprofits make every day in budgeting, compensating, and building. The myths that follow are the residue of scarcity imagination—the first reflex that assumes reserves should be thin and ambitions contained. To debunk them, we have to refuse the story that nonprofits are meant to stay small.

Debunking Myths That Hold Nonprofits Back

Myths that shape nonprofit practice share a common root: equating virtue with deprivation. Although many of these myths came from a desire to do good, they have stopped serving the sector.

Many of these myths are not created by social benefit organizations but by the philanthropic structures they depend on: restricted funding, short grant cycles, overhead caps, and risk aversion in grantmaking. Writers like Edgar Villanueva (*Decolonizing Wealth*), Anand Giridharadas (*Winners Take All*), and Vu Le (*Reimagining Nonprofits and Philanthropy*) have each argued that the structural incentives of modern philanthropy actively produce the scarcity culture the sector is then blamed for living inside. This power asymmetry—where funders set the terms and nonprofits adapt—is the soil the myths grow in. Any critique of scarcity culture that ignores it is incomplete. See Chapter 6 for more information about funding challenges and opportunities.

Much of the conversation around these myths has been shaped by Dan Pallotta, American entrepreneur, author, and humanitarian activist, whose TED Talk and award-winning film *Uncharitable* argue that the sector's fixation on overhead ratios has constrained nonprofit growth and effectiveness. What matters, Pallotta contends, is not how lean an organization runs but the long-term impact of its work. His work, combined with our own research, readings across the sector, and observations from decades of nonprofit leadership and collaboration with practitioners, has informed the myths we share in this section.

Myth #1: Social Benefit Organizations Shouldn't Make a Profit

Many people hear the word *nonprofit* and take it at face value. Maybe it's because we put the prefix *non* in front of *profit*, we think we should make no profits. If nonprofits exist for public benefit, the thinking goes, surely any money generated beyond immediate program costs is inefficient or cause for suspicion. The assumption here is that any surplus is distributed to organization leaders like in for-profits. But if that was the case, where are the big payouts to investors when nonprofits host a successful gala or Giving Tuesday campaign?

In reality, nonprofits should absolutely generate surplus revenue. The National Council of Nonprofits is explicit on this: surplus is necessary for innovation and sustainability, as long as it is reinvested into mission rather than distributed to owners.[5] If you assume you must break even (or worse, run at a slight loss), you may underinvest in growth, innovation, or building the infrastructure that allows you to scale your mission.

Reality: Nonprofits Should Have Operating Reserves

To thrive rather than merely survive, nonprofits need to reframe how they think about money and educate the donors, funders, and board members who hold the old frame in place.

Many of the leaders we interviewed emphasized how critical it is to reinvest in the organization itself. Without reinvestment, growth stalls. We expect businesses to do this, and the same logic applies here. As Kavita Ramdas notes, the assumption that nonprofits are inherently less professional than for-profits doesn't hold up to scrutiny—many for-profit companies don't operate as efficiently as their reputation suggests.

Language matters when speaking with donors and boards. Instead of *profit*, leaders can use terms like *operating reserves*, *surplus revenue*, or *cash on hand*—language that underscores responsibility rather than greed. A surplus is not a luxury; it is insurance for your mission's longevity. Without it, a single downturn forces layoffs, program cuts, and missed opportunities.

Transparency reinforces that language. Organizations that explain how and why they build reserves earn deeper trust from funders. Rather than budgeting to break even—the "zero-balance trap"—successful organizations intentionally budget for a 3–10% surplus to manage funding risk. Clear, written reserve policies should outline the purpose of funds (such as emergency costs or capacity building), target amounts, and specific conditions under which reserves can be accessed. As Propel Nonprofits notes, reserves "should solve timing problems, not deficit problems"—bridging short-term fluctuations without masking structural imbalances.[6]

However, many foundation grants are restricted to specific programs and explicitly prohibit reserve-building—meaning the sector is told to hold reserves by the same system that prevents most organizations from doing so. While having three to six months of cash reserves is aspirational for the sector overall, it is structurally out of reach for many grassroots and BIPOC-led organizations (with less access to unrestricted capital). Building reserves is not simply a matter of discipline; it is a function of what funders allow. Leaders operating inside tighter constraints should set reserve goals that are ambitious but honest, and name the funding conditions that shape what's possible.[7]

Reserves also don't need to sit idle. A financial professional can help structure investments so they grow over time. Surplus revenue isn't a betrayal of mission; it's the infrastructure that lets mission last. A financial strategy grounded in transparency, reserves, and smart investing moves an organization from reactive to durable.

Reflection Questions for Leaders

- How do our staff, donors, and board currently **think about and pursue surplus revenue**? Can we reframe our financial language to emphasize sustainability rather than scarcity?
- Do we have a **written reserve policy** that clearly defines purpose, target size, and conditions for use, and is it aligned with our risk tolerance and growth goals?

- What steps could we take this year to move from "budgeting to break even" toward **building a strategic surplus and investment plan**?
- Are we considering **budget changes and goals** represented in our strategic plan?
- Will our board **step up their fundraising**?

Myth #2: The Best Organizations Have the Lowest Overhead

Few myths have done more damage than this one. The cultural assumption that all costs other than direct program services are wasteful comes from early charity rating and donor-education frameworks that established the overhead ratio as a simple shorthand for stewardship in the 1990s and 2000s. It was easy to compare: "How much of my dollar goes to 'direct program' versus overhead?"

Research challenges this framing. The *Stanford Social Innovation Review* article "The Nonprofit Starvation Cycle" found that many nonprofits under-report overhead in the hopes of achieving an "ideal" 15–20% spend on overhead. In reality, overhead rates of 17–35% are more realistic—accurately reflecting the need to hire and train staff, fundraise, invest in tools, and market an organization's effectiveness.[8]

The damage of the "overhead myth" is real. Underfunding infrastructure—like staff, tech, and operations—cripples effectiveness. Smart investment in overhead leads to greater efficiency and long-term impact. Overhead costs, such as salaries and administrative expenses, are essential for nonprofits to operate effectively and achieve their goals.

Dan Pallotta argues that overhead ratios tell you almost nothing about a charity's impact. What matters, he contends, are the organization's actual goals and accomplishments—not the size of its budget or what share of it goes to programs versus operations. He rejects the notion that public benefit organizations should be rewarded for minimizing spending on essentials like salaries, rent, and insurance.

Kimberlee Riley of Purposeful Philanthropy Advisors points to the real-world cost of this thinking: organizations with the leanest operations struggled most during the pandemic, with some failing to survive because they were financially starved by donors fixated on low overhead percentages. Donor education and briefings are essential to inform funders about what it costs to run a nonprofit.

The burden of this myth is not evenly distributed. A 2020 study from Echoing Green and the Bridgespan Group found that Black-led organizations had 24% less revenue and 76% less in unrestricted net assets than their white-led counterparts, even when controlling for issue area and leader education level.[9] Add a rigid overhead ceiling on top of that, and the squeeze compounds. The organizations most likely to be under-resourced are also the ones most likely to be penalized for investing in their own infrastructure.

Reality: Overhead Is Essential to Mission

The truth is, what we call *overhead* is simply the infrastructure that allows us to do our work well. "Overhead" encompasses the training that makes staff more effective, the systems that keep us efficient, the marketing that brings in new supporters. Leaders must redefine overhead as capacity to sustain our missions. When we make that shift in mindset and language—from "expenses" to "investments"—we start to see overhead as what it is: the foundation that upholds our mission.

To change the culture around overhead, social impact leaders must be educators. Start with teaching your board and then move to your donors and supporters. We recommend a five-step approach:

1. Sympathize with your supporters' desire to use their resources efficiently toward impact, and align with them that that's your goal too. We're all here to create the greatest impact, whether that be lives saved, trees planted, or students educated.
2. Explain the "overhead myth" and reality. Describe how charity rating systems in the 1990s and 2000s popularized the false idea that "low overhead" equals effectiveness. In reality, nonprofits are likely to spend 17–35% on indirect costs to keep operations running. What's more, different organizations have different needs depending on

impact area—so slapping the same 20% overhead target on all nonprofits is a blanket approach that ignores the variance between different nonprofits' needs.[10]

3. Tell a better story, with better language. Demonstrate impact through examples of organizations that invested in infrastructure and saw improved outcomes. Bridgespan's Pay-What-It-Takes Philanthropy study examined 20 of the most successful nonprofits and found that their indirect costs averaged 40% of total costs—roughly double the figure most donors assume is "acceptable." The takeaway isn't that high overhead causes success; it's that the organizations achieving the greatest impact are typically the ones investing seriously in the infrastructure that makes impact possible. Reframe the conversation from "How low is your overhead?" to "What does it actually take to deliver this work well?"[11]
4. Commit to transparency and iteration. Let board members know that you will open a dialogue on which capacity investments are yielding strong returns and which should be reallocated. Follow up with your board to show examples of your mission infrastructure yielding higher impact.
5. Invest strategically and iterate. Stay judicious about where your dollars go—just because overhead is necessary doesn't mean that *all* overhead is necessary. State-of-the-art videos or glossy brochures might be worthwhile for a national awareness campaign, but if your work is hyper-local, it might be wiser to strengthen your outreach staff or CRM system instead.

Reflection Questions for Leaders

- How do our staff, donors, and board currently think about "overhead"? Where in my organization am I **underspending on capacity** due to outdated beliefs about overhead?
- How can we **better educate the board and staff** about our budget, 990, and distribution of operating expenses?

- How can I **reframe my messaging** to show that "smart spending is smart stewardship"?
- What **data and stories** can I use to show donors and board members the tangible returns of investing in our internal strength?

Myth #3: Social Benefit Work Is a Calling, Not a Career, and Compensation Should Reflect That Sacrifice

This myth treats people as the first line item to cut. Because nonprofits are mission-driven, the reasoning goes, staff should accept lower pay, longer hours, and fewer benefits as the price of doing meaningful work. Three forces keep the myth in place: a cultural reflex that treats charity as time donated rather than labor compensated, donor and watchdog pressure to keep overhead low, and competition for scarce funding that pushes organizations to squeeze labor costs first.

Unfortunately, this mindset leads to burnout and high turnover. According to a 2023 survey from the National Council for Nonprofits, 75% of nonprofits have reported job vacancies, with the leading reasons being salary competition and budget constraints or insufficient funds.[12] So many nonprofit staff are underpaid with no career ladder or bonus options. Competitive compensation is critical as it attracts talent and ensures sustainability.

The public benefit workforce skews heavily female and is disproportionately staffed by people of color in direct-service roles—the very roles most likely to be underpaid. When the sector normalizes sacrifice as a professional virtue, it is not asking everyone to sacrifice equally. It is asking those with the least institutional power to subsidize the sector with their wages and well-being.

And the sacrifice is structurally enforced. The funding architecture described in Chapter 1—restricted grants that exclude staff time, short cycles that prevent long-term hiring, the cultural expectation that mission work should cost less—holds salaries down by design.

Many nonprofits assume they can fill labor gaps with unpaid volunteers. Volunteers can be enormously valuable, but they are not a substitute for consistent staff. Volunteer engagement carries real—and often unfunded—costs, including training, supervision, and turnover. Volunteers may also lack the specialized expertise or long-term availability required for complex work. Volunteers can be short-term and juggling their own priorities, making them an unreliable substitute for paid roles. When nonprofits underinvest in staff, they weaken the very capacity they depend on.

This was underscored in our conversation with Dr. Michael Ziccardi, executive director at One Health Institute at UC Davis, who challenged the assumption that altruism alone can sustain nonprofit labor. He described how both employees and volunteers increasingly need tangible returns for their time and energy:

> *"People are stretched already—and especially for. . .volunteers, people are struggling to get by as a whole. So if they're going to spend time assisting in those ways, they need to feel like they're getting something out of it."*

Ziccardi's insight reflects a broader reality: when nonprofits treat labor as something that should be cheap or free, they erode their own capacity.

Reality: We Should Invest in Our People

Compensation is not tied to personal virtue. It is a strategic lever that determines the consistency and quality of your impact. When government-led or for-profit hospitals, schools, or social service agencies underpay staff, outcomes collapse. Nonprofit organizations are no different. Research has repeatedly shown that competitive pay leads to stronger program results, lower turnover, and higher continuity of care. Reducing turnover also yields better financial outcomes: the Washington Center for Equitable Growth has found that turnover costs represent 39.6% of a position's annual wage.[13] Paying people fairly is not indulgent; it is ethical, strategic, and mission-critical.

To shift this mindset, leaders must treat staffing as a core component of organizational strategy. Many successful models blend paid professionals and volunteers with intentionality. Volunteers can bring extraordinary value, especially in advocacy, community connections, and project-based support. The Independent Sector, with the Do Good Institute at the University of Maryland, releases the value of volunteers every year—by April 2025, they updated it to an estimated value of $34.79 per volunteer hour, with variances by state.[14] But volunteers cannot replace the accountability and expertise of trained staff, and managing them well requires significant coordination, training, and oversight—hidden costs that are rarely calculated. For this reason, mobilizing volunteers is not always advisable for small nonprofits that lack the staff capacity to support them.

Effective organizations draw clear lines: staff hold sensitive responsibilities (client and donor information, compliance, financial management, program leadership), while volunteers amplify the mission through roles that align with community voice, passion, and skill. The strongest models are not volunteer-heavy; they are volunteer-smart.

Social impact leaders must confidently make the case for talent investment to supporters who may still hold outdated beliefs about "lean overhead." Push back with data: Bridgespan's Pay-What-It-Takes research, which shows that underfunding staff and infrastructure restricts growth and often harms long-term outcomes.[15] Audit your staffing needs regularly: Which roles require additional investment? Which positions are chronically stretched thin? What skill gaps are slowing down impact? Hold open, honest conversations with your board and team about which labor investments are yielding strong ROI and which are not.

Reflection Questions for Leaders

1. Where have I internalized the belief that **"doing more with less" is virtuous**, and how has that shaped my staffing decisions?
2. Which functions in my organization require **professional expertise**, and where can **volunteers** meaningfully (and sustainably) amplify our mission?

3. How can we **implement or expand training** to increase the effectiveness of our staff and volunteers?
4. How can I have more **effective conversations with my board** to determine where staffing is providing strong ROI, and where it isn't?

Myth #4: Nonprofits Shouldn't Invest in Their Growth Through Expenses Like Marketing, Innovation, or Strategic Planning

Olivia Dodd, executive director of Amplifi Napa Valley, describes this myth as she speaks about a previous organization she led: "We were constantly just trying to survive. And if we did something that didn't work, it was a big deal because we were such a small organization and our reputation was so fragile."

The myth says nonprofits should avoid "business-like" investments—strategic planning, marketing, scaling—and simply deliver programs. The reality Dodd names is what that looks like on the ground: an organization too fragile to risk growing.

It's rooted in a purity narrative: that social benefit organizations are mission entities and that investing in growth is self-interest. Donors often implicitly prefer organizations that appear modest over those intentionally scaling. And the overhead myth compounds the problem: if operations are already suspect, growth spending is doubly so.

This pressure lands differently depending on where you sit. Large, well-networked NGOs have the relationships and unrestricted revenue to fund strategic planning, rebrands, and new systems without asking permission. Grassroots and community-rooted organizations usually do not. They are asked to compete for impact against organizations with ten times their growth budget—and then judged for not growing fast enough.

The short grant cycles laid out in Chapter 1 compound this. An innovative program that fails is a learning opportunity in the private sector and a reputational risk in the nonprofit sector—because funders have historically penalized failure rather than funded it. Risk gets transferred from those who can afford it to those who cannot.

The consequences are tangible. Without spending on marketing, nonprofits fade into the background and their impact goes unseen. Without strategic planning, they flounder, failing to pick a cohesive path forward. Coaching helps leaders stay on target, so capacity building and staff growth deserve a line in the budget too.

Dennis M. Robinson, philanthropic strategist, notes that the sector must move beyond "philosophies of poverty, mentalities of stagnant safety," because you cannot problem-solve while standing still.

Reality: Investing in Growth Is Key to Driving Scalable Impact

Nonprofit leaders often internalize the idea that investing in strategy or marketing is evidence of mission drift. But the opposite is true: strategic investment accelerates mission impact. High-performing nonprofits operate more like learning organizations than lean charities, using planning and investment to drive better outcomes.

High-performing nonprofits invest in or find in-kind support for the following:

- Strategic planning
- Innovative programs that might fail
- High-powered tools and technology systems that increase productivity
- Leadership development, including coaching, training, education, and conferences
- Up-to-date branding, marketing, and communications
- The latest fundraising systems and tools
- Data and decision-making capacity
- Retreats to realign strategy or build space for rest together
- Annual development and marketing

Effective strategic planning is one of the highest-leverage investments a nonprofit can make. In the words of the Bridgespan Group, "Strategy is all about getting critical resource decisions right."[16] If those big decisions are incorrect, organizations can waste months spinning wheels across incoherent priorities or being overly reactive to feedback. Done well, strategic planning reduces internal friction, improves the use of limited resources, strengthens alignment between board and staff, and frees up leaders to spend more time on high-impact activities instead of constant crisis management. It also impacts how donors view the underlying strength and direction of an organization.

Investment in branding and marketing is also essential. Public benefit organizations that have invested in improving their branding and design in the last two years are 50% more likely to have increased fundraising revenue compared to those that did not.[17] This is another instance where reluctance to invest stems from inherited beliefs about immorality. While nonprofits' missions may be different from businesses, the management tools needed to deliver that mission are not.

Reflection Questions for Leaders

- Does my organization have a **strategic plan** and a realistic time frame for revisiting it and monitoring progress in Board and staff meetings? If we have a strategic plan, how well is it serving us?
- What is my nonprofit's **marketing reach**, and how is our **brand** perceived? Is there room to improve branding and marketing?
- How would our impact grow if we treated **strategic investment** as mission-critical rather than optional?
- Are our staff, board and volunteer **job descriptions** up to date?

Myth #5: Bigger Means Better

Is a bigger nonprofit a better one? This myth holds that large organizations are inherently more effective than smaller ones—that scale equals impact, mirroring the corporate growth model. Scaling is celebrated in social innovation discourse, and donors assume that bigger organizations that have more resources, are more professional, are more efficient, and therefore "better."

Beneath this sits a broader illusion: we equate more with better. More revenue, more staff, more people served, more impact. Success becomes synonymous with quantitative output.

Yet the pursuit of "more" often distracts from the deeper question: Are we actually making meaningful change? In philanthropy, this can lead to chasing metrics that are easy to count but shallow in significance—number of meals distributed, number of students enrolled, number of community events, etc. These metrics may reflect volume but not necessarily transformation. Depth, sustainability, empowerment, and justice are harder to measure and therefore often ignored.

Kavita Ramdas notes that nonprofits have absorbed the capitalist notion that "unless you're growing, you're dying," but this growth mindset can lead organizations to prioritize their own survival over their original mission to advance a cause. Joshua Korn, chief development officer at Resurge International, agrees, "Sometimes it can be easy to fall into a trap of 'growth for the sake of growth,' where growth becomes the only true measure of success. . . . The whole organization is so focused on growth that the quality and impact of the programs is ignored."

This pressures nonprofits to scale prematurely or superficially. When we scale, we need to ensure that staffing and financial needs are adequately in place. Instead of focusing on the richness of outcomes, such as how communities were strengthened and what systemic barriers were addressed, organizations may be incentivized to inflate numbers. The more metrics grow, the more "successful" they appear, whether or not the work is actually impactful.

There is also an equity dimension to name. When "scale" becomes the dominant measure of success, the organizations best positioned to claim it are those with the largest existing infrastructure—which, in the nonprofit sector, correlates tightly with historical access to wealth and networks. Community-rooted organizations often do their most important work through depth rather than breadth: trust built slowly, relationships sustained over years, cultural knowledge that does not easily translate into metrics.

A sector that only rewards bigness systematically undervalues the work most likely to reach the communities it claims to serve.

Funders drive this dynamic as much as nonprofits do. Grant programs that ask the question, "How many people will you reach?" reward breadth by design. When the metric itself is set by the funder, the pressure to scale is not really about mission—it is about translating community work into language philanthropy is willing to fund.

True social impact is not just about getting bigger. It is about getting more clear, knowing your priorities well enough to be transformative.

Reality: Scale Doesn't Always Denote Impact

The belief that large nonprofits are inherently more effective often comes from conflating visibility with impact. Bigger organizations have more staff, more polished communications, and more sophisticated fundraising engines, which creates the appearance of more effectiveness. But impact is not a function of organizational size. Research consistently shows that many of the most innovative, high-trust, and community-responsive organizations operate on small or modest budgets. In fact, nearly 90% of nonprofits operate with annual budgets less than $500,000.[18] These organizations often succeed because they are nimble and deeply rooted in community relationships—qualities that large institutions sometimes struggle to maintain as they scale.

Julia Roig, founder of Horizons, cautioned that the pressure to demonstrate impact on large numbers of people often leads public benefit organizations to spread themselves too thin, undermining their actual effectiveness and impact. Nonprofits can "get better without getting bigger," challenging the business-derived growth model that dominates the sector's thinking about success and impact. She discussed "scaling deep" as an alternative approach to measuring nonprofit impact, challenging the conventional wisdom that organizations must continuously scale up and reach more people.

So the challenge is not to become big but to become effective. Effectiveness comes from delivering sustainable impact that is aligned with the actual needs of the people you serve. And to understand those needs, community trust must be built gradually. In fact, rapid growth without intentional grounding in the community of beneficiaries can erode your impact. The right size for your mission is the one that best enables sustainability and empowerment among the people you serve.

Define what *impact* means for you. Metrics matter, but they must be chosen with care. Quantitative indicators (e.g., numbers of people reached, services delivered) are useful but incomplete; they need to be balanced with qualitative measures that reflect deeper outcomes—trust, belonging, empowerment, capacity building, community leadership, long-term change.

Reflection Questions for Leaders

- What metrics am I measuring, and do these **metrics reflect genuine change** or just motion? What deeper indicators should matter for our mission?
- What **advantages** does our current size give us, and how can we strategically leverage those strengths?
- If we were to grow, what **safeguards or investments** would we need to ensure that scale strengthens (rather than weakens) our community connection and impact?
- What do we need and what are **our priorities** for administration, finance, development, marketing, social media program and leadership?

These five myths aren't just misleading. They actively hold nonprofits back from adapting to a changing world. By internalizing them, organizations end up cutting off their own capacity for innovation and long-term impact.

This is by no means an exhaustive list of myths; there are many others. But these myths all share a common root: they equate virtue with deprivation. After years of operating inside that logic, something predictable happens: leaders internalize it. The scarcity stops being a budget problem and becomes a posture. You start believing your exhaustion is evidence of your commitment. That means the redesign cannot stop at budgets and staffing models. It has to include the leaders themselves.

The Leader as a Human: We Bring Ourselves into the Work

Chapter 1 made the case that leadership underinvestment is structural. But the redesign cannot stop at structures. Social benefit leaders are drawn to this work because of our high capacity to give—to take care of others and promote the public good. That capacity is real and worth honoring. It is also where many of the sector's myths take up residence most quietly. The pathway toward sustainable giving runs through understanding our place inside the systems we are trying to change.

Prentis Hemphill, in *What It Takes to Heal: How Transforming Ourselves Can Change the World*, offers a resonant lens for nonprofit and philanthropic leaders. They argue that healing is not only a personal or therapeutic project but a collective practice that shapes how power is held, how conflict is navigated, and how communities endure. As Hemphill writes, "It's through an orientation toward healing and repair for ourselves and others that we recover our capacity for feeling, for relationship, and, with that, the ability to strengthen our bonds and work together."

Hemphill's stories make this tangible. They describe organizers who, under intense pressure, learned to slow down, listen to their bodies, and set boundaries. These actions help leaders take a moment to pause and reorient strategically. In one account, a movement leader realizes that their habit of overworking was unintentionally reproducing the same extractive patterns they were fighting against; by changing how they cared for themselves, they also changed how their team related to one another.

Crucially, Hemphill challenges the myth of the lone heroic leader. "There is a difference between visions that come out of the most individualistic tendencies and those that arise when we are able to admit that we need other people."[19] Hemphill reminds us: your power does not come from being self-sufficient but from your capacity to be in genuine, interdependent relationships. When leaders transform their relationship to themselves with compassion, they simultaneously transform what is possible for their organizations and movements.

Movement strategist Maurice Mitchell, in his article "Building Resilient Organizations," has observed that movements can stumble when leaders unintentionally replicate internal patterns of domination. Read in a hopeful light, this is not a verdict—it is a roadmap. It suggests that when leaders become more self-aware, transparent, and accountable, they can model the kinds of relationships and power dynamics they want to see in the world. Your own growth can become a catalyst for organizational and movement-wide change.[20]

Bringing our whole selves to leadership often means reclaiming what we were taught to set aside. For leaders of color particularly, that can include something as fundamental as play. We spoke with Nikki Dinh, executive director of Leadership Learning Community (LLC). "Many [of our leaders] have talked about growing up and being told not to play at a very young age," she told us, "and so this is a reclamation as well." As Nikki explains, many leaders of color are forced to mature early, learning from a very young age how to navigate and respond to systems. This skill makes them highly effective today.

But that maturity often comes at the cost of rest and play. LLC's work on adaptive leadership treats reclaiming those capacities as essential. Rest, play, and reflection keep leaders curious and resilient, allowing them to navigate complexity.

None of us comes to the work of social change fully healed, enlightened, or built out of steel. To redesign is to evolve from within our own capacities. We are part of the redesign. As we evolve how we lead, we make new kinds of structures possible.

The invitation of this moment is not just to redesign nonprofits but to grow alongside them: becoming the kinds of leaders who can bring a more just, collaborative, and imaginative sector into being.

Who Is Responsible for Changing This?

The truest answer is: everyone who participates in the system. Nonprofit leaders can stop apologizing for operating budgets, reserves, and paying competitive salaries. Boards can stop treating austerity as stewardship. Donors can stop rewarding the leanest organizations and start asking what full-cost funding would actually look like. Funders can shorten the distance between their rhetoric on equity and the terms of their grant agreements. And all of us—as a society that relies on the public benefit sector to hold what markets and governments will not—can stop expecting it to do that work on a diet of scraps.

The good news is that many of these myths and structures are beginning to shift. Trust-based philanthropy is gaining ground, and multiyear general operating support is no longer a fringe practice. The starvation cycle has a name now, and naming it was the first step toward breaking it. The work ahead is to accelerate that shift—and to insist that responsibility for scarcity culture sits with all of the actors who built it, not only with the nonprofits who live inside it.

The nonprofit sector does not need to apologize for its ambition. For too long, social benefit organizations have been treated as auxiliary to markets and government—expected to do more with less and to remain modest in their aims. But nonprofits are where moral imagination and collective action actually meet. They are where communities experiment, where care gets organized, where new possibilities are rehearsed before they become policy or culture. In a moment when old models are faltering, that role is not peripheral. It is central.

Every redesign begins with a meaningful shift: giving ourselves permission to believe that things could work differently—and that we deserve systems built to let us thrive. In each of the chapters that follow, we offer that invitation: to play, to heal, to create, and to be with one another in new ways. We invite you to challenge the status quo, to do your best, to experiment, and to fail in the service of learning. Above all, we extend an invitation to imagine boldly and discover what comes next—for your organizations, for your communities, and for our sector.

Who is Responsible for Changing This?

Chapter 3

Impacting the Great Transfer of Leadership and Wealth

"We are living through a time of great reckoning as wealth and leadership pass into my generation's hands. I believe that wealth inequality, racial violence, and climate chaos are not the final chapter of our families' legacies — something else is struggling to be born."

—Morgan Curtis, Donor Organizer, Solidaire Network

America stands at the edge of the largest intergenerational transfer of wealth in its history. Nearly $125 trillion in assets is expected to move from older generations to younger ones over the next two decades, though rising health care costs for elders will reduce that figure some[1]. Advisors often describe this as a financial event, yet it is much more. It is a transfer of power and wisdom that will be transformational for those who inherit and those whose lives they touch. It is a transfer of power and wisdom that will be transformational for those who inherit and those whose lives they touch.

Trillions of dollars have been accumulating in retirement accounts, investment portfolios, and housing assets. This wealth was built over decades to support aging parents, offset health care costs, sustain families, and provide for the next generation. As that wealth transfers, so does the power to decide where it goes.

Will these resources sustain the current wealth divide, or flow toward something more impactful—affordable housing, the arts, public health, environmental protection, racial and social justice? These are real challenges that resources and collective will have the power to solve.

But whether that wealth reaches the public benefit sector depends on something most organizations and families are still learning to cultivate: intentionally designed leadership that welcomes the next generation in. When elders open the door, offering their wisdom and institutional memory instead of gatekeeping, younger people come to see nonprofits as legitimate destinations for their wealth and energy. The wealth will move regardless. The question is whether it moves through civil society or around it, into the peer-led funds, donor-advised funds, direct giving platforms, and family offices that are already building parallel systems.

Without an intentional hand off that includes planning and intergenerational dialogue, risks compound. Wealth may concentrate without community accountability. Leadership may calcify while younger generations disengage. Civil society may weaken not through any single failure but through a slow erosion of relevance.

The Great Wealth Transfer is a transfer of legitimacy, and legitimacy is not inherited automatically. Institutions that share authority across generations will be the ones still standing when the transfer is complete. This is not a moment for symbolic inclusion: it is a moment for intentional redesign.

The Leadership Transition: Building Bridges Across Generations

The coming wealth transfer coincides with a significant leadership transition. Executive directors from the Silent Generation and Baby Boomer cohorts are retiring in large numbers, and the wealth accumulated by those same generations is beginning to move. These two transfers will shape the nonprofit sector for decades. Whether they strengthen it or sow more division depends on a question many organizations haven't taken a step back to answer: Can the sector build genuine bridges across the generations it contains and serves?

Research consistently shows high levels of cause engagement among Gen Z and Millennials. Many volunteer, donate small amounts online, and organize digitally. But few are entering formal governance roles or executive pathways. According to BoardSource, Millennials and Gen Zers hold less than 17% of nonprofit board seats—despite representing a large share of the social benefit workforce.[2]

For nonprofits to welcome in the next generation's wealth, they must first become places where the next generation sees a meaningful role. Enacting this shift is difficult.

Why Are Intergenerational Bridges Hard to Build?

Traditional news and social media often frame generational tension disparagingly. Millennials are the "Me Me Me Generation." Gen Z is described through a variety of afflictions: loneliness, apathy, digital addiction. In return, Millennials and Gen Zers retort to older generations, "OK, Boomer." These labels create buzz but sow division and oversimplify what is actually happening.

Millennials and Gen Z have come of age in a radically different context, and they often value collaboration and transparency over hierarchy. They expect workplace conditions of diversity, mental health awareness, and equitable compensation. The "entitlement" label often applied to them is a signal that work structures designed for an earlier era no longer match present realities.

But the inverse is also true: younger generations don't always listen to elders. Jan Masaoka, co-chair of the Philanthropy Project, notes that each generation tends to create new organizations rather than take over existing ones: "The sector evolves—every generation reinvents the public benefit sector. And one of the things in that reinvention is they don't listen to the previous generation."

Younger leaders sometimes read traditional processes as resistance when they are actually the result of hard-won judgment. The elders who built the field know things about sustaining organizations through decades of volatility that can't be absorbed from a distance. Bridges are hard to build not because one generation is right and the other is wrong, but because each often values its own viewpoint over the kind of exchange that requires both sides to listen.

Melanie Greenberg of Humanity United describes the posture this requires:

> *"I'm sitting, I hope humbly, where I am in my early 60s, knowing how much I have to learn from every decade of the people that I work with. . . we have to learn from each other. Because the skills and views that people are bringing right from college—it has to be an exchange. It can't just be, 'okay, we've got the leadership reins now, you can have your turn later.' A lot of younger generations don't want to be told how to do things. They're coming in with very strong views about their work-life balance, what's appropriate, what the lines are between their work and their personal values—that we really have to listen to, and that can shape our fields in really important ways."*

Generational Values at a Glance

Exchange starts with understanding what each generation brings. The benefit, as with any form of diversity, is the chance to apply different lenses to the same problems. Understanding generational differences gives organizations a foundation to ask. Who is not engaged? How can we reach populations not yet included? How can we build bridges across ages?

While there are many commonalities, each generation enters social benefit work with a slightly different set of values:

Generation	Birth Years	Ages in 2025	U.S. Population	Common Values and Perspectives
Silent	1928–1945	80–97	15 million	Values duty, tradition, and institutional knowledge

Generation	Birth Years	Ages in 2025	U.S. Population	Common Values and Perspectives
Boomers	1946–1964	61–79	67 million	Brings optimism, confidence, and focus on work
Gen X	1965–1980	45–60	66 million	Pragmatic and serves as a bridge between analog traditions and digital culture
Millennials	1981–1996	29–44	74 million	Focus on collaboration and purpose-driven leadership
Gen Z	1997–2012	13–28	71 million	Demands authenticity, justice, and mental health awareness in leadership
Gen Alpha	2013–2026	0–12	47 million	Will push leadership toward even deeper tech integration and global thinking

[3]*Note:* the population count is not 100% as those few Americans born before 1928 fall outside this chart.

Presence Is Not Power: The Trap of Tokenism

When organizations recognize the need for intergenerational engagement, they typically reach for the most visible structures: junior boards, youth advisory councils, or adding a single young person to a long-standing board. These can be either real intergenerational infrastructure or symbolic holding spaces that signal inclusion without sharing power.

Often, young staff are positioned as implementers rather than co-designers, left out of strategic conversations even when they have real insight to contribute. Youth advisory councils may convene monthly without budget authority, tinkering around the edges of the work. Junior boards often lack clear governance pathways. Over time, this mismatch produces predictable outcomes: rising leaders disengaging from traditional pathways to leadership.

To test whether your intergenerational structures are real or symbolic, ask the following: Who sets the agenda? Who controls the budget? Who has decision rights? Who is mentored, and who is mentoring? Who is compensated fairly, and who is expected to contribute out of passion alone?

If the answers don't include all generations' voices, the structure is likely performative. Young people can tell the difference. This is why symbolic inclusion accelerates the disengagement it was designed to prevent.

What It Looks Like to Build Real Bridges

> *"How can we wholeheartedly offer the next generation our support, mentorship, resourcefulness, and faith in their innovations, dreams, values, and visions? Can we support them to be changemakers and dreammakers, partners and leaders in transforming the nonprofit sector?"*
>
> *—Anonymous parent and family foundation founder*

Designing intergenerational pathways begins with a clear-eyed recognition: eagerness is not preparedness. Many emerging leaders are ready to engage with public benefit and philanthropic leadership, but they may not arrive through the channels older generations took. Younger adults are less likely to inherit civic networks through religious institutions or long-standing community organizations. They may feel out of place at formal fundraising galas. They often seek peer cohorts and mentorship spaces that feel collaborative rather than hierarchical. If institutions want the next generation in the room, the room itself has to be designed for them.

The following commitments share a common logic. They move beyond symbolic gestures and promote real shifts in authority, resources, and relationships.

- **Shared leadership models.** Co-directorship, rotating committee leadership, and distributed executive structures allow authority to be held intergenerationally in real time, rather than transferred in sequence. These models also make executive roles more sustainable: the challenge in the sector is not a shortage of capable leaders but that fewer rising professionals view the traditional executive director role as livable. (See more examples in Chapter 7.)
- **Equitable, inclusive workplace cultures.** For younger generations, diversity, fair pay, mental health awareness, and active attention to burnout are baseline conditions, not aspirations. Organizations that treat them as such will stand out as authentic, mission-driven employers.
- **Competitive compensation, including paid entry points.** Internships and early-career roles must provide living wages and benefits. If nonprofit careers are accessible only to those with independent means, leadership diversity will remain constrained—and the bridge between generations will be built only by those who can afford to cross it. Compensation is also where younger staff most clearly read whether stated values match operating reality.
- **Two-way mentorship.** Structured cross-generational mentorship strengthens confidence, builds continuity, and reshapes the assumption that wisdom flows in one direction. One young staff member put it simply: "Having an elder in my corner has meant everything. I've been exposed to nonprofits my mentor cared about too, and I have met so many new people. It accelerates the learning and feels a lot less lonely." Senior staff who learn from younger colleagues also stay closer to the cultural and technological shifts reshaping the field.

- **Protected professional development.** Better hiring, onboarding, training, and coaching matters, and budgets should reflect that. Too often, a line item for professional development exists on paper but goes unspent or is allocated without input from staff.
- **Visibility for emerging leaders.** The contributions of younger staff and community leaders deserve public recognition. Visibility tells the next wave of talent the door is open.
- **Technology integrated as infrastructure.** Digital storytelling, data platforms, and emerging tools belong in daily operations, not in a separate "innovation" silo. Younger staff often arrive with fluency; building infrastructure around it turns generational difference into operational strength.

One young staff member described what commitment to these principles looked like in their organization:

> *"The organization said they wanted to bring more young people into their nonprofit. But when I arrived, I was the only one. Most of the leaders were in their late forties and fifties, and there was a real undercurrent of adultism—mostly unconscious, but very present. I suggested we bring in someone from Youth on Board or an experienced intergenerational coach to lead a training. I had my own biases and resistance toward older people, but I shared the love of the mission, so it was valuable to learn together. After two training sessions, the organization committed to recruiting three more young people and preparing two of them to serve on the board and on committees. I helped lead that change, and it felt wonderful. I was far less isolated."*
>
> — *Anonymous youth leader*

Building Intergenerational Boards

Boards are traditionally seen as the "older and wiser" cohort that drives public benefit organizations forward. But governance improves when younger community members, wealth holders, and activists bring urgency, digital fluency, and comfort with shared power into conversation with elders' institutional knowledge, donor relationships, and hard-won judgment. The result is not just better decisions but a stronger civic culture.

Some organizations have been building this infrastructure for decades. The Encampment for Citizenship, founded in 1946, works with youth ages 15 to 18, pairing social justice training with intergenerational alumni networks that have followed young people into careers in public service and activism for generations. Youth on Board, which operated for more than 20 years out of Boston, was a leader in training young people for civic leadership and challenging adultism in institutions. New initiatives like Saint Paul's Youth on Boards program are now picking up the thread, placing young people on city boards and commissions where they help shape decisions about transportation, parks, and public safety.[4,5]

But recruitment alone won't solve the problem if the culture isn't ready to receive new members. Ageism on nonprofit boards is real, and it cuts in both directions. The same dynamics show up around gender, race, class, disability, and professional background. Diversity is not just a value statement—it is what makes governance effective.

The following actionable steps can help pave the pathway to intergenerational governance:

- **Recruit beyond the usual pools.** Boards that draw from the same networks year after year reproduce the same demographics and blind spots. Intentional outreach through young professional networks and nontraditional pipelines is what makes generational diversity possible.
- **Start the pipeline before 18.** The legal threshold for voting membership is 18, but readiness is built earlier. Paid training and roles with stipends for 16- to 18-year-olds, modeled on programs like YOB, build the confidence effective governance requires.
- **Create governance pathways with real authority.** Junior boards, advisory councils, and associate roles must come with decision rights over budgetary items and clear timelines for advancement to voting membership.

- **Build financial and philanthropic literacy across the board.** Investment strategy, impact finance, and nonprofit financials are not specialist knowledge—they are the foundation of fiduciary responsibility. Onboarding should equip every member to engage with them confidently.
- **Plan succession as a process, not a single event.** Successful transitions take time and investment to maintain institutional memory and trust. The Women's Foundation of California structured a six-month overlap between outgoing and incoming executive directors, documenting the transition and investing in continuity across staff, board, and funders. The handoff strengthened the organization rather than destabilizing it.
- **Hold the line on diversity, even when it's contested.** Political pressure has made some boards and funders hesitate on equity commitments. Holding the line matters for the communities served and for the credibility of the institution itself.
- **Address ageism in both directions.** Strong boards name these dynamics directly and design a culture that resists both.

Elders as Stewards, Not Gatekeepers

There is a phrase you hear often from experienced leaders in the social sector: "I grew because I had mentors—and because I mentored others." In many cultures, this has been understood through the figure of the auntie, the grandmother, the elder sought out for perspective and the weight of lived experience. These serve as durable sources of wisdom.

And yet the social impact sector, for all its rhetoric about inclusion, rarely makes formal space for elders. Many organizations depend heavily on older volunteers in practice, but few have created intentional roles on boards, in strategic planning, or at convenings that honor what elders bring. There is rarely a seat at the table designated for the person with the longest view.

That is beginning to change. Initiatives like the Elder Academy are training experienced leaders to serve as mentors and advisors in structured ways. The premise is simple: elders add depth, and their involvement should be designed for, not left to chance. This means asking practical questions. Do elders need transportation support or stipends to participate? Is the technology accessible—larger fonts, printed materials, a patient guide through unfamiliar platforms? Genuine inclusion requires accommodation.

Intergenerational power-sharing is a mutual transfer. Elders can teach what experience built, while younger leaders bring what experience can't yet see. The goal is collaboration that treats both presence and perspective as resources too valuable to waste.

Stephanie Roth, principal at Klein and Roth Consulting, names this dynamic directly:

> *"As old people, there tends to be a feeling. . . 'the younger generation, they don't ask us enough questions'. . . And while I share some of that feeling sometimes, I also think it has to be mutual. We have to show an interest in them—what are their ideas, what's their lived experience that they're bringing to it? And then I think there could be more mutuality, because I think there's a lot that can be learned from us, and we still have a lot to learn from the people coming after us."*

Kim Klein, author and lecturer at UC Berkeley, adds, "We don't want them to do it the way we did it. We want them to bring their new innovations and their new ideas."

The Wealth Transition: What Families and Inheritors Face

With those leadership conditions in place, we can turn to the wealth transfer itself and to the families and individuals navigating it.

The Scale and Shape of the Transition

To rank among the wealthiest 3% of American households in 2024, you would need a net worth of roughly \$4–\$6 million. The top 1% now hold nearly a third of all household assets. This represents wealth concentration at its highest level since the Second World War. Of the country's roughly 173 million households, 5.2 million sit in the top 3%—a population large enough to reshape American giving, if adequately supported.[6]

But wealth in America is not evenly held. It is concentrated overwhelmingly in white households, as Table 3.1 and Figure 3.1 show.

Table 3.1 U.S. Median Household Wealth by Race/Ethnicity[a]

Race/Ethnicity	Percent of Total U.S. Population In 2022, 2025	Median Household Net Worth (USD)	Relative to White Households
Asian[a]	5.9%, 6.7%	\$536,000	~1.9× White median wealth
White (non-Hispanic)	58.9%, 57.5%	\$284,300	Baseline
Other/Native American/ Multiracial	4.1%, 2.1%	~\$60,000	~20% of White wealth
Hispanic/Latino	19.1%, 20%	\$62,100	~22% of White wealth
Black/African American	12%, 13%	\$44,100	~15% of White wealth

Federal Reserve SCF 2022 Estimates.

[a] Board of Governors of the Federal Reserve System (2023) *Survey of Consumer Finances 2022.* Washington, DC: Federal Reserve; U.S. Census Bureau (2025) *QuickFacts: United States.* Washington, DC: U.S. Census Bureau. Available at: https://www.federalreserve.gov/econres/scfindex.htm and https://www.census.gov/quickfacts/fact/table/US/PST045224 (accessed 24 May 2026).

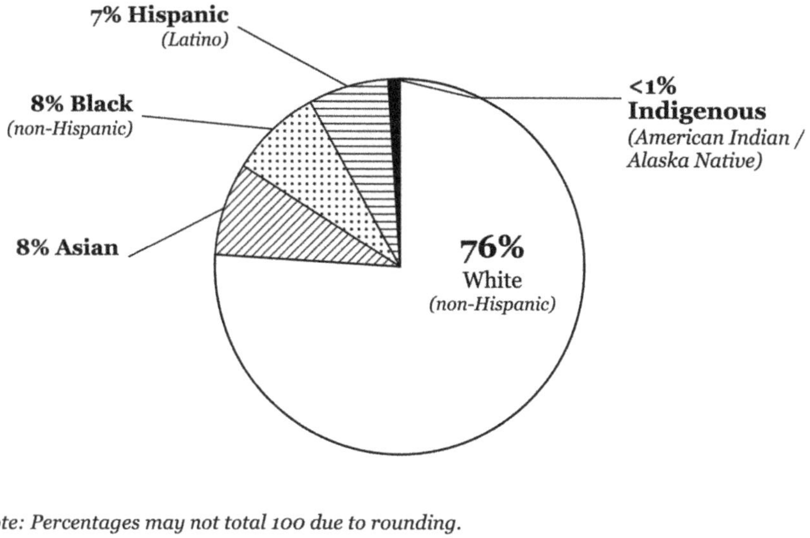

Figure 3.1 U.S. households with net worth over $1 million by race/ethnicity. Percent of U.S. millionaire households. Note: Percentages may not total 100 due to rounding[7]

People of color are steadily building income and assets, but most donor learning communities still draw less than 5–10% of their participants from communities of color, often concentrated among staff, presenters, or activist funders. Even donors and leaders of color deeply committed to redistribution can find these spaces uncomfortable—being among wealth holders as someone with less of it, or with a different relationship to it, is its own kind of isolation.

This matters strategically as well as ethically. Donors and leaders of color bring relationships and grassroots wisdom that make grantmaking more community informed. Many also prefer to give through circles of peers who share their cultural or racial background, where listening and trust come more naturally. Both impulses—joining mixed spaces and forming peer ones—should be supported.

The Inheritor's Experience

The wealth transfer arrives in many different forms, at different moments, for different people. Inheritors receive investable assets at varied times, often after their parents' passing, but sometimes earlier via a trust (for some families, this may mean portions given to inheritors at ages 25, 30, 35, to encourage earlier opportunities to learn about the responsibilities of having, investing, and sharing wealth). Retirees receive distributions when they retire, or at age 72 when required minimum distributions from tax-advantaged accounts begin. And then there can be unexpected windfalls: a gift from an aunt, a collection of art or antique quilts inherited from a friend.

For new inheritors, the money rarely arrives in a vacuum. It comes freighted with questions—practical, ethical, and deeply personal—often at a moment of grief, when a parent or grandparent has just died.

The practical questions alone can be overwhelming. Should I start a business? Buy a home? Set money aside for children I may not yet have? Stay with my family's financial advisor or find my own? Keep working? Hire a planner? What's the maximum I can give away while still benefiting from tax advantages?

Then come the social questions, which can feel even harder. Should I tell anyone? If I grew up working class, what does it mean to be perceived as wealthy in America now? How do I respond when people ask for loans or donations before I've had time to think? Should I give anonymously to protect relationships—or openly, to model generosity?

And beneath all of it, deeply personal questions: How much is enough to keep? What legacy do I want to leave? How do I find people I trust to help me think this through?

Suddenly, an inheritance that looks from the outside like pure good fortune reveals itself as a tangle of decisions and responsibilities. The money may arrive all at once, but learning what to do with it is the work of years.

For nonprofits, next-generation retirees and inheritors are a welcome new stream of potential partners. They have cash flow, excess wealth, and relationships with others of means; with training and support, they can become lead multiyear funders once they see the impact of the work and its alignment with their giving or legacy goals. Organizational leaders should ask past and present boards, advisors, and donors whether they know next-generation people who might want to learn about the agency or join the work. Meeting inheritors also happens at intergenerational events—and one can host them.

And some have earned their money and accumulated wealth without realizing it:

> *"I worked since I was seventeen. The message was clear: produce, earn, get educated, and surpass what my family had achieved. I went to college, became an instructor, and for fifty-three years I saved steadily, spreading my money across four investment accounts with different advisors. Then one of them asked: 'How much do you have across all your accounts? Do you know your total assets?' I didn't. I had paid off my mortgage by sixty. I started with thirty-three dollars in savings. And by seventy, my wealth had grown to four million dollars. I was in shock—but also, suddenly, awake to something new. I could slow down. I could think about how to give and share in ways I never had. I was afraid to admit it: I had 'made it.' And now I could enjoy my life and my giving in ways I never imagined. I was a* 'thrillionaire'*—with choices I couldn't have dreamed of."*
>
> *—Anonymous inheritor*

Family Foundations and Family Businesses: The Relational Core of Wealth Transfer

The questions inheritors face alone become harder when others are at the table. The transfer of wealth is most visible inside families, particularly in family foundations and family-owned businesses. Within these spaces, the most consequential question is rarely about numbers. It is about relationships.

In family philanthropy, tensions often emerge between honoring donor intent and allowing evolving priorities. Older generations may have focused on local institutions, arts education, or traditional civic structures. Younger family members may be drawn toward climate justice, racial equity, or systems-level change. Increasingly, next-generation leaders expect alignment between investment portfolios and grantmaking values. They may question, for example, whether a foundation funding environmental preservation should be invested in fossil fuel extraction.

Without structured dialogue and shared decision-making mechanisms, these differences create friction that feels personal. Families can smooth these issues by investing in education, facilitated retreats, and governance planning before authority shifts, creating stronger long-term cohesion.

Family-owned businesses face parallel challenges. Succession planning is not only about operational continuity; it is about preparing younger leaders to steward both financial and civic responsibility. Some families establish councils, mentorship programs, or next-generation advisory boards where emerging leaders can develop judgment within a supportive framework. Others delay these conversations until retirement or crisis forces decisions under pressure—and siblings or extended family may discover divergent visions too late. Division can become the simplest path forward, but fragmentation often reflects missed opportunities for earlier communication.

> *"I didn't enjoy my family meetings about investing or giving. There was clear control by the older generations. Of course they had created some of the money, but so too had their parents. But then we asked if we could have a share—maybe 25% of the annual amount budgeted to give—and when, after a year of discussion, they said YES, suddenly I felt it was my family foundation too, and wanted to contribute!"*
>
> *—Anonymous inheritor*

What consistently strengthens families across generations is clarity: clear conversations about inheritance, documentation of estate plans, and invitations into stewardship roles well before legal authority transfers.

Younger inheritors frequently demonstrate this clarity themselves. One young woman, traveling extensively for work, completed her own estate planning documents in her late twenties and presented them to her parents, prompting them to update their long-delayed paperwork. Leadership can flow upward as well as downward.

Moving Forward Together: Learning Networks, Traditions, and Civic Infrastructure

The work of the wealth transfer is not done alone. It is done in community: through learning networks, through cultural and faith traditions that teach generosity across generations, and through the civic structures that turn individual choices into collective impact (see Figure 3.2).

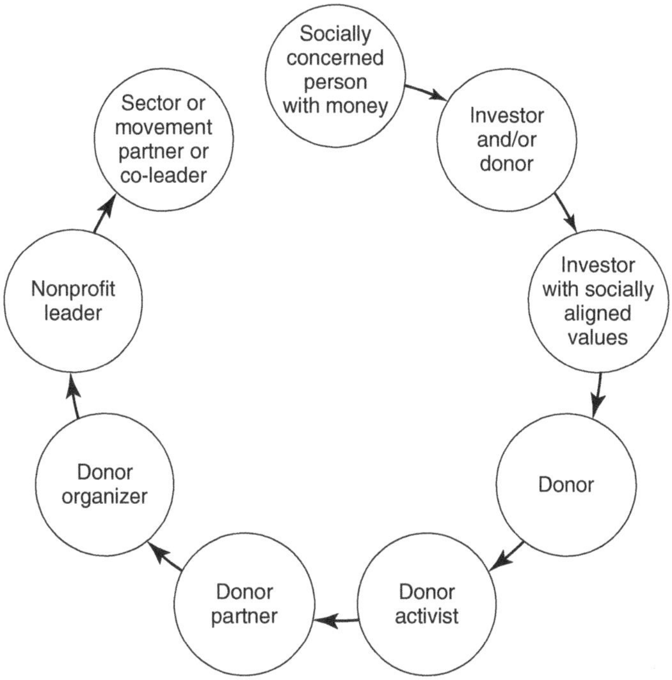

Figure 3.2 Evolution of a donor. *Source:* Unleashing Generosity

Donor Learning Networks as Civic Infrastructure

While many organizations are still wrestling with leadership redesign, next-generation donors and inheritors have been quietly building their own learning ecosystems for decades.

Across the country—and increasingly across the globe—more than 50 donor learning networks convene individuals with inherited or earned wealth to explore how money intersects with identity, responsibility, power, and community. Participants exchange confidentially, with questions such as these:

- What's the source of your money?
- How are you feeling about having inherited or earned wealth at the level you have?
- How much is enough?
- What does it mean to align investments with values?
- How do we partner with communities rather than impose solutions?
- How do we prepare our children to inherit both wealth and responsibility?
- What are great models for team giving or professional support like philanthropic advisors?[8]

These networks function as civic laboratories. They normalize learning, reduce isolation, and create peer accountability around generosity and impact. Participants learn how to give intentionally—with a giving plan, peer input, site visits, and donor briefings—and how to evaluate nonprofits, work in partnership with activists, and share power. Thousands of giving circles worldwide (see givingtogether.org) serve as entry points into deeper practice.

In these environments, wealth holders practice decision-making in community. They sit with activists, learn about impact investing and governance, and experiment with participatory grantmaking. They hear from people who have redistributed significant portions of their wealth and from those navigating complex family dynamics. Some ultimately decide to leave a family business, office, foundation, or investment office when their values are no longer aligned.

The capacity of these networks must be expanded. **Today, roughly 50 donor education networks serve up to 50,000 participants per year**—a meaningful but small fraction of those who could benefit. **In the United States, roughly 4.8 million households hold $5 million or more in assets**—a population that can be mobilized through donor education.[9] Most of these households have no structured support for thinking about giving, governance, or legacy. If 250,000 additional wealth holders were engaged in donor education by 2036, it would represent a meaningful shift; reaching more than 500,000 through ongoing peer learning would be transformative.

Several networks accept inheritors or those expecting inheritances soon, with simple qualification interviews. Others welcome people building wealth or who have received inheritances above certain thresholds ($250,000–$2 million plus is common), with giving commitments typically in the $25,000–$100,000 range. The experience can be transformative. As one member of Resource Generation described it:

> *"I had no idea how wonderful it would feel to be in a community of peers creating change together. I've been involved for over five years, and the training, cultural support, and community have helped me give away more than 25% of my inheritance. I have a clear plan for my annual giving and legacy, even though I'm in my early thirties. We also experiment with giving alongside allies who don't have wealth—that's a stretch, because so much is about power and control, but we are learning together."*
>
> —*Anonymous member of donor network Resource Generation*

Narratives of transformation have long catalyzed action among wealth holders. In the 1990s, *We Gave Away a Fortune* by Anne Slepian, Christopher Mogil, and Peter Woodrow helped spark a wave of wealthy activism by showing what redistribution looked like in practice. In the 2000s, Bolder Giving's *Inspired Giving: 100 Stories* extended the tradition with interviews about journeys toward more intentional generosity. The anthology *Free the People, to Free the Money, to Free the People*, published in 2025 and edited by Michael Gast, Marian Moore, and Alex T. Tom (each of whom shares their own story alongside others), picks up the thread for a younger generation, collecting diverse stories of what it means to align wealth with values.

Gast has spent two decades in this work—organizing with Solidaire Network, writing the field's history through his project Organize the Rich, and supporting donors, inheritors, and newly wealthy people of all ages. He sees in it the early outline of something historic. Reflecting on a half-century of wealth holders organizing for justice, he writes:

> *"In so many ways, over the last 50 years, we've seen that it's possible for wealthy people to be organized, together, to meaningfully contribute to movements for equity and justice. We've seen wealthy people advocate together for higher taxes on the rich, and fund grassroots groups in states like GA, WI and AZ that made a key difference in recent elections. . . Wealthy people, through social justice philanthropy and investing, through reparations and divestment, have taken steps to become full partners in cross-class movements where they are not the lead strategist or the boss. . . The reality is that we are seeing the emergence of the largest movement of wealthy people, attempting to work alongside poor, working and middle class people, for equity and justice, in the history of class societies."*
>
> *—Michael Gast, '5 things I want you to know about wealthy people', Substack, 2023*[10]

Cultural Traditions and the Formation of Generosity

Across cultures and faith traditions, the transfer of wealth is inseparable from the transfer of values. Teaching children to care, save and give from an early age, volunteering together as a family, inviting young people into decisions about charitable dollars—these are not primarily financial exercises. They are lessons in responsibility and belonging.

The traditions take different forms. In Jewish communities, *tzedakah* frames giving as obligation, not charity. In Muslim communities, *zakat* and collective service initiatives root generosity in faith. Christian tithing embeds proportional giving into household rhythms. Secular families develop their own rituals—regular volunteering, foundation visits, and shared conversations about money and meaning. The through line is consistent: generosity is not inherited. It is learned through noticing needs and differences, considering ways to help, and taking action with others.

And yet participation requires intention. Bringing children to nonprofits early, encouraging weekly service before schools impose their own requirements, making civic engagement a family habit—these choices shape how young people understand their place in the world. In an era when the average child spends several hours a day online outside of schoolwork, the case for hands-on service is developmental, not sentimental. The earlier young people are invited into conversations about money, purpose, and impact, the more confident and capable they become as future leaders.

Youth Civic Education as Infrastructure

From grade school onward, young people can get a head start on community engagement. A K–12 curriculum on philanthropy and the nonprofit sector—Learning to Give, launched in 1997 by the Council of Michigan Foundations—has been freely available and regularly updated for nearly three decades. Every state should have a comparable curriculum on nonprofits and service.[11]

Some of this infrastructure already exists. AmeriCorps volunteers enter service with clear aspirations and a hunger for professional development. Graduates of Michigan's youth service programs leave high school with weekly habits of engagement cultivated since grade school. Maryland has required 75 hours of service learning for high school graduation since 1992, the first state to do so; Arkansas adopted a similar requirement in 2023, taking effect with the class of 2027. Other states leave the question to local school districts, which impose varying requirements, or none at all.[12,13]

The result is a patchwork. In states with strong expectations, young people emerge with experience and a sense of agency. Elsewhere, civic identity is left largely to chance. A national service requirement, even if modest, would deepen the pipeline of future nonprofit leaders and cement civic participation as foundational.

> *"We are fourteen and sixteen years old. Since grade school, we've been inspired by Greta Thunberg and other young leaders to do what we could for the environment. We chose an issue—plastic microparticles and the damage they are causing worldwide—and we've become speakers at global conferences and daily activists, working to inspire others. We can't imagine a better way to spend our time. When we show up at conferences where nearly everyone is an adult, people are often surprised by our commitment, our research, and our directness in asking policymakers to act. Sometimes our youth is what moves them. We remind them of their own grandchildren, of the generations who will inherit whatever decisions they make—and that seems to change the conversation."*
>
> *—Zara Hawkins and Ashton Hawkins*
> *(www.hiddenplastics.org)*

Social Benefit Organizations and Donor Networks as Partners

A growing number of next-generation funders are seeking organizations that demonstrate transparency, measurable impact, and genuine community partnership—or simply organizations whose missions match their giving plans. When traditional institutions feel slow or opaque, newer donors are increasingly comfortable moving funds through peer-led vehicles and collaborative funds instead.

Public benefit organizations can view this shift as either competition or as partnership. The redesign move is to treat donor networks as strategic allies rather than funding pools: co-hosting learning sessions where donors and community leaders learn together, inviting network members into time-bound roles with real responsibility (campaign committees, rapid-response fund design teams, participatory allocation pilots), and building engagement pathways that include site visits, briefings, governance exposure, and shared decision-making. When donors are invited into meaningful responsibility, generosity expands alongside trust.

One practice worth borrowing: panels and conversations that invite inheritors, family foundation members, and donors of color into open storytelling—*what's your money story, and how are you involved in making change?* The Encampment for Citizenship has run intergenerational programming of this kind, and the format translates easily to board meetings, donor-education sessions, or staff convenings.[14]

A Just Transfer Requires Policy, Too

For the Great Wealth Transfer to happen justly, reasonable and fair taxation must help. Chuck Collins offers one model of what individual action looks like alongside policy advocacy: the great-grandson of Oscar F. Mayer and an heir to the meat-processing fortune, he gave away his inheritance of roughly $500,000 in his twenties to social justice organizations and has spent his life since building nonprofits and advocacy initiatives to make taxes and foundation payouts more fair. He now directs the Program on Inequality and the Common Good at the Institute for Policy Studies, where he co-edits Inequality.org, advocating for increased taxation on the ultra-wealthy to narrow the widening income inequality. He is the founding member of the initiative Patriotic Millionaires, which offers similar opportunities for new inheritors or earners to advocate for reasonable taxation.[15,16]

Stepping Up to Steward a New World Together

In the next few decades, the Great Wealth Transfer will happen. Assets will move, leadership will change hands, capital will flow. The question is whether we can meet this shift with shared power and values stewarded across generations. As we pass the torch, we must intentionally redesign how the torch is held, by whom, and to whom.

What that redesign looks like in practice can be seen in the story of Marta Drury.

Marta's father grew up poor in Richfield, Minnesota. When Marta was 6, he and Marta's mother decided to start a new business on a simple premise: people always need their garbage collected. He stayed with his mail carrier job in the morning and hauled garbage each afternoon, while Marta's mom ran the office from their small bedroom. All vacations were spent following garbage trucks in new cities, with the kids expected to work in the business.

When Marta was in her thirties, she was living in Northern California on welfare as a single mother. Unbeknownst to her, her family continued to grow their wealth. She was brought up to work hard and make a difference, so she juggled two jobs and started a toy shop. Her parents had spent decades growing their business into what would eventually become part of the largest waste management companies in the world.

In 1986, Marta's father called her and said he was sending each child $3 million, along with a piece of advice, "You'd better learn about money." Marta, knowing that one day she might inherit more money, had saved a paragraph from *Ms. Magazine*, about a nonprofit in San Francisco supporting women to learn about financial education.

Marta jumped in. She volunteered with Resourceful Women and its project, the Women Donors Network. She became a successful investor and shared her returns with her learning community peers. She was diligent in aligning her investments with her values and found advisors who did so. When her parents died, she received another $11 million. While not in her family of origin's tradition, she learned to donate and became passionate about having good relationships with activists. She found mentors and became one. She joined boards, including the Women's Building and *Ms. Magazine.* She traveled supporting nonprofits worldwide and became a skilled, bold, donor activist. Over time, she became one of the leaders of the women's funding movement, giving most of her inheritance to programs supporting women and girls in the United States and globally through the Global Fund for Women and Urgent Action Fund and her own Heart and Hand Fund, which for 23 years supported LGBTQ initiatives for Peace in the Balkans. Today she and her spouse, Kerry, an exemplary leader and community organizer, work on a project at Standing Rock reservation with volunteers and schoolteachers.

For more than four decades, Marta built a community of peers, donors, organizations and activists. She modeled donor activism for her daughter, Gita, who joined Resource Generation in her twenties and learned alongside other young inheritors. Gita is a cofounder of the Making Money Make Change conference and a philanthropic advisor with a family of her own, including a daughter who is growing up with strong generosity and giving values.

Marta's granddaughter does not have to be told that wealth comes with stewardship. She will have watched it her whole life. This is what the Great Wealth Transfer can be—not just an event but an inheritance and community of shared values and dreams for a better world, lived across generations.

Chapter 4

Harnessing the Shift Online and Growth of AI

"I dream about a near-term future where AI provides operational ball bearings to mission-led organizations so they can make a much bigger dent in the universe on their cause. . . . If they could be 20% more productive and efficient, that's 20% more people that get fed or kids that learn to read."

—Darian Rodriguez Heyman

Living in Digital Nativity

In the last few decades, we have watched the Internet reshape how people build community. In the last few years, we have seen AI reshape how people and organizations work. These two technologies are transforming the two things nonprofits depend on most: human connection and human judgment.

Let's start with connection. The communities nonprofits serve and the supporters they depend on increasingly live their social lives on screens: sending emojis across group chats, navigating cities by GPS, consuming content an algorithm has arranged. Where organizations once gathered people in brick-and-mortar spaces like churches or community centers, they now compete with Internet creators and corporate ads for attention in a digital environment engineered to fragment it. This digital world feels both more connected and more distant. We can reach one another instantly, yet so much time alone has fueled an American epidemic of loneliness.

On top of this transformed landscape, a second wave has arrived. Generative AI has entered workplaces with startling speed, with major technology companies promising their tools can compress days of labor into minutes. That value proposition could not be more attractive to nonprofits operating under relentless pressure to do more with less.

But it deserves a harder look—because alongside AI's productivity gains comes something researchers call *cognitive offloading*. AI can automate tedious tasks and augment decision-making. When we use it for the latter, we can offload pieces of our human judgment to machines. For nonprofits whose decisions affect people's housing, benefits, and safety, that raises questions about accountability that most organizations have barely begun to ask.

These two shifts—the digitizing of human connection and the rise of AI—are now converging on a sector that has the fewest resources to spend on technology yet the most responsibility for implementing it ethically.

We can't afford to look away from any of this. The communities we serve are already shaped by these technological realities, and the institutions we build must adapt to them. Nonprofits carry an obligation that Silicon Valley startups do not: our purpose isn't efficiency for the sake of margins or scale. It is to strengthen communities, nurture relationships, and advance the common good. That obligation means approaching these tools with a different set of questions than the ones the market is asking:

- How do we use digital platforms to **widen access to community** without hollowing out the deeper bonds that sustain it?
- How can we use digital strategies to break through our divisions, coordinating efforts for **greater collective power**?
- How do we harness AI by maintaining **cognitive sovereignty** instead of surrendering human judgment?
- How might we redesign our organizations so that technology **increases our efficacy** instead of layering AI onto existing workflows that don't actually work?
- Finally, how can we make sure technological adaptation **prioritizes our humanity**—rather than replacing it?

The answers won't just determine how social impact organizations operate in the coming decades. They will shape the kind of society we build into the future.

Digitizing Connection: How the Internet Has Reshaped Community Building

Our social lives are reorganizing around digital spaces. We start relationships, build trust, and host team meetings online. "It's great to e-meet you!" our email responses exclaim. For nonprofit leaders, the implications of this run deep. Community is at the heart of what we do—and the basic conditions under which community forms have fundamentally changed.

For many people, social platforms aren't just entertainment. Pew has found that for 42% of Americans, social media is important for getting involved with social or political causes.[1]

This means a huge portion of Americans—roughly 150 million of us—are looking to create real social or political impact via the avenue of social media. What if public benefit organizations could coherently and persuasively tap into this group? We can see who follows our nonprofit social media, Facebook, and other pages, but are we using these contacts as fully as we should?[2]

Easy access doesn't always result in deeper connections. Digital environments have reshaped three structural ingredients of community—attention, participation, and proximity—in ways that make movement-building harder to sustain.

Attention is now mediated by algorithms built to capture and monetize it. The economist and Nobel laureate Herbert Simon saw this coming more than 50 years ago. Writing in 1971, well before the Internet existed, he observed that "a wealth of information creates a poverty of attention." That scarcity now defines the landscape nonprofits are trying to operate in.[3]

Participation has tilted from contribution toward consumption. The "1% rule" is a colloquial term that estimates 1% of users in an online community create content, a small share reacts, and the vast majority watches. The digital public square is more of a concert hall than a town hall.

Proximity, once a necessity for community, has been replaced by distantly networked connection. While our reach is now global, the cues that build trust—eye contact, spontaneous conversation, subtler signals of presence—are stripped away.

A newer pattern is emerging too: people increasingly turn to AI for the conversation, support, and problem-solving they once sought from other people. Writing for Workday, Chief Impact Officer Carrie Varoquiers notes that the junior employee who once swiveled their chair to ask a veteran colleague now asks ChatGPT instead. The percentage of professionals who report feeling isolated has nearly doubled in a year. For a sector whose work depends on human-to-human trust, the tools we're reaching for to save time may be eroding the connections we most depend on.[4]

Eric Solomon, founder of the Human OS™ and an organizational psychologist with executive experience at YouTube, Spotify, and Instagram, offered a blunt assessment when we spoke: the trajectory points toward more screen time and more isolation.

For nonprofits, these aren't just cultural observations—they have profound implications on how we work. In our sector, our currency is altruism. We rely on behaviors that are inherently social: volunteering, donating, showing up to events, collaborating, and listening to participants rooted in their communities. Altruism grows when people feel connected to something meaningful. When social life migrates onto platforms optimized for speed and entertainment, those feelings become harder to cultivate.

Digital spaces are no better or worse than physical ones. Both have their strengths. As we think about how to consciously redesign to leverage strengths of both spaces, several questions arise: How can we better cultivate digital spaces to engage and retain new communities around social causes? In what situations should we foster digital communities, and where do we need physical presence? How do we manage the co-existence of digital and physical spaces?

For public benefit organizations, the stakes are high. Organizations that intentionally design for both digital and in-person environments can rebuild community within these new conditions. Our future isn't in retreating from digital life. It's in engaging with it deliberately—as a pathway toward greater access and not a substitute for the deeper human bonds that sustain collective care.

The Age of AI: The Technology Reshaping Productivity and Decision-Making

Let's talk about the technology that has hit the world like a thunderclap.

Generative AI—short for generative artificial intelligence—has leapt into everyday use at a pace that has caught even its creators off-guard. A 2025 survey by Elon University found that roughly half of all Americans now use large language models like ChatGPT, Claude, or Gemini.[5] Other data suggest that 61% of American adults have used AI in the past six months, with nearly one in five using it daily.[6] By any measure, this is one of the fastest-diffusing technologies in history.

Yet for all that speed, the trajectory is far from settled. Sam Altman, the CEO of OpenAI, has himself cautioned that we may be in a speculative boom—that many of the assumptions driving today's AI enthusiasm could turn out to be wrong or exaggerated.[7] At the other end of the spectrum, figures like Kai-Fu Lee, the former president of Google China, argue that AI will bring lasting, structural transformation to how humans and machines work together. The truth is probably somewhere in between. But even a moderate version of AI's promise is enough to reshape how organizations operate.

What makes this moment feel different from previous waves of technology is that AI seems to *infer decisions*. Unlike any previous technology, AI outputs look like fully fledged products that a human could have made: well-researched essays, strategies, or emails.

AI systems like ChatGPT, Claude, or Gemini are "large language" statistical models that produce text, images, or code by identifying patterns in enormous quantities of data. They are prediction engines, forecasting which word, phrase, or image is most likely to follow a given prompt. The results are often remarkably fluent and useful, but they can also be wrong. AI's guiding principle is probability, not truth—which is why the field uses the term *hallucination* to describe outputs that sound confident but are factually incorrect.

AI models appear to be thinking and reasoning critically, but this is a common misconception. AI models do not have human brains. Instead, they are projecting likely responses from the large quantities of data they are trained on. These models are also opaque: they don't tell us how their outputs were generated.

When humans receive and act on AI outputs, we are transferring our critical thinking away from ourselves and toward these incredibly sophisticated tools. We are asking a machine to make these decisions for us. The stakes of that trade vary. Instructing AI to draft an email is one thing; asking it to design an outreach plan for an underserved community is another. And at scale, this can create meaningful impacts in how decisions are made inside an organization.

Nikki Dinh, E.D. of Leadership Learning Community, puts the challenge well: as people begin to automate their decision-making, leaders have to grapple with the difficult calibration of determining when to trust machines versus when to trust people and communities. As Nikki puts it, "This is going to be an embedded system that will be useful and harmful at the same time, and we release a little bit of our survival whenever we get a little bit more sophisticated in our technology."

The Dividend of Time

Before we get to the risks, it's worth talking about what AI does well—because the gains are real, and they go beyond productivity. AI can be an incredibly effective tool for automation and saving time on administrative tasks. Beyond this, it can also function as a cognitive partner: a research tool that helps us reason, explore, and refine ideas.

Nonprofit consultants Beth Kanter and Allison Fine put a number on the time-saving potential for automation in their book *The Smart Nonprofit*: roughly 30% of social benefit staff time goes to administrative tasks—scheduling, data entry, reporting—much of which could be automated. They call this recaptured capacity the "dividend of time," and their vision for it is hopeful. That freed-up time, they argue, should go toward the things only people can do: building relationships, dreaming up new solutions, strengthening communities.[8]

Darian Rodriguez Heyman, a nonprofit strategist and author of *AI for Nonprofits: Putting Artificial Intelligence to Work for Your Cause*, makes a similar case: AI provides "operational ball bearings" for mission-led organizations. Make a nonprofit even 20% more productive, he argues, and those gains translate directly into serving more people.

But here is the question that separates a good AI strategy from a misguided one: What do you actually do with the time you get back?

If the dividend gets reinvested into *human actions* like deeper listening and real community stewardship, it compounds mission impact. If it gets absorbed by more busywork, or faster but less reflective decision cycles, it will only manufacture a false sense of productivity and lead to higher levels of burnout.

Kanter herself has warned that the sector risks getting "sucked into the big AI company narrative around automation and efficiency"—a narrative that offers short-term relief but ignores long-term consequences. Eric Solomon seconds this concern, questioning whether technology will genuinely free up time for meaningful work or whether the cultural pull toward constant busyness will simply fill that time with more tasks.

In a 2026 keynote, Kanter laid out two futures. The first future is one where AI simply accelerates bad practices, causing workers to "do more work faster." The alternative is a future where organizations first give those bad practices what she calls "a joyful funeral" and then redesign their work from the ground up.

To chart a path toward the better future, Kanter proposes the SHIFT framework:

Save time through automation.

Hold that time rather than filling it with more work.

Use it for **I**mpact.

Apply AI to help staff **F**lourish and develop new skills.

And **T**ransform organizational culture in the process.

The Risks We Can't Automate Away

The productivity story, compelling as it is, covers only half the ledger. Generative AI also introduces a set of ethical risks that public benefit organizations must weigh as our sector's work touches vulnerable communities and questions of equity.

Bias and discrimination. AI models learn from biased historical data, which means they can reproduce inequities nonprofits exist to fight. Addressing this requires scrutinizing where your data comes from, prioritizing inclusive sources, and involving diverse stakeholders in the design and review of AI-assisted processes.

Privacy and data misuse. AI systems can be fed sensitive personal information and use it in ways that can be difficult to trace. Nonprofits working with vulnerable populations need strict data governance and clear compliance with privacy regulations.

Accountability gaps. When an AI-generated recommendation causes harm, someone has to be responsible. Organizations need clear lines of human accountability and agreed-upon policies for when a human must be "in the loop."

Job displacement. AI will automate some job functions, particularly administrative, creative, and knowledge-adjacent ones. Nonprofits can respond by upskilling staff, using AI to augment rather than replace human capacity, and creating more positions for relational and creative work.

Environmental costs. Training large models requires enormous amounts of energy and clean water. Organizations can be selective about which tasks warrant AI, choose lower-impact models where possible, and advocate for sustainable computing practices.

Hallucination. AI systems generate outputs based on probability, not truth, and can produce confident-sounding statements that are factually wrong—fabricated statistics, invented sources, misattributed quotes. Social impact organizations can guard against this by fact-checking AI outputs before they reach external audiences and being especially rigorous with research, reporting, and any public-facing claims.

Misinformation. Generative AI makes it easy to produce convincing false content. Nonprofits can invest in media literacy and transparent communication to protect the trust they've built with their communities.

Cognitive dependency. The same tool that functions as a cognitive partner can also become a crutch. When we consistently outsource thinking, we risk eroding the very capacities that make our work sharp. Emerging concerns around "AI psychosis," in which heavy users lose confidence in their own judgment or develop distorted thinking patterns through prolonged AI interaction, underscore the stakes. Nonprofits can protect against this by treating AI as a collaborator rather than a substitute, preserving space for unaided reasoning and creativity, and being especially cautious in work that requires an ethical stance or original insight.

Hovering above all of these is always the question of *human oversight*. How much judgment must remain in human hands? How do we audit what AI produces?

Finding the Balance

Generative AI can feel overwhelming in both its promise and its risks. Darian Rodriguez Heyman identifies this as a major friction point: the opportunity is significant, but many nonprofits and foundations feel overwhelmed and lack capital to invest in responsible implementation.

Kanter offers a useful way to cut through the noise. She identifies three postures organizations are currently taking toward AI: outright resistance, rapid adoption, and balanced adoption. Her recommendation is the third path. Nonprofits are already poised to adapt to AI from an ethically and socially responsible lens. In this moment, nonprofits have an opportunity to model what responsible AI adoption looks like, rather than boycotting the technology or implementing it blindly. That includes pushing for systemic accountability: water usage standards for data centers, fair labor practices for the workers who train AI models, and regulatory frameworks that allow time for proper testing before deployment.

Jensine Larsen is the founder of World Pulse and a leader of multiple nonprofit initiatives that explore the intersection between social impact and technology. She builds upon Kanter's point: "Also, it includes building and resourcing the alternative technology the sector needs. There are many tech-centered non-profits in the US that are building—but often without adequate resources." Larsen has conducted hundreds of interviews with social change leaders who are grappling with these tools, and she has found that many of these leaders feel they are in a catch-22 even when taking the balanced path. "They want to use the mainstream AI and social media tools because they are accessible and easy to use, but feel ethically torn because they don't want to compromise their communities or their data. Yet the well-intentioned social impact tech is often less-resourced, less user-friendly, and harder for their communities to adopt."

The critical reframing for nonprofit leaders is this: AI adoption should be treated as more than an IT project. It is complex and deeply human. Workflows, decision rights, training protocols, quality control, and ethical guardrails all change when machine-generated outputs enter core work. Adoption must be treated as an organizational transformation—with human judgment, autonomy, and community accountability at the center.

Redesigning Social Impact for the Two Shifts

So we are caught between two massive shifts at once: the Internet has reshaped community building, and AI is changing how organizations make decisions and get work done.

But they land on the same desk. For nonprofits operating with thin margins and deep obligations to our communities, these shifts can have massive implications. Organizational redesign starts with one deceptively simple question: Where must humans remain at the center, and where can automation help?

Frameworks and Tools for Creating Digital Community

One thing is unquestionable: the Internet broadens access to community. A person in a remote town can find forums, affinity groups, and networks of shared experience that geography once made impossible. For public benefit organizations, this has been useful for identifying new supporters, coordinating collective action, and running the daily machinery of meetings, file sharing, and communications.

But access is not the same thing as connection. And it is not evenly distributed. Sarah Hobson, philanthropic advisor and former foundation executive, draws from recent work in rural India. She observes that technological advancement often benefits the top 10% of a population while leaving many behind.

Online giving to nonprofits is easy, but the long-term commitment behind those gifts is less deep than what grows from real-world relationships. Although virtual fundraising kept the sector afloat during the pandemic, the share of donors who continued giving to the same organization year over year declined by 4.1% between 2019 and 2020.[9] The same pattern shows up in activism. Digital platforms make it easy to express support for a cause, but that ease can mask a shallower commitment, a pattern often called *armchair activism* or *slacktivism*.

Techno-sociologist Zeynep Tufekci argues that movements that gain momentum online can scale faster than ever before—yet when they skip slower, relational work such as building leadership structures, honing negotiation skills, and fostering collective decision-making, they lose staying power. The result is that social movements are easier to organize, yet harder to win.[10]

Committed altruism and committed activism come from building a feeling of closeness over time. This is harder to cultivate through posts that can be scrolled away in the blink of an eye, or on virtual calls where microsecond drops in connection puncture the illusion of presence.

In-person gathering has great strategic value for nonprofits. Still, the Internet remains a powerful front door—a first point of contact to draw people toward deeper engagement—and digital tools are essential behind the scenes, with virtual meetings reducing geographic friction for staff, boards, and working groups. The goal is complementarity, not competition: in-person gatherings as the core that builds trust and drive, digital spaces as the connective tissue.

Designing for Hybrid

Hybrid community is about designing a coherent system where online and offline participation each do what they are best at.

Susan Tenby, who has run online community programs for nonprofits for two decades and serves as global director of community at TechSoup, points to this design principle: not every activity belongs in every format. Lectures translate well to hybrid and online formats. Design thinking, brainstorming, and ideation work best in person, where walls and sticky notes still outperform their digital equivalents. Breakouts are the trickiest of all—they tend to work fully online or fully in-person, but rarely split between the two.

As in-person touchpoints have become uniquely precious, it is important to prioritize in-person time for human-centered tasks—deep relationship building with donors, listening to your community stakeholders, high-level strategy, and convening volunteers and beneficiaries.

As for our online ways of working, governance matters: Wikipedia's long survival as a trusted platform demonstrates that durable online communities depend on transparent norms and human moderation. Privacy and data transparency are the first principles of nonprofit-led digital spaces. And online communities can be designed for both bonding and bridging—both connecting like-minded people and creating structured opportunities for constructive dialogue across differences.

The common assumption is that it's not easy to form deep relationships online. But Tenby notes that they absolutely can—she has worked with colleagues for years through video calls and digital messaging platforms and sometimes forgets they have never met in person. The harder thing to reproduce digitally is not depth but spontaneity: unplanned "water cooler" chats or the chance of bumping into the CEO in the elevator. Tools like Zoom and Slack now offer random pairing features to recreate some of that serendipity.

Hybrid systems can sustain community under conditions that require adaptability. Free Minds Book Club & Writing Workshop, a Washington, DC, nonprofit, builds community with people incarcerated as adults, often in federal prisons hundreds of miles from home. Free Minds recognized early that maintaining contact across distance was vital to helping members redirect their lives throughout incarceration and reentry. The community moves fluidly across channels: a handwritten letter answered with a digitally drawn response, a member-led magazine mailed to people scattered across the federal system, a weekly virtual book club. Each channel does a small part to carry the whole relationship. The digital tools extend human presence into spaces a visit can't reach. The model has had resounding success: Free Minds reports that 97% of members home from prison are employed, in school, or in vocational training, and 92% do not return to jail or prison.[11]

Hybrid Strategies That Work

Effective digital outreach is distinguished by a few design principles: favor intimacy over scale, treat large events as on-ramps rather than endpoints, and invest in storytelling that evokes genuine empathy.

Small, well-moderated virtual circles build psychological safety and effective teamwork. A CEPR study co-authored by researchers from Stanford and the University of Nottingham found that online meetings are more efficient for smaller gatherings of 2–4 people, while in-person meetings are preferred for gatherings of 10 or more with a steady decline in virtual meeting effectiveness as group size grows.[12]

Large online meetings still have their place in the work. Big digital events can act as a funnel to bring people into volunteer work, in-person events, or direct action. The Brookings Institution (2022) recommends that organizations integrate hybrid face-to-face and digital volunteering options.[13] Indeed, this seems like a promising pathway. The U.S. Census Bureau and AmeriCorps found that in 2023 virtual and hybrid volunteers reported engaging in more hours of service per year (95 hours) than those who volunteered solely in person (64 hours).[14]

To recruit volunteers through digital channels, nonprofits have to invest in digital storytelling. The decision to volunteer begins with emotion rather than information, so online outreach should be designed to reach people there. Short video, live testimony, and personal narrative consistently outperform slides and statistics in moving people to act.

Rajasvini Bhansali, E.D., Solidaire Network, points to the shift required here. The sector historically relied on in-person conferences to exchange information, but those mechanisms are evolving: "Our members have such vibrant stories to tell—[for example], how they have won a massive internal battle and now have access to a billion new dollars that they're going to put into racial justice work. The mechanisms by which we tell those stories are still old [and] are no longer working. And so we're now investing in some more capacities so that our team can support our members in their storytelling."

Devising Your Tech Toolkit

Selecting the right tools is harder than it sounds. Jensine Larsen describes nonprofits as stranded between options: "Nonprofits know they need the technology, but they don't really want to use existing mainstream platforms like Meta or TikTok or Palantir, because they are so dangerous and not values-aligned. So we're 'in between trapezes' right now—where what the social impact sector needs from technology still needs to be built. But we do need these communities to be a part of building it." Larsen points to hopeful emerging alternatives that are building digital sovereignty: federated platforms, open-source infrastructure, and community-owned tech.

But aiming to choose (or build) a 100% ethical platform can cause paralysis. Amy Sample Ward, CEO of NTEN, offers a useful corrective. Because three major companies own roughly 75% of the technology stack most organizations access, perfectly ethical options are often simply unavailable. Instead of chasing moral purity, Ward advises focusing on transparency—communicating clearly to staff and community members what guardrails are in place and what trade-offs have been made. NTEN's commitment is surprisingly simple: "We will never sell your data to anyone at any price at any time," Ward says. This straightforwardness indicates community-first values and builds trust.

In practice, a nonprofit's digital toolkit is a set of our capabilities, including document and file management, synchronous meeting tools, email and messaging platforms, donor customer relationship management (CRM) tools, AI tools, social media platforms, and content creation tools. This "stack" of tools should be governed by clear norms, including data safety, password and phishing protection, and content integrity standards. When tools are added or removed, this should be supported with clear training and governance.

Models Worth Watching

A few examples illustrate what intentional digital design looks like in practice. These nonprofits and movement builders are paving the way for conscious digital communities and infrastructure:

New_ Public is doing some of the most ambitious work in this space. A nonprofit R&D lab co-founded by Eli Pariser—the activist and author who introduced the term *filter bubble*—New_Public describes itself as "digital urban planners," building healthy public spaces online the way cities build parks and libraries. Their two-year Signals research project surveyed more than

20,000 people across 20 countries to identify the qualities that make digital spaces flourish, and they've translated those findings into a public design playbook that any organization can use. They also build their own prototypes—most recently Roundabout, a tool for local community forums designed as an alternative to Nextdoor and Facebook groups. For nonprofits, New_Public offers a values-aligned source of both research and working models for what better digital community infrastructure can look like.[15]

Project for Awesome, run by the Green brothers' Foundation to Decrease World Suck, uses YouTube videos and social sharing as digital entry points and then channels that energy into a concentrated 48-hour livestream fundraiser where donations, challenges, and real-time interaction drive collective giving. The digital, synchronous event allows fans of the Green brothers to interact with them in a more human way and generates urgency.

Ben's Friends is a network supporting dozens of peer-support communities organized by rare disease or chronic illness. For many members, these forums are the primary community—low friction, available around the clock. They emphasize that since rare disease patients are geographically distributed, connecting online is their best alternative.

Giving Tuesday, now well-known across the social impact sector, demonstrates how digital infrastructure can synchronize a global wave of generosity. A hashtag serves as both rallying cry and organizing tool, transforming diffuse online goodwill into a single coordinated moment of action. In 2023, U.S. participants donated an estimated $3.1 billion in 24 hours.[16]

Queer in AI uses digital platforms for onboarding, discourse, and collaborative projects, but regularly convenes in-person meetups primarily tied to academic AI conferences, to build collegial collaborations. Their model shows that digital on-ramps can successfully bridge to in-person collaboration.

What these examples have in common is that intentional human systems sit behind the technology. Each of these is a coherently designed organization that takes advantage of digital on-ramps and prioritizes creating human connection.

Putting AI to Work Toward Your Mission

What does it actually look like when a public benefit organization starts using AI responsibly? It starts with a commitment and policy.

The commitment comes first. It is a simple promise to each other to *figure this out together*. That means across generational lines, across roles, across backgrounds. In most nonprofits right now, it is often younger staff—people who grew up with screens in their hands—who are diving into these tools and helping their colleagues adapt. That generosity should be named and reciprocated.

But the commitment also runs in the other direction. How an organization decides to use AI—where it's welcome, where it isn't, what it's allowed to touch—cannot be a decision handed down from leadership or delegated to whoever happens to be most comfortable with the tools. It has to be collectively stewarded. That means asking your staff, your board, and the communities you serve a set of open questions: What are we not willing to give up? What values must remain central to how we work? The answers are the foundation of AI policy and adoption.

A policy is the next necessity. Policies can be lightweight and adapt to emerging needs. A recent Center for Effective Philanthropy report found that more than half of nonprofits now use AI in some capacity—for drafting, content creation, data analysis—yet fewer than 10% have a formal policy governing that use.[17] Staff are already experimenting. The question is whether the organization has decided what's acceptable and who is accountable for AI use.

An AI policy needs to answer a few essential questions:

- What is AI being used for, and by whom?
- What data is it allowed to touch?

- Who is accountable when something goes sideways?
- Where do we want a human being making the call, no matter how good the machine gets?
- How will the policy evolve as the technology and the regulatory landscape change?

Cheryl Contee, co-founder of Change Agent AI and co-author of *AI for Nonprofits*, recommends starting with an all-staff conversation before anyone drafts anything, then a small task force to write it. A co-created policy is stronger, because "the people who are writing the policies might not have as much experience with AI as the people who are using the AI."

Jensine Larsen emphasizes that social impact organizations need members with technological expertise on their governance boards to create these frameworks well. Initiatives like Board.dev are working to connect nonprofits with that kind of knowledge, moving beyond ad hoc approaches toward genuine governance capacity.

Where to Start Using AI

The most reliable early value from AI comes from augmentation—drafting, summarizing, triaging, and accelerating analysis. A Stanford HAI and Project Evident survey found that around 80% of AI-using social impact organizations have deployed these tools in supportive functions: finance, HR, communications, and donor engagement, while only about 60% deploy AI for mission-related work.[18]

Function	Tasks to Start With	Example Prompt
Communications and outreach	Drafting newsletters, social posts, and press releases; analyzing engagement metrics; generating visual content for campaigns	"Draft a 200-word donor newsletter update on our fall food drive. Use a warm, grateful tone. Here are the key facts: [paste]."

Function	Tasks to Start With	Example Prompt
Fundraising	Drafting grant proposals and donor letters; identifying lapsed donors from CRM data; suggesting personalized outreach timing and messaging	"Here's a list of donors who gave in 2022 but not since. Group them by giving level and suggest a re-engagement message tailored to each tier." (Consider your policies around donor data privacy before using this prompt.)
Program evaluation	Summarizing qualitative feedback from interviews and open-ended survey responses; surfacing themes and trends across program data	"Review these 40 participant survey responses and identify the top three themes. For each theme, pull two representative quotes." (Consider your policies around participant data privacy before using this prompt.)
Translation and accessibility	Translating program materials, intake forms, and outreach into multiple languages—including languages historically underserved by translation services	"Translate this two-page program flyer into Spanish, Vietnamese, and Mam. Keep the reading level at 6th grade."

Across all of these examples, human review is paramount. AI outputs should be checked for accuracy, tone, and mission alignment before they reach the people you serve. A 2025 Candid study found that when AI and human experts analyzed the same set of community interviews, both surfaced similar thematic patterns—but the human reviewers caught cultural nuance and intersectional context that the AI missed entirely. The lesson here is that AI is a highly capable first pass, but it can't be the final word, especially in deeply human work.[19]

Keeping Humans in the Driver's Seat

Cognitive offloading is a real risk—as we get more comfortable with generative AI tools, our reliance on them can turn into dependence. Beth Kanter offers a useful framework: there are zones where AI collaboration increases our capacities—first drafts, routine communications, information formatting, data gathering. Then, there are zones where reaching for AI can erode our abilities: creative problem-solving, community relationships, ethical decision-making. One of the dangers is generating "workslop"—mindless productivity that creates more noise for your team to parse without improving anything that matters.

She recommends a simple set of questions before reaching for an AI tool:

- Will doing this task myself strengthen the abilities I need for leadership?
- Does this task require my unique judgment or creativity?
- Am I reaching for AI because I don't want to think through this myself?

When a tool does the thinking, the person managing the tool often learns less. A 2026 Anthropic study put numbers to it. Fifty-two engineers, all regular Python users, were asked to learn an unfamiliar library—half with an AI assistant, half with only documentation and search. The AI group barely saved any time, and the small edge they gained wasn't statistically significant. But on a quiz taken minutes later, they scored 17% lower than those who had coded by hand—nearly two letter grades. How people used the assistant mattered as much as whether they used it: those who simply handed off the work retained the least, while those who interacted with the output—asking for explanations, working through the concepts, pushing back—held onto far more. The lesson is to bookend AI with human judgment: shape the task at the start, let AI move the middle along, and verify, question, and learn at the end.[20]

The "bookend" discipline protects your own capability. A second safeguard protects the people your decisions affect: keeping a "human in the loop." This is the principle that AI should assist and inform decisions but that a human being must remain accountable for the outcome. The higher the stakes—anything involving client eligibility, safety, benefits, housing, legally sensitive decisions—the more rigorous that human review needs to be.

Link Health, a nonprofit that helps people in East Boston enroll in public benefits like SNAP and WIC, learned this firsthand. The organization invested in AI-powered chatbots designed to answer eligibility questions and guide enrollment. The goal of this initiative was to give its student volunteers an instant policy reference and reduce their cognitive load. In practice, the chatbots proved useful only for the simplest questions. As one patient navigator put it, immigration policy changes constantly, and the AI was never quite current enough to answer the questions that mattered most. What Link Health found instead was that AI worked best as a first step, not a last word: a chatbot might get someone 60% of the way there, but it took a person to help them cross the finish line. Their takeaway is a practical statement of the human-in-the-loop principle: offer human help early and often, in partnership with technology.[21]

The Funding and Investment Gap

Investing in technological capability isn't free. The nonprofit sector's chronic underinvestment in technology makes the AI transition harder than it needs to be. Larsen points to a stark gap: while the business sector typically invests 5–7% of its budget in digital infrastructure, nonprofits often invest less than 1%. She recommends that every social impact organization allocate a "digital dividend" of at least 5% to technology infrastructure and development. This takes into account both the tools and the training it will take boards, staff, and volunteers to onboard.

NTEN data tells a similar story. Nearly half (45%) of surveyed organizations describe their technology spending as "too little," with available budget as the most cited barrier. Additionally, training—arguably the most important investment in an AI moment—amounts to a mere 1% organizations' technology budgets.[22]

Fast Forward CEO Kevin Barenblat puts it plainly: "I feel like the social sector always eats last at the table when it comes to technology and innovation."[23]

But the portrait this sentiment paints is overly negative. Amy Sample Ward challenges the anxiety behind it. Nonprofit professionals, Ward observes, constantly express feeling "behind"—and that narrative often serves external interests, specifically vendors with billions invested in AI.

"Behind who?" Ward asks, noting that nonprofits are frequently ahead of small businesses in integration. More importantly, Ward pushes back on the idea that innovation means buying expensive technology. True innovation means experimenting intentionally with new changes—like shifting organizational power dynamics by putting program participants on boards, rather than purchasing another corporate tool. Contee points out that this is not new ground for the sector. The NAACP built its early organizing on the telegraph, so a community facing violence could raise an alarm quickly enough to get help. They were "early adopters," she says, "of what was then new, pioneering technology." Larsen sees the same pattern holding now: "Nonprofits are ahead of where the tech needs to go. They are laboratories that shape the tech that will serve—not harm—society. They are bringing vital use cases and ingenuity that will define how tech evolves in the future."

Building the Airplane While Flying It

The regulatory landscape is moving fast. The EU AI Act entered into force in August 2024 with phased obligations; U.S. frameworks like the NIST AI Risk Management Framework and the Blueprint for an AI Bill of Rights provide guidance on trustworthiness, accountability, and human oversight. Civil society is organizing too—in late 2025, a coalition called Humanity AI committed substantial philanthropic funding to center human needs in

AI development, framing the technology's future as "design, not destiny." With this rapid speed of development, and the risks it entails, some socially minded people and organizations tune out AI entirely.

But social benefit organizations need to think strategically: if the social sector doesn't help set norms and accountability structures for AI, that work will be done by commercial interests whose priorities are more self-serving than ours.

Eric Solomon suggests this is a moment to slow down to speed up—taking strategic pauses now to ensure that when you do move forward, you're accelerating toward goals that actually matter: "As hard as it is and as time-starved as you feel—if you want to go faster, you might want to take a pause." In a world that feels nonstop, AI only accelerates our pace. Nonprofits should, in our enthusiasm for creating a better future, also create guidelines and standards to ensure balance and protect against burnout.

Nonprofits don't need to adopt AI wholesale overnight. But they do need to start playing with it, and speaking with their organizations and beneficiaries about it. We can build better organizations by treating technology as an organizational transformation—with human judgment and community accountability at the center.

Conclusion

How we work and how we build community will look very different in 10 years. Navigating these shifts can feel daunting. But the nonprofit leaders we spoke with kept returning to the same point: these new technologies are here to stay. And they are tools that take the shape of the hands that wield them.

The organizations that approach AI and digital community building with intention will define what responsible technology use looks like for everyone else. That means that we should bring care to adoption: investing in governance, protecting human judgment, designing for genuine connection rather than frictionless engagement, and strengthening human capacities and relationships outside of these tools.

We are living through a period of democratic backsliding, media platform capture by concentrated wealth, and the global defunding of civil society. The for-profit world is optimizing for speed and scale. Government is struggling to keep pace with regulation. That leaves civil society—those of us stubbornly committed to putting people first—as the sector most likely, and most obligated, to demonstrate that technology can deepen democracy rather than erode it. How social impact organizations govern AI and design digital communities is a question about who gets to shape the civic infrastructure of the next generation.

Nonprofits have more agency in shaping that outcome than we tend to believe. May we bring our full humanity—our judgment, our relationships, our stubborn commitment to one another—to help shape our technological future.

Chapter 5

Expanding Collaboration, Diversity, Partnerships, and Mergers

"If you want to go fast, go alone. If you want to go far, go together."
—Attributed as an African Proverb

There are many strategies for engaging, uplifting, and transforming the ecosystem of the social benefit sector. In this chapter we focus on moving away from the challenges of working alone to pursuing collaboration, diversity, partnerships, and mergers to strengthen impact, be more inclusive, improve sustainability, and help organizations meet rising community needs more effectively. The social benefit landscape is increasingly resource-constrained, and working together allows organizations to do more with less while expanding reach and resilience. Collaboration and partnerships are an antidote to competition and to the old dysfunctional funding models.

The health of a democracy often depends on the quality of collaboration within it. When collaboration breaks down—polarization, mistrust, or refusal to engage—democratic institutions struggle to function. When collaboration is strong, democracies tend to be more stable, inclusive, and effective. Both rely on people sharing power, working together, and making decisions collectively rather than having authority concentrated in one place.

Collaboration helps nonprofits pool strengths, reduce duplication, and respond to growing demand for services. Yet in the pressure-cooker environment that is the mainstay of many nonprofits, collaboration (though celebrated in theory) can feel like a luxury. It's not that you don't want to network with other local public benefit organizations, set time to speak with your beneficiaries one-on-one, or discuss the needs of your municipal and business community. It's that when your nonprofit's survival depends on meeting immediate needs, building partnerships with others feels like the last item on an already overextended to-do list.

This pressure is reinforced by the funding system itself. As we've covered before, nonprofits are often measured by their individual outputs. Grant applications reward quantifiable, organization-specific results rather than collective outcomes. And the competition for funding pits organizations against each other, which again leads to isolation. The unfortunate and unintended consequence has been a sector where organizations are laser-focused on proving their own value to funders, sometimes at the expense of stepping back to ask how they might be part of a larger whole. Too often, this means missing out on opportunities to listen deeply to the diverse communities they serve and to learn from peers tackling similar challenges.

Yet no mission can be achieved by a single organization. The lofty societal changes we aim to enact, whether addressing climate change, expanding access to the arts, or ending homelessness, require a full community's—sometimes, a full society's—support. We need the perspectives of our beneficiaries and the wisdom and experience of other nonprofits. We need the insights of funders and philanthropists and the resources of businesses and local institutions. And in each of these pieces, we need diversity. We need to embrace and learn from the full richness of the communities we aim to serve.

Diversity is not just a nice-to-have—it is essential. Diversity here is not limited to demographics; it also encompasses the multi-textured mosaic of roles, expertise, and lived experience that, when brought together, create solutions with staying power.

The question, then, comes: How can social benefit organizations embrace collaboration when they remain accountable to the narrow, scrutinizing eye of a funder? This is a genuine tension, but it is not an insurmountable one. In fact, we are beginning to see a shift: funders increasingly recognize collaboration as a marker of adaptability and a deeper commitment to lasting impact, as exemplified in the following example.

In 2023, three nonprofits—an environmental advocacy group, a youth education nonprofit, and a local health organization—joined forces to launch a community resilience program addressing climate-related health risks in underserved neighborhoods. Instead of applying for separate grants, they submitted a joint proposal to a regional foundation. The funder not only approved the grant but increased the award size, citing the collaboration as a sign of strategic adaptability and a shared commitment to long-term impact. The foundation noted that the partnership allowed for cross-sector expertise, reduced duplication of efforts, and created a more holistic solution to a complex issue.

Funders increasingly understand that shared outcomes demand shared effort. The challenge for nonprofits is to navigate the balance: meeting funder requirements while also carving out the time and intentionality to link arms and strategize with others. When they do, the result is a sector more capable of collective impact, more responsive to community needs, and more aligned with the big visions that inspire the work in the first place.

Melanie Greenberg of Humanity United explained that funders are generally receptive to collaborative proposals when they emerge organically among grantees, sharing examples of successful collaborations funded by Carnegie Corporation, MacArthur Foundation, and Humanity United.

So, how do we collaborate with other organizations in a way that captures the diversity of the community we serve?

First, we must accept that many nonprofits are working alone to run their programs and keep their organizations afloat. Many have not explored the potential of collaboration or partnerships with other nonprofits. This was exacerbated during the pandemic when we all needed to isolate. Many leaders indeed felt isolated, which often led to a sense of overwhelm or despair. We're still recovering from this time and the uncertainty of the economy makes it challenging to plan ahead.

Yet we don't have to go it alone. Many nonprofits don't have all the skill sets, people power, or resources to be effective on their own. Increasing collaboration, partnership, and diversity can be powerful strategies for success within and across organizations: by partnering with other nonprofits, organizations can tap into new supporter bases, increasing their reach and impact in the community.

For example, when multiple organizations collaborated on homelessness, they created a more comprehensive support system, from immediate shelter needs to long-term housing solutions. It led to increased visibility and credibility and the organizations attracted more attention from donors, volunteers, and community members.

Yet organizations have to overcome certain obstacles. "One of the most significant obstacles to collaboration among nonprofits is the scarcity mindset, which assumes that resources are limited and that one organization's gain must come at the expense of another," cites the Fund for NGOs. This mindset can stifle innovation and prevent organizations from exploring collaborative opportunities that could lead to greater impact.

To overcome this, nonprofit leaders must shift their focus from competition to cooperation. "This requires a cultural change within organizations, encouraging staff and board members to view collaboration as an opportunity rather than a threat. Nonprofits can foster this mindset by engaging in open dialogues about their goals and challenges, creating an environment where sharing knowledge and resources is seen as a pathway to mutual success rather than a zero-sum game," the Fund for NGOs explains.

Another obstacle to successful collaboration is dealing with differences that can turn into conflict. It's important to respect the wisdom, perspective, and experience of the partners, especially when different from your own. When collaborating, we often encounter varied approaches or opinions—that can be stressful, but it does not need to stop progress as it can deepen the connection when handled well. A third-party facilitator or coach can also be helpful when needed. The advantages of partnership can be exponentially exciting.

A Framework for Collaboration

Collaboration is one of the nonprofit sector's most overused and under-defined words. Too often, it gets tossed around as a vague aspiration. How should leaders and their organizations think about collaborating and understand its goals and opportunities? If we want collaboration to be more than rhetoric, it helps to break it down. We believe meaningful collaboration entails three interconnected practices: listening, exchanging, and weaving.

1. **Listening** helps us tune our mission toward what is truly needed and effective. This is an often-overlooked dimension of collaboration. Every nonprofit is driven by a mandate to achieve its mission. Yet the truth is, many of us don't know if the strategies we employ are truly the most effective ways of fulfilling that mission. We do what feels right, or what we've always done, but we rarely pause to ask, is this the best way forward?

   CEO of Candid, Ann Mei Chang reminds us of the importance of experimentation in her book *Lean Impact*. Just as startup companies test, measure, and iterate to ensure they're providing meaningful value to their customers, nonprofits can cultivate a discipline of listening and adapting. Crucially, this kind of listening must be inclusive. It requires seeking out the voices of those who represent the full diversity of our beneficiaries—the people whose lives we are trying to improve.[1]

   The risk of overlooking listening is high: we have sometimes seen nonprofits that spend effort and resources without truly reaching the populations they aim to benefit. If you are a board member, social benefit leader, or funder, it is your duty to ensure your nonprofit is connecting deeply and adapting intentionally to their beneficiaries. We recommend leaders ask the following questions:

   - Is your nonprofit hosting focus groups, recruiting staff and board members with diverse backgrounds from the communities you serve? Do you seek feedback and administer surveys?

- Do you talk about what you've learned after a program or season is over?
- Do you relate programmatic outcomes to your mission?

Listening with humility and being willing to adjust as soon as a better approach reveals itself are at the core of producing needed social change.

2. **Exchanging** is the second dimension and is what we often think of when we think of "collaboration"—how can we share resources with other people, nonprofits, businesses, or institutions? To get more holistic with this dimension and develop lasting partnerships, we must look both inward and outward.

   Every person and organization has differentiators—the skills or resources they have in abundance—and also areas where they struggle or lack capacity or interest. Perhaps your public benefit organization has a strong marketing team but no affordable access to meeting venues. Or maybe you have a deep bench of volunteers but lack the financial expertise to design a sustainable budget.

   Collaboration allows us to match these pieces. By naming our differentiators (organizational strengths and resources) clearly, we put ourselves in a position to contribute them generously to others. By being transparent about our gaps, we give others the chance to step in with their strengths. This mutual exchange can look very practical: sharing office space, trading technical know-how, contributing staff time, or offering pro-bono support. But more than filling logistical holes, it builds trust. When nonprofits and their communities consistently show up for one another, they create a culture where resources circulate more freely and everyone is better equipped to advance their mission.

3. **Weaving**, the third dimension, goes deeper. Weaving is about spending time with each other: attending the events of other nonprofits, going to political gatherings, and being patrons at local businesses.

> This requires stepping outside our own organizational silos and spending real time with other nonprofits across diverse issue areas, with funders, with government leaders, with local businesses, and with community members themselves—with or without a goal in mind. Over time, this generates trust and mutual understanding. This "spending time" becomes something larger than any one organization: a collective vision and warmth for each other.
>
> This vision works in both directions. As we embrace the goals and missions of our partners, they also begin to embrace ours. Our mission expands beyond our social impact organizations and becomes not just ours—but owned across our ecosystem. The intersectional issues our communities shoulder call for intersectional solutions. Thus, collaboration through weaving has untold value, increasing the resilience, embeddedness, and widespread impact of our mission.

Listening, exchanging, and weaving provide a three-pillar framework for collaboration that exists as more than a side project or an occasional partnership but as a core way of operating. Collaboration is not about losing your identity as an organization. It's about recognizing that the problems we seek to solve are bigger than us. By listening openly, exchanging resources with each other, and weaving unity, nonprofits can drive sustainable, collective impact.

Collaboration in Practice

In practice, strong collaboration usually combines all three dimensions of the collaboration framework. Collaboration within and across nonprofits has many benefits and can help to foster innovation.

Ann Mei Chang suggests reframing collaboration discussions by asking, "What would we do if we were divisions of the same company?" This approach helps identify opportunities for resource sharing, functional realignment, and leveraging organizational strengths. She explains that by identifying organizational synergies and being willing to transfer programs, social benefit organizations can ultimately better serve the sector by reaching more communities with needed resources.

Sarah Hobson, former E.D., West Marin Fund, recommends that organizations include collaboration and impact measurement in their core values, suggesting this clarity helps inform staffing, board composition, and funding strategies. The most successful nonprofit efforts involve multiple partners with crystal-clear goals and realistic timeframes. Sarah emphasizes the urgency of the moment, suggesting organizations focus on 10-year rather than 30–50 year timelines. Successful collaboration requires funding for infrastructure and visioning work. Though it may take more time than independent initiatives, collaborative efforts often yield tenfold results compared to disconnected individual projects.

Sarah emphasizes the need to be realistic about what collaboration actually means, what it will accomplish, and what it will cost. She cautions that nonprofits can become territorial about their work, which conflicts with the goal of better serving their missions.

Another perspective is network-based social change, which is an approach to creating social impact by mobilizing relationships, connections, and distributed leadership rather than relying on a single organization or top-down authority. It treats change as something that emerges from networks of people, organizations, ideas, and even technologies working together. It recognizes that social impact grows when many interconnected leaders coordinate, share information, and act collectively. Network thinking shifts us away from linear, hierarchical models and toward ecosystem-based approaches. It transforms isolated efforts into coordinated, scalable, and resilient movements.

David Ehrlichman is a prominent figure in the field of networks and collaboration. He has written about the importance of networks in driving systemic change, including three types: learning, action, and movement networks. He talked about the need for network leadership to be inclusive, diverse, and open. He saw networks as a modern approach to solving global issues, emphasizing intentional design and relationship-building as core components of effective impact networks.[2]

There are many ways to build internal collaboration, including the following:

Framework Theme	Collaboration Tactic	How to Use This Tactic
Listening	Transparent communication	Use shared communication and information platforms (e.g., Slack, Microsoft Teams) for real-time updates and discussions. Hold regular all-staff meetings to establish joint goals and celebrate successes. Engage your board, key volunteers, and advisors on your plans and progress.
	Internal workshops	Host internal workshops or lunch-and-learns where teams share insights and best practices.
	Mentorship	Create pathways for mentorship or sharing across departments to build relationships and knowledge.
Exchanging	Cross-departmental projects	Create task forces or working groups that include members from different departments. Encourage joint ownership of initiatives like fundraising campaigns or community outreach. Bonus points if community stakeholders or board members can join.
	Collaborative goal-setting	Involve staff from all levels in strategic planning.

(continued)

(continued)

Framework Theme	Collaboration Tactic	How to Use This Tactic
	Shared performance indicators	Set shared performance indicators that require interdepartmental cooperation. Performance indicators are most successful when they are SMART (Specific, Measurable, Achievable, Relevant and Time-bound), as they help project managers create clearly defined mission objectives that can help ensure success.
Weaving	Shared work spaces	Create shared workspaces, collaborative learning hubs, and moments for spontaneous connection.
	Culture of trust and safety	Promote safety so staff members feel comfortable sharing ideas and concerns. Establish a "concern box" so people can share concerns anonymously, or encourage staff to elect a representative who can share concerns. Recognize and reward collaborative behavior.

Similarly, there are many avenues for external collaboration between organizations. The following are some examples:

Framework Theme	Collaboration Tactic	How to Use This Tactic
Listening	Peer learning	Host regular roundtables or forums to exchange ideas and challenges. Participate in nonprofit associations or affinity groups.

	Data and knowledge sharing	Create shared databases or research repositories. Publish joint reports or case studies to inform the sector.
Exchanging	Joint programs or services	Partner on initiatives that serve overlapping populations or missions. Share resources like staff, coaches or consultants, space, or technology to reduce costs and increase reach.
	Co-funding opportunities	Apply for grants together to show funders a united front and broader impact. Pool funds for shared projects or community investments. Evaluate your impact together for exponential benefits.
	Memoranda of understanding (MOUs)	Formalize partnerships with clear roles, expectations, and accountability. Use MOUs to build trust and structure long-term collaboration.
Weaving	Coalition building	Form alliances or networks around shared causes (e.g., homelessness, climate action). Coordinate advocacy efforts to expand policy influence. Participate in nonprofit associations and affinity groups.
	Shared work hubs	Work in the same cafe, community center, or nonprofit hub. Build space for spontaneous connection.

It's helpful to start small. Pilot a project or host a joint event before diving into deeper collaboration. Be sure that values and goals are compatible to avoid friction. Sharing wins publicly can build momentum and attract more partners. Effective change requires collaboration across sectors, including government, healthcare systems, and other institutions, with public benefit organizations serving as one tool within a larger ecosystem of change.

Wisdom on Collaboration

Jensine Larsen, founder of World Pulse, shared experiences from the women's rights and gender justice space, noting that many organizations want to collaborate but often lack capacity. Most receive individual organizational grants rather than ecosystem funding. More than $20 million was tracked in one-off technology investments where organizations tried building their own platforms and backend infrastructure, resulting in duplicative efforts and inefficient use of resources. Current funding patterns incentivize organizations to compete rather than collaborate, with foundations often requiring nonprofits to demonstrate uniqueness instead of complementary strengths.

Jensine observed that shared infrastructure based on common topics or missions could benefit multiple organizations simultaneously. Most nonprofits, for example, struggle with PR, marketing, and storytelling due to limited resources, which could be shared through collaboration. She recommended new social impact leaders do thorough research and seek collaboration with existing organizations before launching something new, starting their own initiative only if they identify a genuine gap with little partnership potential.

Rajasvini Bhansali, the executive director of Solitaire Network, emphasized that effective collaboration requires hard work beyond good intentions, including checking one's ego and organizational sense of supremacy to be a good partner to others. She described their most successful collaboration as the Women Donors Network's "Block and Build Funder Coalition." They attributed the success in just one year to several factors; having the right staff members who aligned politically and to living feminist principles where they lifted each other up, shared credit, and openly discussed conflicts when they arose. She observed that many organizations give up on collaboration over minor issues that hurt feelings, noting it takes discipline and practice to work through difficulties when the whole is greater than the sum of its parts.

Zafra Lerman, the founder/president of Malta Conferences Foundation, described strategies for collaboration she used when designing the Malta Conferences, which bring together scientists from all Middle Eastern countries regardless of political conflicts, to collaborate with Nobel laureates for five days. These include (1) Creating unity through shared purpose. Find a subject that unites people—science can serve as this unifying factor even for participants from countries at war. (2) Focus on collaborative issues that cross borders, like water management problems that span multiple countries where underground aqueducts don't follow political boundaries. (3) Establish equality—everyone from graduate students to Nobel laureates is treated equally. (4) Build genuine connections. Show participants that there is much more that unites them than what separates them. Create a "Malta family" atmosphere where people celebrate each other's successes even during times of regional tension.

Melanie Greenberg said that given the interconnected "poly-crisis" challenges, nonprofits should develop better cross-sector collaboration rather than addressing climate, women's issues, and health separately. Umbrella organizations could play a greater role in weaving these efforts together. Funders could help create spaces for joint strategy, visioning, and sense-making where organizations within sectors could develop collaborative approaches and pilot projects. Universities could serve as platforms for nonprofit engagement and provide spaces where diverse groups could collaborate. New digital platforms could also help conceptualize the nonprofit ecosystem as more of an interconnected tapestry.

Julia Roig, founder of Horizons, advocated for a cooperative model where public benefit organizations share operational resources like financial management, professional writers, and communications expertise rather than each organization developing all capabilities internally. She shared her positive experience with a model where 80 organizations share a communications team, noting that this collaborative approach works much better than individual organizations duplicating efforts.

Sarah Hobson discussed the Agroecology Fund as a successful collaboration model. It was founded in 2013 with just two executive directors who persuaded their boards to invest and then grew to include 42 foundations collaborating to support grassroots agroecology initiatives. The fund exemplifies successful collaboration, demonstrating how well-structured partnerships can effectively multiply impact.[3]

Olivia Dodd, CEO of Amplifi Napa Valley, said that unlike corporations that compete for market dominance, nonprofits benefit from collaboration because they're incentivized by mission impact rather than becoming the biggest organization in their space. She feels that nonprofits should explore a full range of collaboration options to better leverage resources and increase impact across the sector.

Why Valuing Diversity Is Critical to Collaboration and Sustainability

The workplace is becoming increasingly diverse as the face of America is rapidly changing. Minorities, currently representing a third of the U.S. population, are expected to become the majority by around 2045, according to the U.S. Census projections.[4] It is also diverse by age, with Gen Zers entering the workforce, leading to five generations interacting daily. Women now make up almost half of the labor force, and there is increasing religious, gender and sexual identity, and other diversity.

The nonprofit sector houses more women and people of color; however, social impact leadership is typically whiter and more male than the staff it oversees. The gap widens as organizations get larger, as shown in Figure 5.1. Women of color lead a disproportionate share of the smallest nonprofits—those with the tightest budgets, the thinnest staffing, and the least access to the unrestricted funding that makes organizations resilient—while the largest, best-resourced organizations remain predominantly led by white men. As Ann Mei Chang notes, white-led and male-led nonprofits tend to receive more funding partly due to bias but also because of better networks, more privilege, and funder familiarity bias.

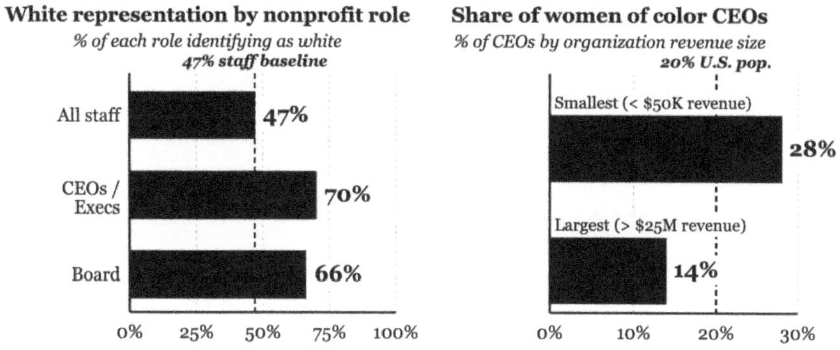

Left chart: dashed line marks the 47% staff baseline. Right chart: dashed line marks women of color as a share of the U.S. population (~20%).

Figure 5.1 Nonprofit leadership representation, 2024[5]

Establishing and valuing diversity is increasingly important for all public benefit organizations to be effective and connected within their communities. Diversity is connected to legitimacy, effectiveness, and responsibility, and strengthens collaboration because it expands who is listened to.

When leadership and staff reflect the communities they serve, programs become more culturally relevant. Outcomes improve and innovation follows. It can strengthen fundraising, as donors increasingly support organizations that prioritize equity. The reverse is also true: when an organization doesn't reflect its constituency, trust erodes, blind spots multiply, and credibility suffers.

It's important to avoid tokenism. It is not enough to put one woman or one person of color on a board and think this shows diversity. The opportunity is to ensure there is enough diversity in terms of gender, ethnic groups, race, age, physical ability, religion, and other factors that are representative of the community. The real questions are—who is at our table, and do we respect and value their contributions? And who is not included and why?

"One of the biggest challenges nonprofit boards face is the confusion around the meaning of diversity, where it is often seen only as the difference of race, color, or religion. When used to describe people and population groups, diversity encompasses many factors—color, age, gender, race, ethnicity, ability and/or disability, sexual orientation, religion, education, socioeconomic class, geographical locations, professional background, marital and parental status, learning and communication styles and diversity of thoughts. While the social impact sector is known for caring, serving, and empowering diverse communities, boards need to seek out leaders that look like the communities they serve," says Sahar Andrade, Forbes council member.

Unfortunately, diversity, equity, and inclusion (DEI) programs have been under attack in current policy shifts with many programs being defunded and required to close. This has been a big challenge for universities, companies, and nonprofits. It has created an atmosphere of fear to the point that some foundations and nonprofits have edited DEI language off their websites. Yet we can't shy away from something so critical to our organizations or to the core value of respecting diversity in our country. Promoting and valuing diversity within organizations should remain a strategic path as it leads to more inclusive, innovative, and effective organizations. A diverse workforce better understands and serves a diverse customer base. Inclusive cultures attract top talent from all walks of life. Diverse organizations are more adaptable to change and uncertainty and thus are more resilient.

There is often a pipeline problem limiting diversity in nonprofits. Many nonprofits and businesses offer summer internships that are unpaid, which restricts entry to those who can afford to work without pay. Paid internships and junior staff positions are potential solutions. The government is proposing to reimburse companies $3,500 per new apprenticeship to turn around the lack of entry-level manufacturing jobs, with a goal of one million new jobs. The government, foundations and individual funders could fund paid internships and public benefit apprenticeships as well, ensuring a diverse pool of job or internship applicants with a living wage.

Here's how nonprofits and their advisors, funders, and coaches can foster diversity across their teams, programs, and leadership:

- **Embed diversity in core values and strategy**
  - **Make it explicit:** Include diversity in your mission, vision, and strategic plans.
  - **Board-level commitment:** Ensure DEI is a standing agenda item at board meetings to keep it top of mind.
  - **Ground actions in values:** Align diversity efforts with the nonprofit's core beliefs to ensure authenticity and sustainability.
  - **Develop a statement of purpose:** Your statement should showcase your commitment to diversity and connect not only with the organization's workforce but with the communities you serve.
- **Foster inclusive hiring and leadership**
  - **Diversify recruitment channels:** Go beyond traditional job boards—use community networks, affinity groups, and culturally specific platforms.
  - **Inclusive job descriptions:** Use language that welcomes diverse applicants and avoids bias.
  - **Leadership pathways:** Create mentorship and advancement opportunities for underrepresented staff and volunteers.
  - **Avoid the "cloning effect":** Trustees tend to seek out those from their immediate circles of influence, almost cloning themselves, which creates a homogeneous board that is often disconnected from its communities.
- **Engage communities authentically**
  - **Partner with grassroots organizations:** These groups have often developed trust and relationships with marginalized communities.

- **Use culturally responsive outreach:** Tailor messaging and materials to reflect the language, values, and lived experiences of different groups.
- **Participatory decision-making:** Involve community members in program design, evaluation, and leadership roles.

- **Create a safe and inclusive culture**
  - **Psychological safety:** Foster an environment where staff feel safe to express themselves and challenge norms. Respectful communication matters.
  - **Ongoing dialogue:** Encourage honest conversations about race, identity, age, and inclusion across all levels of the organization.
  - **Training and education:** Offer DEI workshops, anti-bias training, and cultural competency development. There are many trainers who can offer this training.
- **Measure and evaluate progress**
  - **Set DEI goals and performance indicators:** Track metrics like staff diversity, board composition, and community representation.
  - **Conduct equity audits:** Assess policies, practices, and culture for barriers to inclusion.
  - **Share results transparently:** Communicate progress and challenges with stakeholders to build trust.
  - **Welcome the next generations,** to fill important positions and to bring their creativity, new perspectives, and skills.
- **Sustain and evolve the work**
  - **Celebrate diversity:** Highlight diverse voices, stories, and contributions in communications and events.
  - **Adapt and learn:** Stay open to feedback and continuously refine your approach.
  - **Network and learn from others:** Join DEI-focused nonprofit coalitions or advisory groups.

Funders can be a barrier to collaboration when they only fund individual organizations, discourage shared infrastructure, or require unique program branding. True inclusivity requires an "outsized investment" of time and resources to build relationships with new communities and to educate donors, requiring patient funding that allows organizations to take risks and develop authentic connections.

Olivia Dodd describes how well-intended but misguided diversity efforts often fail. She outlines some strategies to address diversity:

- **Move beyond surface-level efforts:** Avoid treating diversity as a "check the box" exercise with superficial measures like demographic percentages or basic translation services.
- **Make outsized investment in relationship building:** True inclusivity requires significant time and resource investment to build authentic relationships slowly with new communities. This demands patient funding that allows organizations to take risks and develop genuine connections.
- **Address institutional barriers:** Recognize that grassroots community groups often aren't formalized nonprofits due to institutional barriers, distrust, and the complex bureaucracy of nonprofit formation. Funders want to support organizations of color, but these groups may need different approaches to access support.
- **Include community input in programming:** Avoid creating culturally themed programming without community input and then concluding "they must not want it" when targeted communities don't attend. Authentic engagement requires involving communities in the design process from the beginning.
- **Acknowledge leadership limitations:** Olivia noted that nonprofit leadership has historically been dominated by white females who, despite good intentions, often lack the lived experiences to understand diverse communities. Organizations need to address this gap through intentional leadership development and community partnership.

Daphne Scott, community development leader, emphasized that diversity and respect cannot just be policy statements but must be built into the design of operations, focusing less on board representation and more on redistribution of power and voice. Respect naturally arises when people have genuine agency—when those closest to the work and communities served help shape decisions rather than just implementing them.

Vanessa Daniel, former E.D. of Groundswell Fund, identified five primary barriers that undermine leaders who are women of color (WOC): glass cliff invitations, assumption of incompetence, expectation to mother or mammy, zero margin for error, and abandonment when they are attacked. She described three ways funders make leadership difficult for WOC: pausing funding when WOC leaders are hired, requiring more scrutiny for less money than white male counterparts, and withdrawing support when leaders face criticism.

Nikki Dinh, E.D., Leadership Learning Community, addressed the burnout during the pandemic specifically among Black women and other marginalized leaders who have historically been excluded from culture-defining and systems-defining spaces. She noted that corporatized DEI systems leave out the whole person—they're primarily about data and statistics, focused on closing equity gaps. True diverse leadership, she explained, would incorporate beauty, art, and culture that helps communities persist despite systems of oppression.

Gary Lucks, author and environmental attorney, described the benefit of collaboration, explaining that his nonprofit functions as "part of a constellation" of organizations that become a brighter universe through collaboration, with each group having a specific role.

Valuing and practicing DEI means grounding the work in the organization's core mission rather than in slogans or programs that can be easily targeted. It becomes about protecting the dignity, safety, and full participation of every employee—something that strengthens performance, reduces risk, and builds trust—while being thoughtful about language, framing, and implementation. Leaders should focus on evidence-based inclusion practices, such as fair hiring, equitable access to development, transparent decision-making, and respectful culture norms, all of which are legally sound and fiscally responsible. This approach keeps the spirit of DEI alive without exposing the organization to unnecessary scrutiny or defunding threats, and it signals to employees that inclusion is a non-negotiable part of how the organization operates.

Partnerships as a Structure for Collaboration

Collaboration and partnerships are often used interchangeably, but they are slightly different. Collaboration is typically informal and short-term with a lower level of commitment, while partnership is usually formal and long-term with shared responsibilities and risks. Often the purpose of collaboration is to achieve a specific goal by pooling resources, ideas, or expertise, whereas partnerships pursue shared interests or business goals over time. Partnerships can build deeper trust, mutual investment, and sustained collaboration. Both will help social benefit leaders and funders imaginatively redesign the sector through new mindsets and structures for funding, tech, leadership, and collaboration, so we can collectively meet this moment.

Partnerships with businesses, government agencies, and other nonprofits can unlock funding, expertise, and visibility. It can help reach new audiences and expand your impact. Government partnerships can help shape public policy and secure support. And partnering with local organizations builds credibility and cultural relevance.

Partnering with other nonprofits allows organizations to reach broader audiences and address more complex social issues. Nonprofits can pool resources, such as financial capital and human capital, to enhance their programs and services. By working together, nonprofits can amplify their effectiveness and achieve more than they could alone. Partnerships can widen the community of supporters.

We recommend you create a visual chart with your current and established partnerships and hold a meeting of leaders, board, staff, and donors to discuss and build your partnership and collaboration plans. Notice what questions come up and see what next step actions there might be to build relationships.

As you advance your collaboration and partnership work, be sure to keep files, saving the history of what your committee or team discovers and commits to document your progress. Be sure you document commitments made and that they are approved and expectations are mutually understood. An MOU can be enormously helpful.

Here's a toolkit to help public benefit organizations increase partnerships:

1. **Clarify your values.**

   Before reaching out, be clear about what your nonprofit brings to the table:

   - **Mission:** What cause do you serve, and why does it matter?
   - **Unique strengths:** Do you have deep community ties, specialized expertise, innovative programs, or something else?
   - **Mutual benefit:** What can you offer a partner (e.g., visibility, shared impact, access to networks)?

2. **Increase visibility and outreach.**

   - **Attend local events:** Conferences, roundtables, and workshops are great for networking.
   - **Host community events:** Invite other organizations to co-host or participate.
   - **Leverage social media:** Share success stories and tag potential partners.
   - **Publish thought leadership:** Articles, blogs, or reports that showcase your work and invite collaboration.

3. **Build relationships strategically.**

   - **Start with warm connections:** Board members, donors, and volunteers often have networks you can tap.
   - **Use LinkedIn and professional networks:** Reach out to leaders in aligned organizations.

   - **Offer informal meetings:** Coffee chats or virtual introductions to explore synergies.

4. **Create win-win proposals.**
   - **Co-design initiatives:** Invite potential partners to shape the collaboration from the start.
   - **Be flexible:** Tailor the partnership to their goals and constraints.
   - **Show impact:** Use data and stories to demonstrate what you've achieved and what's possible together.

5. **Formalize and strengthen partnerships.**
   - **Draft MOUs or partnership agreements:** Clarify roles, expectations, and shared goals.
   - **Set joint performance indicators:** Track progress and celebrate successes.
   - **Maintain regular communication:** Schedule check-ins and updates to keep momentum.

6. **Nurture existing partners.**
   - **Acknowledge contributions:** Publicly thank partners and highlight their role.
   - **Invite deeper engagement:** Engage partners in co-funding all the way to co-advocacy.
   - **Ask for referrals:** Happy partners often know others who'd be a great fit.

Additional ideas:

- Create a "partnerships lead" role, or someone dedicated to building and managing relationships.
- Launch a partner advisory council: Bring together key allies to guide strategy.
- Offer partnership titles, like "Community Ally" or "Impact Champion" to recognize different levels of engagement.

Developing good partnerships involves trust, respect, courage, openness, shared purpose, deep listening, relationship building, and good collaboration skills. It means moving from the concept "this is mine" to "this is ours," not letting ego get in the way. It means valuing diverse perspectives and practices and thinking about what's best for the whole. It can open up new channels of funding, outreach, and project management not previously thought possible.

What Real Collaborative Ecosystems Look Like

There are many examples where collaboration, partnerships, and diversity helped nonprofits to grow and thrive, building resilient, impactful organizations that are trusted by the communities they serve. Across these examples, the pattern is similar: organizations listened to community needs, exchanged assets or expertise, and wove relationships strong enough to sustain shared work. Here are a few examples:

- **Public health nonprofit + local government: childhood obesity initiative.** A public-health nonprofit partnered with a local government agency to tackle rising childhood obesity rates. The social benefit organization contributed community trust and program design; the government contributed data, school access, and policy levers. Together they implemented school-based nutrition and activity programs that neither could have scaled alone. It worked because of combined grassroots credibility with institutional authority, shared data enabled targeted interventions and joint messaging increased community adoption.
- **Asian Youth Center + Parent and Youth Leadership Program.** The Asian Youth Center acquired the Parent and Youth Leadership Program, allowing both to expand their cultural advocacy and youth empowerment work. The youth center gained a stronger empowerment focus; the leadership program gained access to more schools

and families. It worked because the mission aligned around youth empowerment, there was shared cultural expertise and it expanded geographic and demographic reach.

- **Multiple arts nonprofits** in Santa Fe, New Mexico, collaborated to host a vibrant festival featuring visual and performing arts, culinary experiences, and local artists and community groups. By pooling resources and promoting them collectively, they attracted a broader audience, increased revenue, and celebrated cultural diversity in a more public way.
- **Museums** across the United States partner with the Smithsonian Institution to access traveling exhibitions, share educational resources, and offer professional development. This partnership strengthens local museums, boosts public engagement, and opens up access to world-class content.
- **Accessia Health,** a nonprofit focused on chronic disease support, partnered with organizations specializing in housing, food security, and mental health. They built integrated care models that addressed not just medical needs but also social determinants of health. This collaboration had a positive impact—they delivered more holistic care to underserved populations, improved health outcomes by addressing barriers like housing instability and food insecurity and strengthened advocacy efforts for policy change through collective action with other nonprofits.
- **Room to Read,** a nonprofit focused on literacy and gender equality in education, partnered with local governments and communities in developing countries. They emphasized inclusive education by tailoring programs to cultural and regional needs and collaborated with schools and families to ensure sustainability and relevance. This resulted in reaching more than 32 million children across Asia and Africa, improved literacy rates and educational access for girls, and demonstrated how community-driven collaboration can scale educational equity.

These examples show how social benefit organizations can multiply their impact when they embrace collaboration, build diverse partnerships, and center equity in their work.

Michael Ziccardi, E.D. of One Health Institute at UC Davis, emphasized the success of building collaborations and partnerships with other organizations rather than competing with them. The Oil Wildlife Care Network was designed as a collective of agencies, nongovernmental organizations, and universities. It began 30 years ago with more than 20 organizations working together in a structured system for oil spill response and has since grown to 45 participating organizations. Early challenges included competition, distrust, and concerns about fundraising conflicts. Over time, organizations realized that collaboration actually increased the total funding available rather than dividing limited resources.

To maintain trust, they implemented a proactive information strategy ensuring partner organizations receive proper recognition—including branded apparel, social media mentions, publication credits, and approved language for communications. This collaborative approach provided multiple benefits: emergency response capabilities, staff/volunteer training, and marketing opportunities that partners can leverage for their own fundraising during nonemergency periods.

Michael observed that nonprofits often overlook partnership opportunities with universities, typically because universities haven't historically reached out or demonstrated the value they could bring to such collaborations. Universities have evolved beyond the "ivory tower" model focused solely on education and research; they now prioritize service opportunities and community engagement that align with nonprofit missions. Universities can offer nonprofits expertise, resources, and research capacity while social impact organizations provide universities with real-world applications, community connections, and potential funding opportunities.

He cited the Gorilla Doctors program as a successful partnership model between UC Davis and the Mountain Gorilla Veterinary Project, where the university provides veterinary services while the nonprofit handles fundraising for nonprofits interested in university partnerships. Michael recommended finding faculty champions already working on aligned projects, inviting them to events, and building individual relationships that can lead to broader institutional collaboration.

Mergers: Another Form of Structured Collaboration

Social benefit organizations are motivated to merge for a variety of reasons. It could be because of financial instability where the leaders realize that by combining resources they can reduce overhead and strengthen long-term viability. It could be due to a leadership vacuum or the founder wants to retire and merging is the only way to keep the mission alive. Or it could be because two organizations realize their potential is much greater when they combine.

There are many advantages to merging. A merger can allow nonprofits to offer a broader set of programs, or reduce duplication: merging can eliminate overlapping efforts, free up resources, and collectively seek innovative funding sources. This is important in today's environment since we are seeing a longer-term decline in corporate and government support of the nonprofit sector, including in 2026, the revoking of USAID funds. This speaks to a loss of major funding streams with few new prospects on the horizon.

Some of our interviewees felt there are simply too many public benefit organizations today and merging would be a way to streamline and focus efforts more effectively. The number of nonprofits has grown dramatically over the sector's roughly 100-year history. In 1940, there was approximately one nonprofit for every 2,590 Americans; by the 1970s, that had risen to one per 848. Today there are more than 1.9 million registered nonprofits in the United States—close to one for every 175 people—and the count continues to climb toward two million.[6,7] The question this raises is unavoidable: How many nonprofits can the country meaningfully sustain?

Jason Franklin, founder and principal at Krisis Capital, advocates for more social impact mergers while acknowledging they are challenging because, unlike the for-profit sector, nonprofits lack ownership incentives to merge or acquire. He believes funders shouldn't force mergers due to the nuances involved, but should offer incentives. He shared that the Foundation Center and GuideStar merger (becoming Candid) exemplifies two successful organizations merging to improve their work rather than due to financial necessity, highlighting strategic rather than crisis-driven consolidation.

How the merger process works: first, leaders from both organizations discuss goals, values, and whether a merger would truly advance their missions. Often this includes a formal feasibility study. Second, they conduct due diligence. This includes reviewing finances, evaluating programs, checking legal obligations, and assessing staff and leadership structures. Third, all mergers need board approval. Because nonprofits are governed by boards, both boards must vote to approve the merger. This is a legal requirement in most states. Additional legal steps, depending on the state, may include filing merger documents with the state, updating bylaws, notifying the IRS and transferring assets and liabilities.

The real work happens with integration planning. Combining staff and leadership, aligning programs, merging cultures, and communicating with donors, clients, and the public. Once the merger takes place, the organizations officially operate as one entity, with unified branding, systems, and governance.

There are various types of nonprofit mergers:

- **Full legal merger:** Two nonprofits become one new organization.
- **Absorption:** One nonprofit joins another and ceases to exist as a separate entity.
- **Parent–subsidiary structure:** A larger nonprofit becomes the parent organization while the smaller one retains some autonomy.
- **Strategic alliance:** Not a full merger—organizations share services or collaborate deeply without legally combining.

What makes social benefit mergers unique is that they're mission-driven, not profit-driven; the boards play a central role; donor relationships and community trust must be carefully managed; and cultural alignment matters just as much as legal alignment.

If we want to support mergers, foundations and donors need to be willing to fund them for a minimum of two to three years. Fifteen years ago only one foundation in the United States funded mergers. While more foundations support it now, we need to keep expanding the possibility and support of mergers.

Wisdom on Mergers

Ann Mei Chang suggests that unlike the for-profit sector where mergers offer financial incentives, nonprofits have little motivation to merge as the board and executives of the acquired organization typically lose autonomy without gaining any clear benefits. As a result, most nonprofit mergers happen under financial duress when an organization is struggling and seeking to preserve their work, rather than from a position of strategic strength.

Kimberlee Riley described coaching two organizations serving abused women that were required to merge by government funders but faced challenges due to leaders already invested in their separate organizational identities.

Olivia Dodd advocates for shutting down nonprofits that are no longer effective rather than perpetuating them, wishing more organizations were comfortable saying "This lived its life" instead of continuing for the sake of continuation. She sees value in strategic mergers and has experienced two nonprofits folding into her organization to combine resources and create greater impact.

Conclusion

As we've shared, collaboration, partnership, and diversity are essential to a nonprofit's ability to create meaningful and lasting impact. At their best, social benefit organizations create change by listening deeply, exchanging generously, and weaving durable relationships across communities and institutions. Working collaboratively allows organizations to combine strengths, share resources, and tackle complex challenges more effectively than they could alone. Strong partnerships expand reach, deepen community trust, and open doors to new opportunities, funding, and expertise. Embracing diversity ensures that a nonprofit's decisions, programs, and leadership reflect the varied experiences of the communities it serves, leading to more inclusive, innovative, and equitable outcomes. Together, these elements strengthen a nonprofit's capacity to fulfill its mission and drive sustainable social change.

Elizabeth Sheehan, MPH, of the Valerian Fund, sums it up, "The future will be shaped not only by what we fund but by how boldly we work together."

Chapter 6

Reshaping the Funding and Fundraising Worlds

My heart is moved by all I cannot save:so much has been destroyed. I have to cast my lot with those who age after age, with no extraordinary power, reconstitute the world.

—Adrienne Rich

Imagine if giving at every level reflected courage, care, and consciousness of community needs. Picture two donors. MacKenzie Scott has redistributed more than $26 billion over seven years in large, unrestricted gifts that arrive without warning and without strings. Oseola McCarty, a laundress in Mississippi, saved for eight decades and gave $150,000 in scholarships for African American students at the University of Southern Mississippi after retiring at age 86.

These are merely two points in a spectrum of giving. Between them sit millions of Americans who give what they can in many ways: religious tithes, online gifts, monthly recurring donations, mutual aid networks, giving circles, bequests, volunteer hours, and the everyday generosity of neighbors helping neighbors. In a single recent year, Americans gave more than $617 billion. Individuals accounted for the vast majority, as detailed in Figure 6.1.

What organizations and issue areas did this generosity go to? Religion led the recipient list, followed by human services, education, foundations, and health, as seen in Figure 6.2.

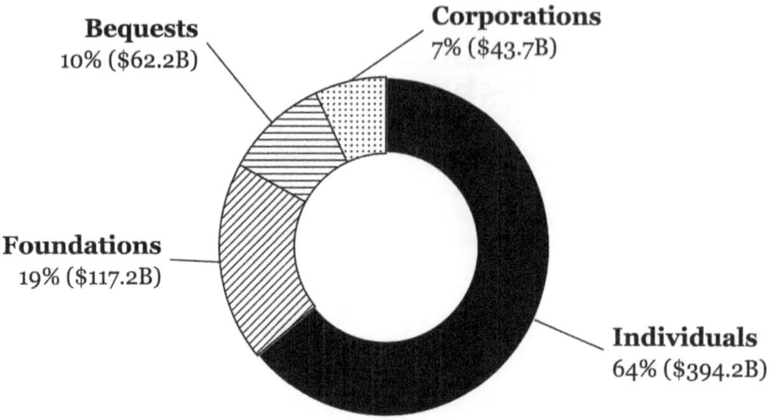

Figure 6.1 Where giving comes from, 2025.[1] *Source:* Giving USA Foundation and Indiana University Lilly Family School of Philanthropy (2026) Giving USA 2026: the annual report on philanthropy for the year 2025. Chicago, IL: Giving USA Foundation

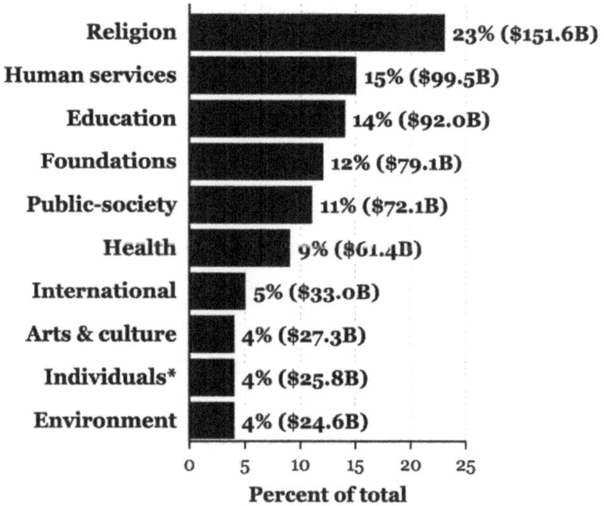

Figure 6.2 Where giving goes, 2025.[2] *Source:* Giving USA Foundation and Indiana University Lilly Family School of Philanthropy (2026) Giving USA 2026: the annual report on philanthropy for the year 2025. Chicago, IL: Giving USA Foundation

Generosity is one of the defining civic practices of American life. As Maryse Durand, a donor from France, observed: "Americans are so much more generous and caring than we, in many parts of Europe. You get out and help each other, and we remain quite separate. You all fund strangers, get to understand and know their problems, and try to help. Bravo!"

Global leaders like Chef José Andrés with World Central Kitchen, responding to crisis after crisis in real time, and social entrepreneurs like Jeff Skoll and the Skoll Foundation's World Forum, show us what is possible.

Funding Is Not a Finite Resource: Creating Pathways for Generosity

The conversation about nonprofit funding usually begins with scarcity: funding is always running out, and organizations are competing for slices of a limited pie.

This framing isn't entirely wrong. Nonprofits set our funding goals to match the needs of our communities, and the need is enormous—large enough that even a fully reformed funding system would not close the gap. Setting our ambitions higher than our means is part of what makes this work worth doing. But scarcity as a *starting assumption* can hold us back. It shapes how nonprofits write proposals, scaling ambitions down to what funders are presumed to accept. It leads boards to treat fundraising as awkward rather than essential. It allows foundations to preserve themselves rather than serve their missions. And it leaves donors holding back, uncertain whether their giving will be enough or last long enough to matter.

The funding pie can grow. It can move faster. And it can reach more of the people who need it. We cover three levers of funding redesign:

- **Move it.** Release the charitable capital that already exists but sits parked in funds.
- **Grow it.** Bring in new givers, new wealth, and new pathways into generosity.
- **Ground it.** Send what flows to the communities and leaders closest to the need.

Each lever has social, cultural, and structural elements. Before turning to them, we start by examining the current conditions of funding.

Our Funding Predicament: The Challenges We Face

Social benefit organizations today are operating under pressures unlike any in recent memory. The strain comes from three directions at once: a public sector pulling back, a slow-moving philanthropic sector, and a corporate sector that gives meagerly.

Government support has become less predictable, less generous, and more politicized. Hundreds of programs have been cut in 2025 and 2026—including Medicaid, food programs, and USAID—many serving the most underserved communities. Contracts are uncertain, public agencies are weakened by layoffs and abrupt reorganization, and executive orders targeting DEI have led foundations to quietly scrub websites and soften language. Nonprofits are increasingly asked to absorb needs that public funding once addressed, without the capital or staffing required.

Darian Rodriguez Heyman, author and founder of Helping People Help, has emphasized that government funding cuts dwarf what individual donors or foundations can replace—even the largest funders are making hard triage decisions amid the $50 billion being cut from USAID alone.

Many funders remain slow, inequitable, and overly procedural letters of intent, proposals, tailored narratives, customized portals—consuming hours of staff time smaller organizations cannot afford. Foundations are often understaffed relative to their assets, particularly family foundations that depend on family member time, leaving them unable to keep pace with the requests they receive.

A persistent gap also remains between what funders say they value and what their grantmaking communicates. Many speak of equity, innovation, trust, and partnership in their public materials; their processes have been slower to catch up. Latonya Slack, founder and principal of Slack Global Consulting, has named the deeper dynamic underneath these patterns.

"The relationship between philanthropy and nonprofits is an unholy alliance," she has said, "set up for a lot of problems and reflecting unspoken power dynamics in class and race. There are good people in philanthropy, but it's the system. Everyone seems afraid to talk about and challenge the system that is in place."

Corporate funders sit in a related category of underperformance. Corporate contributions to nonprofits remain modest, and many sponsorships serve marketing over mission. Sponsorship is useful, but it is not a substitute for civic responsibility. Corporations benefit from public infrastructure, an educated workforce, and stable communities, and should have a stake in the sector. The business case is also stronger than many companies realize: Millennial and Gen Z employees increasingly choose where to work based on a company's community engagement and corporate social responsibility practices.

These conditions are real, and need conscious thought and collective effort to challenge. But focusing only on the strain misses something equally real: the opportunity for funding to grow.

The Opportunity of Untapped Generosity

Consider what is already designated for charity but moving slowly. By 2026, donor-advised funds held roughly $328 billion across 3.6 million accounts, growing faster than the rate at which money is granted out of them. Private foundation endowments compound year after year. By some estimates, more than three-quarters of already-charitable assets remain parked, invested, and growing rather than being released to organizations serving urgent needs. Asset managers earn fees on capital under management; no required timetable compels timely distribution from donor-advised funds to working nonprofits. The incentives are misaligned with the urgency communities face.

The funding world is wider than most people realize. Figure 6.3 maps the landscape: foundations of every kind, donor-advised funds, bequests and trusts, giving circles, online giving, earned income, sponsorships, scholarships, and the government support that surrounds it all. Each ring represents a different layer of how charitable capital flows—and each holds room for growth.

Now consider that the largest intergenerational wealth transfer in American history is currently underway. Tens of trillions of dollars are moving from one generation to the next over the coming decades. Some of that capital, if we are specific in our planning, will flow into public benefit organizations through legacy gifts, bequests, trusts, and retirement funds. Far more could, if the sector stewards it well (Chapter 3 takes this up in depth).

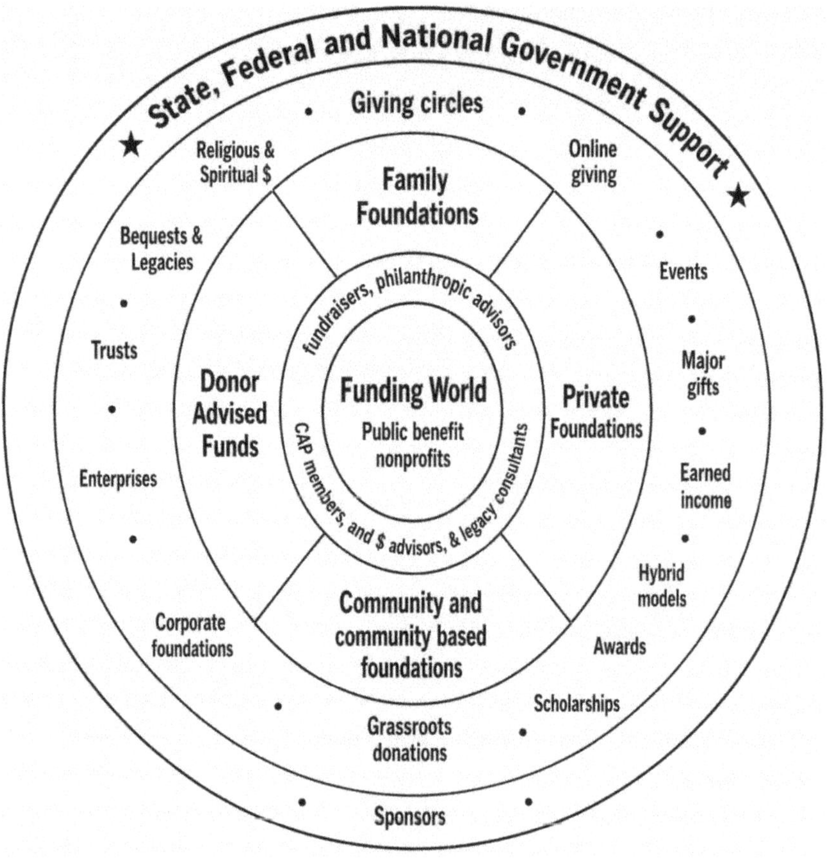

Figure 6.3 The Nonprofit Funding Ecosystem

Most inheritors have received no education in giving, and many financial advisors are trained to preserve assets, not deploy them. Women now control a rapidly growing share of household wealth and are emerging as the demographic most actively reshaping how giving happens. Online giving has lowered the floor of participation so that a first-time giver can become a recurring monthly donor, a volunteer, or a board member. Accessible giving circles also grow exponentially. Giving circles have arisen in the United States, engaging donors collectively. Earned income, mission-aligned investing, and nonprofit loan funds represent capital streams that barely existed a generation ago.

Finally, consider in-kind giving and mutual aid. Across the United States, communities organize food, childcare, and legal support. Unpaid caregiving for the sick and elderly represents one of the largest forms of generosity in American life and almost never appears in philanthropic accounting. Caring for our neighbors and communities and expressing it, during hard times, is what makes us so positive as a country.

Each of these is a place where funding and support can actively grow. The question is whether the sector is equipped to advocate for this capital, create pathways to it, and steward it well—not only its largest, best-staffed institutions, but the small and midsized organizations closest to communities. The first step is releasing capital already designated for charity back into the system.

Move It: Moving Existing Charitable Capital

Chuck Collins, author and senior scholar at the Institute for Policy Studies, estimates that roughly $1.4 trillion in charitable assets sits warehoused in private foundations and donor-advised funds rather than reaching the communities that need them. Most foundations distribute only the minimum 5% payout each year.

This money has already been raised, designated for charitable purposes, and granted its tax benefits. It is charitable money in every legal and moral sense. Why isn't it moving? The rest of this section lays out how to release dormant capital from foundations, donor-advised funds, and endowments back into the work it was meant to fund.

Donor-Advised Funds

A donor-advised fund (DAF) is a charitable account held at a sponsoring institution that allows donors to set money aside for charity, take an immediate tax deduction, and recommend grants to social impact organizations over time. The structure was designed as a flexible bridge between contribution and grant. Used well, DAFs are helpful tools. Used poorly, they function as warehouses rather than waterways.

By 2024, DAFs held roughly $328 billion in assets, with grantmaking from DAFs reaching $64.89 billion that year. Fidelity Charitable, Schwab Charitable, the National Philanthropic Trust, and a wide network of community foundations and sponsors manage these assets. Donors receive immediate tax advantages upon contribution. But no required timetable compels distribution from a DAF to a working nonprofit. Meanwhile, asset managers earn fees tied to the size of the assets under management—a structural incentive that rewards holding rather than moving.[3]

Reform proposals include requiring DAF payout within a fixed timeframe—three to five years is a commonly proposed window—and banning or limiting the practice of private foundations donating to DAFs as a way to delay their own payout obligations. The Half My DAF initiative (www.halfmydaf.org), founded by Jen and David Risher in 2020, encourages DAF holders to deploy at least half their funds, with the Rishers themselves matching grants made by donors who do. It's a meaningful effort to shift norms from the bottom up—but voluntary commitments alone are unlikely to move hundreds of billions now in DAFs. Legislative reform is needed too.

The levers here are concrete:

A minimum payout requirement for DAFs—modeled on the 5% rule that already applies to private foundations, or stronger—would establish a floor for how quickly designated charitable capital must reach working organizations. Several policy proposals along these lines have circulated in Congress in recent years and deserve sustained attention from the sector.

Sponsor-level transparency would let donors, advisors, and the public see how quickly different DAF sponsors actually move money. Some sponsors distribute aggressively; others let assets sit. Right now there is little public information to distinguish them.

Donor-led norm change through initiatives like #HalfMyDAF, which invites donors to commit publicly to moving at least half of what sits in their accounts.

Advisor practice matters too. If financial and philanthropic advisors routinely asked clients not only how much they wanted to contribute to a DAF but how quickly they intended to distribute it, donor behavior would shift. Most advisors don't ask that question. They could.

Foundations

Private foundations in the United States are required to distribute at least 5% of their assets each year. Many treat that floor as a ceiling.

In a moment of compounding crises, that posture is harder to justify. Foundations exist to serve their missions, but many have become preoccupied with perpetuating themselves. A foundation that preserves its corpus while the communities it was created to serve are starved of resources has drifted from its purpose.

Some are responding by choosing to spend down or "sunset"—deliberately distributing their assets over a defined period rather than existing in perpetuity. The Atlantic Philanthropies, the S.D. Bechtel, Jr. Foundation, the Beldon Fund, the Gates Foundation, the Merle Chambers Foundation, and others have shown that a finite lifespan can concentrate impact and force harder, clearer decisions about what matters most.

Others are staying in perpetuity but giving well beyond the minimum. The Marguerite Casey Foundation, in Seattle, has committed to grant at least $500 million over the next decade—a 50% increase over its previous decade's average, and an annual floor of $50 million—on the explicit principle that the 5% requirement is a floor, not a ceiling.[4]

Care must be taken to not leave out of consideration new grantees with opportunities, and solutions, for funding. Others advocate for increasing payouts. The MacArthur Foundation has issued a call to foundations to "Set it at Six," raising its baseline payout to 6% for the next two years.[5] In times of crisis, philanthropy must act like risk capital, not a savings account. And grantees need cash flow loans and capital as they scale and merge. These dollars are very scarce and should be expanded by many funders.

A separate question is how actively foundations engage the communities and donors they serve. Community foundations stay rooted in their actual communities when they treat donors as active learners rather than pass-through clients. Megan Hyman, CEO of the Dallas Jewish Community Foundation, has built such a model. The foundation has grown to more than 650 donors and convenes them in small "Minyan groups" of 10 for sacred discussions about what they are funding and what their communities need.

The contrast matters: at the country's roughly 900 community foundations, an estimated 80% of donor-advised contributions pass through without foundation engagement. Where sponsors invest in donor formation, capital moves with greater knowledge.

Other levers exist for foundations:

Raise the private foundation payout rate. Going from 5% to 7% or 10% during sustained periods of high need is a defensible exercise of fiduciary judgment, not a violation of it.

Mission-align the endowment. The 95% of foundation assets not granted out each year are invested somewhere. If those investments contradict the foundation's mission—for instance, funding fossil fuels while granting for climate work—the foundation is working against itself with most of its money.

Fund what nonprofits actually need. Multiyear, unrestricted, general operating support remains the most useful form of grant capital. Trust-based philanthropy practices exist precisely because the field knows what works and has been slow to adopt it at scale.

Get civically involved. NCRP recommends that at least 25% of philanthropic funding support advocacy, organizing, and civic engagement. Fewer than 10% of foundations meet that threshold.

Expand staffing. Investing in more paid staff can help streamline processes, deepen connection with grantees, and expand opportunities for funding.

Endowments

Beyond foundations and DAFs, vast charitable capital sits in institutional endowments—at universities, hospitals, museums, and large social benefit organizations. Most of these institutions preserve their principal and spend only a small percentage of investment returns each year.

This norm deserves more scrutiny. Endowments were built by donors who hoped to support a mission, not to fund the perpetual existence of a balance sheet. As many of these institutions face direct attacks on their work, they may need to draw down endowment principal to continue advancing their mission.

Two things have to shift. The first is cultural: trustees treating endowments as resources for the present, not only insurance for the future. The second is fiduciary: boards revisiting spending policies set decades ago under very different conditions.

Policy Recommendations

The deepest levers for moving dormant capital are public policy. Charitable giving in the United States is shaped by tax law in ways that most donors and even many nonprofit leaders do not fully see. A few areas where policy redesign could meaningfully accelerate flow:

Restore and expand the universal charitable deduction. When current nonitemizers can deduct charitable gifts, giving from middle-income households increases. The temporary universal deduction during the pandemic showed measurable effects; making it permanent and meaningful would broaden the donor base. Donors itemizing decreased from 30% to an estimated 12%. Lilly Endowment reported that as much as $20 billion annually was not being given by middle- and upper-income families after the change in the tax law in 2015, as one incentive, tax deductibility had been removed.

Reform DAF payout rules. As noted earlier—a minimum distribution requirement, calculated at the account level, would close the gap between contribution and grant.

Strengthen private foundation payout requirements during sustained crises. Temporary adjustments to the 5% payout, as stated previously, during periods of acute need are worth serious examination.

Close loopholes that convert charitable vehicles into tax shelters. A small share of DAFs and private foundations function more as estate-planning tools than as philanthropy. Tightening definitions and reporting requirements would protect the integrity of charitable status.

Fund the IRS's nonprofit oversight capacity. The agency responsible for overseeing the sector has been chronically under-resourced. Stronger oversight protects donors, beneficiaries, and the legitimacy of charitable status itself.

These are not small reforms. They are structural redesigns that reliably direct charitable capital toward charitable use.

Charitable Capital Is a Civic Resource

Policy and culture have to move together. As long as donors believe their generosity ends at the moment of contribution, as long as advisors define their job as preservation, as long as foundations measure success by endowment size rather than impact—the money will continue to sit. Charitable capital is not a savings account. It is a civic resource. Holding it indefinitely is a choice with consequences for the communities waiting on the other side.

Grow It: New Pathways to Giving

The previous section was about releasing capital that already exists. This section is about growing the pool itself.

Individuals make up the majority of Americans' charitable giving, as detailed earlier. Living donors and bequests together account for 74% of all charitable contributions.[6] But that base is shrinking. Individual giving as a share of total philanthropy has been declining for decades, even as total giving has grown. The everyday donor is encountering a tax structure that no longer rewards their generosity, economic pressure on household budgets, and a sector that has come to rely increasingly on a smaller circle of high-net-worth donors.[7]

This is the largest opportunity in the redesign. Restoring the individual giving base is the single highest-impact lever for the future of the sector. Four shifts are reshaping who gives and how: a generational wealth transfer underway, women emerging as the demographic most actively reshaping giving culture, online platforms lowering the floor of who can be a donor, and earned income opening revenue streams that didn't exist a generation ago. Each represents a place where funding can grow—but only if the sector builds the pathways to receive it.

The Great Wealth Transfer

The largest intergenerational wealth transfer in American history is happening right now, as discussed in Chapter 3. This is the single largest opportunity and risk for the philanthropic sector in our lifetimes. If inheritors are met early with strong donor education and peer learning communities, a meaningful share of that capital can flow into civic life.

The lever here is *donor development*—the work of helping wealth owners become confident, strategic, and relational givers. This development often happens in donor learning communities. The Women Donors Network, Solidaire Network, Resource Generation, Threshold Foundation, Women Moving Millions, and dozens of others, bring donors together for sustained learning, peer accountability, socially impactful investing resources, and collective giving decisions. Resource Generation has built a support network for younger inheritors that combines political education and concrete giving practice. These communities reduce the isolation that often keeps wealth holders from giving, replacing it with relationships that make giving feel possible and joyful.

Rajasvini Bhansali, executive director of Solidaire Network, has described what this isolation looks like in practice. A Solidaire survey found that people often have more access and power over wealth than they realize, but the absence of a supportive community keeps them from acting on it. "A lot of what my team does is matchmaking," Bhansali has said, "helping people meet other brave people who've either done it before or are in the process of doing it, so they don't have to go at it alone." Networks like these provide community, courage, and trusted advisors who support liberating wealth toward justice.

Maya Angelou's observation captures what these communities know in practice: "I have found that among its other benefits, giving liberates the soul of the giver." Giving changes the giver when done in community.

As Darian Rodriguez Heyman has noted, individual philanthropists can magnify their impact "10 or even 100×" by engaging peers through collaborative funding rather than acting alone. Bring family members, friends, and inheritors into giving and learning communities. Generosity is contagious, and donors who invite others to the table multiply their own impact while lifting others.

Individual donors and donor activists have also begun designing their own infrastructure for moving capital quickly. Ari Nessel founded the Pollination Project in 2013 with a simple practice: give $1,000 every day to early-stage changemakers around the world. More than a decade later, the project has supported more than 6,500 leaders in more than 120 countries, and Nessel has helped catalyze parallel funding networks like Farmed Animal Funders. The model has had a huge impact and is a reminder that the redesign can start small and grow over time.

Women as the Demographic Reshaping Giving

A significant portion of the wealth transfer described earlier will pass through women. Of the projected $124 trillion intergenerational transfer in the United States, roughly $54 trillion is expected to move horizontally to surviving spouses, 95% of whom are women, with another $47 trillion passing to women in younger generations.[8]

Women's control of wealth is already growing rapidly. In the United States, assets controlled by women rose from about $10 trillion in 2018 to roughly $18 trillion in 2023, and McKinsey projects women will assume control of an additional $16 trillion by 2030 (see Figure 6.4).[9] Decision-making is

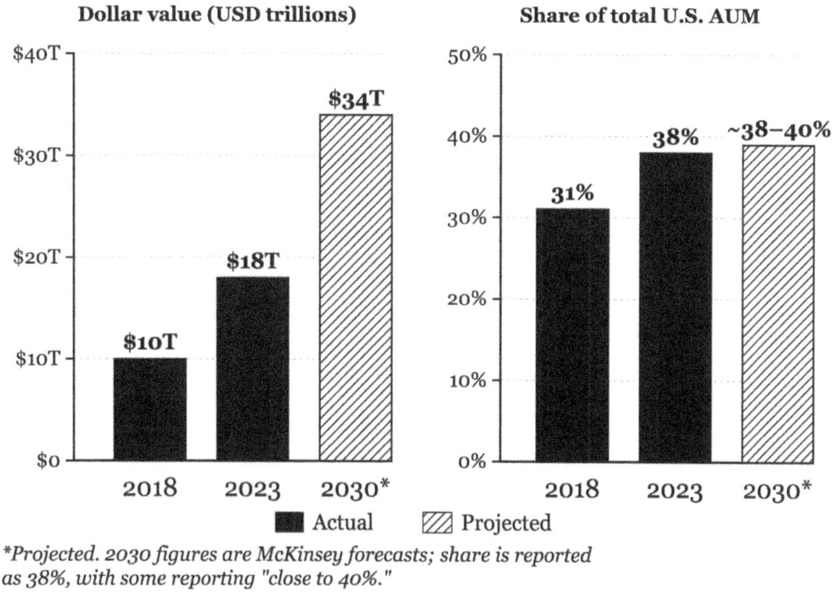

Figure 6.4 Women's share of U.S. assets under management (AUM) 2018–2030 (projected).[10] Dollar value of assets controlled by women (left) and share of total U.S. AUM (right)

shifting in parallel: women are now the sole or co-equal decision-maker on charitable giving in the large majority of high-net-worth households. The patterns describe a demographic that is not only giving more but deciding more.

Research on women's giving consistently shows a few patterns: women tend to give more relationally, to learn before giving, to give in community, and to combine giving with volunteering and advocacy. They are more likely to give in pooled or collective vehicles, more likely to follow the work of organizations they support over time, and more likely to bring others into giving alongside them.

Giving circles—pooled, peer-driven funds, initially sparked and documented by author Sondra Shaw-Hardy—have grown to nearly 4,000 in the United States. Between 2017 and 2023, they engaged more than 370,000 people and granted more than $3.1 billion to causes around the country.[11] Members typically contribute anywhere from $50 to $25,000 a year, with the amount set by each circle and agreed on by its members. Women have led this growth. The model works because it solves several problems at once: it lowers the barrier to entry for new givers, builds relationships that sustain giving over time, and generates collective learning that turns first-time donors into long-term ones.

Women's funds—starting in the mid-1970s, with the Astraea Lesbian Foundation for Justice, the Ms. Foundation for Women, the California Women's Foundation, Mama Cash, and Women's Way, anchored by networks like the Women's Funding Network and Prospera International—have built institutions that not only move money to women and girls but model practices the rest of philanthropy is now adopting: participatory grantmaking, trust-based funding, community-led decisions, and accountability to those most affected.

Megan Hyman has offered a sharp account of why women's giving practices look the way they do. "Women weren't allowed to have their own bank accounts," she notes. "I think one of the reasons women are so good at philanthropy is that we don't have this inherited bias that we need to have control—because we know what it's like. . .to have every aspect of our life dictated by someone else. We have a really special perspective about what it means to have a trust-based relationship with a nonprofit."

Social benefit organizations and foundations that adapt to how women actually give will be positioned to receive significantly more of the capital that is moving.

Online Giving: Making Generosity More Accessible

Twenty-five years ago, asking a stranger to enter their credit card information online was a hard sell. Today, giving by phone or computer is normal, widening access to everyday donations.

Crowdfunding platforms have built a flourishing ecosystem of generosity, supporting not only nonprofits but also individuals, families, mutual-aid responses, medical crises, and memorial funds. GoFundMe alone has raised more than $40 billion since its 2010 launch, connecting more than 190 million people globally.[12] Millions have given through these platforms to causes that would never have reached them through traditional fundraising. Giving Tuesday, local giving days, recurring monthly programs, and peer-to-peer campaigns have widened the circle of participation in ways earlier generations of fundraisers could barely imagine. This is one of the most democratized forms of giving available today.

A first-time $25 gift can become a recurring monthly donor, a volunteer, a board member, and, 20 years later, a major or planned giving donor. But this pipeline works only for nonprofits that treat digital giving as the beginning of a relationship. Too many organizations spend heavily to acquire first-time online donors and never invite them deeper. Virtual giving still requires relational follow-up—welcoming, thanking, and involving online donors so their generosity becomes sustained participation.

Online giving also widens the geography of philanthropy. Donors can now support organizations far from where they live, with diaspora communities supporting work in their countries of origin, climate-concerned donors funding frontline communities they will never visit, niche causes building national constituencies that would have been impossible to reach a generation ago.

Earned Income as a Revenue Stream

The pie also grows when social impact organizations generate revenue that previously did not exist. Earned income—through training, consultation, performances, licensing, workshops, space rental, social enterprises, and mission-aligned products and services—has expanded substantially in the last two decades. The average U.S. nonprofit now earns about 20% of its revenue through program services like fees, ticket sales, tuition, patient fees, dues, and product sales, according to Independent Sector.[13]

Earned income is not right for every organization, and the risk of mission drift is real. But where it fits, earned revenue strengthens independence, reduces dependence on annual fundraising cycles, and generates flexible capital that no grant will fund. A nonprofit earning 30% of its revenue through mission-aligned services is structurally more resilient than one dependent entirely on contributed income.

Mission-aligned investing and nonprofit loan funds are a parallel development. Foundations, community development financial institutions, and aligned investors have begun building capital infrastructure the sector has long lacked—facility loans, growth capital, working capital lines, and bridge loans that let nonprofits weather cash flow gaps the way any business does. These tools let organizations scale and invest in their own infrastructure without waiting for the next grant cycle.

The opportunity is to expand this infrastructure further. More funders could establish loan funds, as some community foundations already do. Public benefit organizations deserve the same financial tools any business relies on to survive and grow.

The Role of Advisors

A thread runs through all four shifts: advisors are central, underused, and capable of unlocking enormous giving when trained well.

The evidence from the field is striking. Phil Cubeta, CAP and founder of Philanthropy Offerings, has pointed to Omaha as a working model. A Chartered Advisors in Philanthropy (CAP) study group there grew from 10 advisors to roughly 100 over a decade, collectively facilitating $9.2 billion in philanthropic giving that would not otherwise have moved. The local community foundation tracked the results and found that CAP-trained donors gave gifts roughly three times larger than non-trained donors. The initiative was inspired by Warren Buffett's stated goal of making Omaha the most generous city in the country. The sentiment to "give where you live," does make giving tangible and is a great way to get involved and follow the changes in the nonprofit you have funded. You can always give a small donation to be included in their mailing list and keep up with them at events and through newsletters and annual reports. But there are many solutions that come from regional and national organizations, and advisors and donor learning communities can help donors find them.

Financial planners, estate attorneys, philanthropic advisors, accountants, and wealth managers are in the rooms where capital moves. They are there when businesses are sold, inheritances are received, estate plans are drafted, and DAFs are established. What they ask in those moments shapes how much of that capital flows toward charity. Yet most are not trained to ask the giving questions. Financial advisors often view philanthropy as a niche specialty rather than a core part of wealth planning. Estate attorneys default to templates that minimize charitable provisions. Accountants and planners often treat charitable giving as a tax benefit rather than a value or community engagement path, giving to their client and themselves greater purpose, passion, and connectivity.

This is changing. The CAP curriculum and designation, dedicated philanthropic advisory practices, and values-based financial planning all reflect the shift—but it is not nearly fast enough for the wealth transfer underway. Decision-making for clients is often a long process. Sparking the excitement with a question about lifetime or legacy giving often speeds up the planning process. Clients completing and signing or updating their documents is key, and delays can mean valuable assets may not be designated to family or nonprofit causes or donor-advised funds. Advisors help immensely. Nonprofits can help with legacy clubs and events.

Advocating for Increased Funding and Public Support

There is one more lever worth naming: civic advocacy. Funding moves—or is blocked—through policy. Tax law, DAF and foundation payout rules, the charitable deduction, government contracting, and program funding all shape what resources nonprofits can access. The sector's voice on these policies is one of its most underused levers.

The case for using it has rarely been more urgent. As Figure 6.5 shows, U.S. billionaire wealth has grown more than fivefold since 2010, while charitable giving has barely doubled. The gap is widening at an accelerating rate.

This divergence is the result of policy choices. Federal tax rates on the wealthy have declined steadily since the 1960s. Recent administrations have intensified that trend, reducing taxation on the top, loosening regulation, and elevating individual billionaires as cultural and political figures. America now has its own class of billionaires whose influence rivals that of foreign

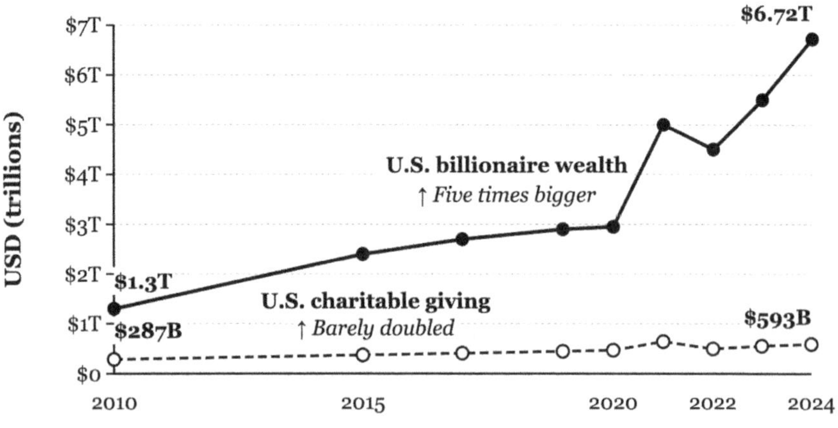

Figure 6.5 America's widening wealth-giving gap.[14,15] *Source:* Giving USA Foundation and Indiana University Lilly Family School of Philanthropy (2026) Giving USA 2026: the annual report on philanthropy for the year 2025. Chicago, IL: Giving USA Foundation

oligarchies—a fact that would have been unimaginable a generation ago. Much of the underlying wealth creation is genuine: AI, technology, financial markets, and a diversified economy have produced real innovation and broad stability. But the gains have concentrated so steeply at the top that the question is no longer whether the system is generating wealth, but for whom, and what the rest of us are entitled to ask of those who hold it.

Chuck Collins gives the case for advocacy: he notes that for every dollar a billionaire gives to charity, taxpayers subsidize up to $0.74 through lost income, estate, and gift tax revenue. He has proposed capping the deductible amount at $500 million per donor, with anything above that taxed. Whatever the right policy mechanism, the underlying point holds: charitable capital is not purely private money. Since it is untaxed, it carries a public subsidy, and the public has a legitimate interest in how quickly and how well it moves.

Organizations like the National Committee for Responsive Philanthropy, the Philanthropy Project, and Inequality.org, led by advocates such as Aaron Dorfman, Jan Masaoka, and Chuck Collins are working to change individual and corporate tax rates and payout levels for foundations and DAFs. Tax rates on the wealthy have steadily decreased since the 1960s. Redesigning taxation to ensure the ultra-wealthy contribute their fair share is essential to a more equitable future.

Just because nonprofits are nonpartisan does not mean we must be silent. 501(c)(3) organizations have substantial legal room to educate, organize, testify, mobilize constituents, and defend the policies their missions require. Letters to the editor, social media campaigns, coalition work, and convenings are all legitimate uses of nonprofit voice. Organizations with affiliated 501(c)(4) capacity can do more, including direct lobbying within legal limits. The Alliance for Justice offers training to help boards and staff understand what's possible. Donors and nonprofits are also showing up directly—through Funders on the Hill days and growing congressional advocacy efforts that pair training with dedicated budgets for higher impact. Across both designations, there is far more room for advocacy than most nonprofits use (see Figure 6.6).

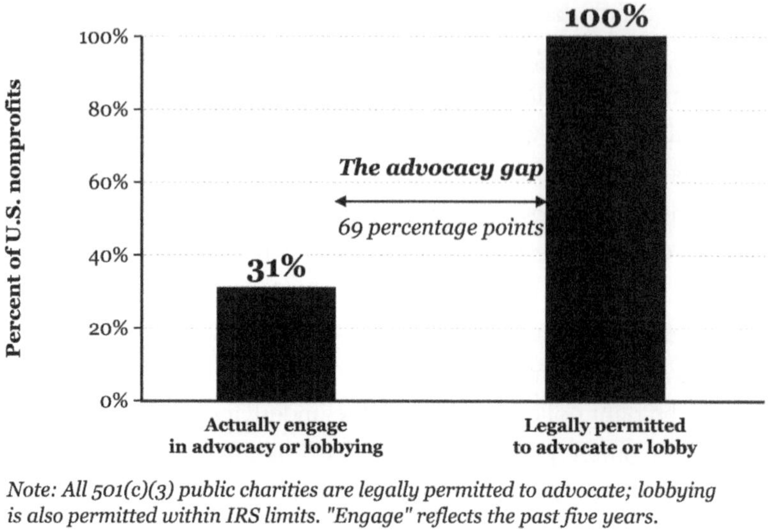

Figure 6.6 The nonprofit advocacy gap.[16] *Source*: Giving USA Foundation and Indiana University Lilly Family School of Philanthropy (2026) Giving USA 2026: the annual report on philanthropy for the year 2025. Chicago, IL: Giving USA Foundation

If public policy is harming the communities a public benefit serves, speaking up is part of the mission. And if the sector wants better tax policy, more public investment, fairer treatment of nonprofits, and protection for vulnerable communities, those changes will only come through its collective voice.

Ground It: Aligning Capital Closer to Needs

Growing and moving funding matters. But neither resolves the deeper question this chapter has been circling: Who decides where the money goes?

For most of American philanthropy's history, money flowed from wealth holders to causes they selected, on the terms they allowed. Communities were meant to be grateful beneficiaries. That arrangement is changing slowly and not without resistance. But it is an imperative to make this shift because, simply, *proximity to the issue produces wiser funding*. People closest to a problem usually understand it better. They know which leaders are credible and which are performing, which solutions look good in proposals and which hold up over time.

Grounding capital means connecting it to the people, communities, and lived experience closest to the need. The practices below put that principle into operation.

Trust-Based Philanthropy

The clearest articulation of this shift is the trust-based philanthropy movement, which has codified six funder practices from more than a decade of organizing:

- Give multiyear, unrestricted funding.
- Do the homework.
- Simplify and streamline paperwork.
- Be transparent and responsive.
- Solicit and act on feedback.
- Offer support beyond the check.

Each practice corrects a specific habit in the old funding culture. Together, they describe how a respectful, capable partner would behave. They change the emotional climate of philanthropy, reducing subservience and cutting wasted time, and signaling to nonprofit leaders that their judgment matters.

The clearest large-scale demonstration of these practices in recent years has been MacKenzie Scott's grantmaking. Since 2019, Scott has distributed more than $26 billion in unrestricted gifts, including roughly $1.2 billion to historically Black colleges and universities and significant endowment-strengthening grants to organizations long underfunded by traditional philanthropy. She emphasizes speed, due diligence done by her team rather than by grantees, and trust in nonprofit leadership to deploy the funds well.

Meanwhile, leaders working at the front edge of equitable philanthropy are asking the framework harder questions. Vanessa Daniel, former E.D. of Groundswell Fund, has argued that trust-based philanthropy can sometimes defeat its own purpose. "Trust-based philanthropy can center the comfort and the ego of the donor wanting to feel good about what they're giving and how they're giving, shirking their responsibility to actually do proper due diligence."

Daniel's point is not that trust-based philanthropy is wrong. It is that trust without rigor defaults to existing networks, reproducing inequity. She counters that asking for proof of impact remains essential. "If you're doing voter engagement, you should be able to show how many voters you talked to and how many people cast ballots. If you're a base-building organization, you should be able to talk about how many new people and new leaders you've brought in. You should be able to speak to how your work has delivered improvements in the material conditions of people in the communities you serve, and how those people have more power because you existed. Organizations that are accountable to the communities they serve should be able to share information about impact with their constituents first and foremost, and then pass it along to their funders too."

Jason Franklin, founder of Ktisis Capital, frames this as a shift in what accountability looks like. "The new edge in trust-based philanthropy is to talk about what mutual trust means. It doesn't mean carte blanche—'here's money, I don't care what you do, there's no accountability.' It means there's a different way you hold each other accountable. There's a different relationship that you enter into that is trusting from both sides."

In this fuller version, trust is rigor practiced relationally—a mutual commitment to seeing the work through.

Participatory Grantmaking

Trust-based philanthropy redesigns the relationship between funder and grantee. Participatory grantmaking redesigns who decides where that funding goes.

In a participatory model, grant decisions are made by members of the communities the funding is intended to serve. People with lived experience review proposals and make funding decisions, folding in communities like disability rights advocates, formerly incarcerated leaders, immigrant organizers, BIPOC leaders, youth leaders, and frontline climate activists. Foundation staff may facilitate the process; they do not control its outcome.

Community panels are often more rigorous than outside reviewers. They distinguish quickly between organizations genuinely rooted in their communities and those that are not and recognize emerging leaders traditional grantmaking consistently misses.

The Disability Rights Fund, the FRIDA Young Feminist Fund, the Red Umbrella Fund, and a growing number of community foundations have built durable participatory practices over years. The model requires real authority for community decision-makers, fair compensation for their time, and a foundation board willing to share power rather than merely consult.

Participatory grantmaking is not right for every grant or every funder. But for the many issues where lived experience is central, the question is increasingly hard to avoid: Why are decisions about communities still being made primarily by people who do not live in them?

Equity-Rooted Philanthropy

Some of the most consequential philanthropy reforms have been led by communities that traditional philanthropy has historically underfunded. These funds are considered community-based giving as donors, activists and community leaders identify issues and then solve them together with grants, technical assistance, advocacy, and training.

Women's funds, as listed earlier, sparked a movement. Now, more than 180 women's foundations worldwide—connected through networks like the Women's Funding Network and Prospera International—have moved billions of dollars to diverse women and girls while modeling participatory, trust-based, and community-grounded practice for the rest of the field.

BIPOC-led funds have done similar impactful work. Groundswell Fund, the Solidaire Network, NDN Collective, Donors of Color Network, the

Black-Led Movement Fund, the Latino Community Foundation, AAPI-led funds, and Indigenous-led funds globally have demonstrated what becomes possible when funding decisions are made by people whose lives are shaped by the issues being funded. These funds consistently identify leaders, organizations, and strategies that traditional philanthropy overlooks. They move money faster and partner deeply, sustaining relationships over years.

Faith-rooted philanthropy is its own deep tradition. Tzedakah in Jewish practice, zakat in Islam, tithing in Christian denominations, and interfaith giving circles and federations all rest on theological commitments to mutual obligation and community accountability—commitments that have organized substantial charitable resources for centuries.

Equity funding has lineage. Beginning in the 1970s, a network of activist and donor-led foundations called the Funding Exchange—including Vanguard Public Foundation in San Francisco, the Haymarket People's Fund in Boston, and Liberty Hill in Los Angeles—pioneered an approach they called "Change, Not Charity": grantmaking decisions made jointly by donors and grassroots organizers, site visits to fund the work directly, and grants that supported organizing rather than service delivery. The contemporary trust-based, participatory, and community-led funds named above extend that tradition.

When communities build their own philanthropic infrastructure, they empower themselves from multiple angles. Donors and foundations who want to redirect how charitable capital flows should resource BIPOC-led funds, women's funds, LGBTQ+ funds, and disability-led funds at the scale of their work.

Flow Funding

Flow funding is a practice where a donor or foundation identifies activists, healers, artists, organizers, or community leaders they trust, and hands them the resources and responsibility for making grants themselves.

The Indigenous Women's Flow Fund of the Kindle Project, a donor and activist funding circle, is one of the clearest examples. Indigenous women activists serve as grantmakers, bypassing the institutional habits that have kept philanthropy distant from the communities it claims to serve. The model assumes that lived experience produces better funding decisions than institutional processes.

Flow funding is a creative additional way to give. It was begun by a member of the Rockefeller family, Marion Weber, who sought partners in her giving. It has many heartfelt results. It does not scale as easily as other models. It depends on relationships, on the donor's willingness to genuinely cede authority, and on the recipient's capacity to take on the work of grantmaking. But where it works, it proves the section's underlying claim: capital is best directed by those closest to the need. Often when wealthy people have a birthday, they can share their wealth by giving friends money to redistribute. This is a common way to do "flow funding" that can include convening people to listen to what they learned, and who and how they funded.

The Kindle Project and the website flowfunding.org offer entry points for funders curious about the model.

Mutual Aid and In-Kind Support

Not all generosity travels through 501(c)(3) infrastructure. During COVID, mutual aid networks raised emergency funds, delivered food, made masks, organized childcare, and protected elders. These networks operated faster and with greater cultural fluency than formal institutions. As immigration enforcement became a greater threat in 2026, communities organized legal support and sanctuary through informal networks that operated below the radar of conventional philanthropy. Unpaid caregiving for aging parents, disabled family members, and loved ones with serious illness is one of the largest forms of generosity in American life and almost never appears in philanthropic accounting at all.

Mutual aid is not a substitute for durable institutions, and it is not philanthropy in the formal sense, but it still represents generosity that scales. Funders can support mutual aid networks where they exist through fiscal sponsorship, rapid-response grants, and infrastructure support—without trying to formalize them out of their effectiveness. Social impact organizations can recognize mutual aid as a partner and a peer, not a competitor. The sector as a whole can expand its definition of where civic generosity lives.

Next Steps: Reshaping Funding Together

The redesign described in this chapter depends on specific people in specific roles changing our habits together. Below is what the three levers ask of each actor in the sector.

Foundations: Move More and Adopt Trust-Based Practices

Foundations sit closer to the redesign than any other actor. They hold the dormant capital, set the cultural norms for institutional grantmaking, and shape the experience of thousands of nonprofits at once.

- *Treat 5% payout as a floor, not a ceiling*—and consider whether the times call for a higher rate, a defined spend-down, or a structural shift in how the foundation thinks about its lifespan. Join in the new trend toward "spending down" limiting foundations to a 5–25 year lifespan, thus giving more annually and often in multiyear grants.
- *Adopt trust-based practices in full,* including giving to known grantees, for more than one year. This streamlines applications, and if one funds operating support as the default rather than the exception, a great deal of stability in grantees and hires they need or programs can happen with greater ease. Grantmaking processes and applications must be streamlined.
- *Invest in your own staffing,* because more paid staff is the precondition for being a useful partner to grantees and potential grantees, not bureaucratic bloat. Educate your board and finance committee on reasonable expenses for staff and consultants needed.

- *Mission-align the endowment*, since the 95% of assets not granted out each year are invested somewhere, and values-aligned investments can further the foundation's work.
- *Resource community-led infrastructure*—BIPOC-led funds, women's funds, disability-led funds, LGBTQ+ funds, and participatory grant-making initiatives—at the scale of their work.
- *Be accessible to your community*, engaging in site visits and opening doors for grantees to other possible funders.
- Fund start up nonprofits. (See the Smart Family Fund, who fund $25,000–$100,000 first-time grants; https://smartfamilyfund.org.)

Donors: Give What's Parked, Plan, and Learn

Donors at every level make the cumulative decisions that shape the field.

- *Create a giving or legacy plan now*, and consider moving some of what you intend as a bequest into your lifetime. Get financial and planning advice from a certified CAP, your own financial advisor, or an advising team.
- *Move what's parked* by distributing from your donor-advised fund, ideally through a public commitment like #HalfMyDAF.
- *Give earlier and make multiyear, unrestricted contributions*, because if you trust the organization enough to fund it, trust it enough to fund it well.
- *Join a donor learning community.* See suggested networks listed throughout the chapter.
- *Be trained and become a donor organizer*, or invite others to give and learn with you.
- *See Transformative Donor Organizing: The Developing Theory and Practice*, by Isaac Lev Szmosnko for Solidaire Network, 2026.

Advisors: Steward the Process

Financial planners, estate attorneys, philanthropic advisors, accountants, and wealth managers are the most underused lever in the funding redesign.

- *Ask the giving question in every wealth conversation*—sale of a business, inheritance, estate plan, retirement plan, DAF setup—rather than treating it as a footnote.
- *Get philanthropically literate* through the Chartered Advisors in Philanthropy designation or peer learning communities.
- *Help donors move money, not only contribute it*, by closing the gap between facilitating contributions and facilitating distributions. DAF assets should be distributed, as communities need these already tax deducted funds now, not later.
- *Align investments with values*, because donors increasingly want their portfolios and their giving to point in the same direction, increasing their impact.
- *Reframe legacy planning around lifetime giving*. Help clients live their legacies—giving meaningfully while they're alive, to a wider range of causes than the alma maters and anchor institutions that already capture most bequest dollars.

Nonprofits: Fundraise Consciously and Advocate for Your Needs

The redesign also asks social benefit organizations to *fundraise* differently, not just receive funding differently.

- *Ask for what you actually need*—operating support, multiyear commitments, reserves, technology, coaching, capacity building, communications staff—rather than trimming asks to fit assumed funder preferences.
- *Diversify revenue* across annual giving, major gifts, monthly donors, earned income, sponsorships, bequests, DAF grants, and selected institutional support.

- *Treat first-time online donors as the start of a relationship*, with deliberate welcome, thanks, and progressive invitations to deepen connections and share about the nonprofit.
- Get fundraising training and coaching for the board, development team, and staff. Invest in your success.
- *Build relationships with advisors*, because the professionals who guide your donors' largest decisions should know your work.
- *Use your advocacy rights*—nonpartisan does not mean silent, and speaking up when policy harms your communities is part of mission, not a detour from it. Most 501(c)(3) organizations have far more legal room for advocacy than they use, and the sector's collective voice is one of its strongest levers for funding redesign.

Boards: Steward Donors Responsibly and Champion the Sector

Boards are where governance meets fundraising, and the redesign asks them to take both seriously.

- *Treat fundraising as a fiduciary responsibility*, because sustainability is governance. Grassroots and major gift fundraising takes training, planning and advocating.
- *Orient new board members*, donors, and volunteers in fundraising, messaging, and financial training, coaching, or mentorship.
- *Give first, every year*, since 100% board participation signals to every other funder that the people closest to the organization believe in it.
- *Steward and engage donors, not only solicit them*, through thank-you calls, site visits, and introductions. Host house parties and donor briefings for new prospects.
- *Champion the sector publicly* in your community, your professional networks, and with policymakers.

Policymakers and Public: Recognize Social Benefit Organizations as Civic Infrastructure

Some of the deepest levers are not held by anyone inside the sector.

- *Restore and expand the universal charitable deduction* so nonitemizers can deduct charitable gifts.
- *Establish a minimum payout requirement for DAFs* to close the indefinite gap between contribution and grant.
- *Strengthen foundation payout requirements during sustained crises*, recognizing that the 5% minimum was set under different conditions than the ones the sector now faces.
- *Fund nonprofit sector oversight and legal advocacy*, because the agencies responsible for protecting the integrity of charitable status need the resources to do that work.
- *Recognize nonprofits as essential civic infrastructure* in public language, public policy, and public investment.

Businesses and Corporate Foundations

Businesses benefit from public infrastructure, an educated workforce, and stable communities. Supporting the nonprofit sector that sustains those conditions is both civic responsibility and sound strategy.

- *Commit a set percentage of pre-tax profits annually*, encouraging the CEO and board to formalize this commitment publicly and report against it.
- *Sponsor and contribute to nonprofits* as a core part of community and employee engagement, not only as marketing.
- *Expand your corporate employees' matching gifts* and spark their volunteer activism representing your business.

- *Partner with nonprofits on substantive projects*, getting to know the organizations working in your industry's geography and field.
- *Lend what your business already has*—employee time, professional expertise, equipment, meeting space, technology, and trainings—to nonprofits that need them.
- *Build a culture of employee volunteering*, educating employees about volunteer opportunities, offering paid volunteer time off, and connecting employees to causes they care about. This benefits the nonprofit sector and strengthens employee retention.
- *Set up donor-advised funds* (DAFs) as a benefit for management or high-achieving staff.

Conclusion

We have more choices with our money and giving. Charitable capital that already exists and simply builds up can move sooner. New capital will replace it. And what flows can reach the communities closest to needs. Given cutbacks and changes, it can seem overwhelming, but every effort to move, grow, and direct funds will bring more impact and change.

There is joy in this work. There is relief in seeing resources arrive where they are needed and in helping a social impact organization become stronger than it was. There is excitement as a board comes alive, a donor finds courage, a foundation shifts practices, a volunteer becomes a giver, a young inheritor becomes a thoughtful steward, a grant moves faster, a new partnership forms. Through these actions, a community says, we are not alone.

Most of us can give more. It is up to us how we spend our money, how we think about what matters now, and what we want our legacy to be. We have so much "stuff." Isn't it time to lift others more? Do our heirs really need so much? A simple codicil can make charitable change in your will. Spend time reflecting on your assets and your budget, how you spend your money, and what more you could do as a household in your lifetime and beyond. Invest in this powerful sector that brings joy and hope to so many.

This is, finally, what the redesign is about: not money for its own sake, but money put to service for each other. As Edgar Villanueva, founder of the Decolonizing Wealth Project, has put it: "If we could use money in a different way, toward a healing, reparative purpose, then money can actually be sacred—something that could be used as medicine." What Melinda French Gates calls "using whatever resources you have at your fingertips and applying them to improving the world" is exactly this: building a community of compassionate generosity.

John Hagel describes what this kind of work requires: an Opportunity Narrative, a frame compelling enough that people feel pulled forward by it even when the hard realities are at our door. Martin Luther King's dream was one. The redesign of funding asks for another: hold the hard realities honestly, and pull the field toward a larger possibility with greater charitable investment.

Generosity is one of the defining civic practices of American life. If we advocate for it, create pathways for it, and steward it well, the whole society moves with it.

Readers interested in the practices and resources discussed in this chapter can explore further through the Trust-Based Philanthropy Project, the Women's Funding Network, Prospera International Network of Women's Funds, the Donor Advised Fund Research Collaborative, the Kindle Project (Flow Funding), and inspiredphilanthropy.org. *Engaging in work by Sondra Shaw-Hardy, Joan Garry, Stephanie Roth, and Kim Klein is a useful starting point. Find and share more resources at* redesigningnonprofits.org.

Chapter 7

Emerging Models of Leadership and Governance

"Leadership is strongest when it is collective, when it lifts up the voices of those closest to the solutions."

—Ai-jen Poo

When we sat down with Amy Sample Ward, CEO of NTEN (a nonprofit that connects people who use technology equitably for social change), they recalled a moment with us when a staff manager told them: "No one else can talk to my staff."

The manager had a history with NTEN. Like her colleagues, she was hired from the community the organization serves. She shared NTEN's values, but now that she was on staff, she struggled with its culture.

NTEN has a collaborative, flat leadership structure. Staff build their own budgets, join project teams at will, and make decisions through consensus. Amy Sample Ward describes their role as CEO as a facilitator who "breaks the wind" so the rest of the team can do the work. NTEN had taken years of deliberate effort to transform itself into an organization where all voices were heard.

In consensus-building meetings, though, this manager lost patience. "Let's stop discussing this, Amy. You just make the decision," she said. Ward answered, "It's not my decision to make. I can support this conversation. If people are still in disagreement, we can work toward consensus. But I don't have a veto card." The manager was testing NTEN's distributed leadership structure. Would the organization bend to her pressure?

The final test came when staff who reported to the manager asked to join a cross-functional team that the manager wasn't on. This was when the manager put her foot down: "No one else can talk to my staff." Amy reminded her that NTEN's staff were welcome to join initiatives they had passion and skills to contribute to. The manager, frustrated, left NTEN of her own accord. The model wasn't for her, and that's okay—not everyone thrives in a distributed environment.

There was a trade-off here: NTEN lost a valuable member of the staff. However, this moment cemented NTEN's commitment that no single opinion can trump others, and that shared power is critical to the way NTEN enacts social change.

NTEN challenges a contradiction that runs through the nonprofit sector. While many social benefit organizations are built to redistribute power, they are often still structured in a way that concentrates it. While leaders aim to empower communities from the ground up, we often model hierarchical organizational structures. We champion the lone heroic leader, corporatized hierarchies, and governance models that center wealth and tradition over community and shared decision-making.

Equitable advancements can't come from executing this playbook better. But there are other playbooks that we can imagine and enact. What follows are stories and structural blueprints of what is possible.

Why We Still Have Hierarchical Leadership Structures

The myths we've named—scarcity and undervaluation of care work—become implicit answers to these organizational questions: Who holds power? How do we work together? There are three ways these mindsets contribute to hierarchical cultures.

The "lone hero" executive director (E.D.): The single, tireless executive director is a hallmark of our sector. They are extremely capable leaders, and both credit and blame flow to them. Often, they're women—particularly women of color—answering society's calls to "do it all" with a commitment to lead, inspire, and do good in the world.

Many E.D.s work 70-hour weeks and don't have anyone they can fall back on. For the majority of nonprofits, having a staff of just one E.D. maximizes tight finances. But it begs the question: How can we build structures that support these leaders' ambitions, even within tight constraints?

When we chatted with Nikki Dinh of the Leadership Learning Community, we asked her what structures the nonprofit sector is ready to release. She said this: "I'm ready to compost the idea that there needs to be a lone hero kind of leader. Planting more seeds for ecocentric leadership, I think, is my main emphasis these days." Nikki's alternative is liberatory leadership: collective leadership that centers love, humanity, joy, and play as it fights oppression. This is a step further than *equitable* leadership, which seeks to minimize harm within current systems. *Liberatory* leadership seeks something outside current systems.

The lone-hero model persists within a larger story baked into American civic life: benefactors are saviors and beneficiaries are passive recipients. In this mythology, our leaders are the embodiment of the mission's moral weight. Mathis Wackernagel, cofounder of the Global Footprint Network, explains: "If people start to talk about 'my NGO,' then we know you're on the wrong track. Because the NGO belongs to the public. And you just have the fiduciary responsibility to follow the mission."

The pressure to "professionalize": Public benefit organizations have long been called on to "professionalize" our sector. Speak to anyone who hasn't worked in a nonprofit (and some who have), and you'll hear the age-old "Oh, nonprofits are *so inefficient*." Where does this adage come from?

Mandi J. Stewart, nonprofit researcher and associate professor at NC State University, conducted a systematic review of professionalization: the adoption of business-like practices in public benefit organizations. She found that professionalization tips the balance from an organization's "expressive logic" (values, civic roots, and community orientation) toward an "instrumental logic" focused on performance metrics and operational efficiency. Professionalizing produced a paradox: while adding more instrumental practices gave greater autonomy to executive leaders and made nonprofits look more attractive to funders, it resulted in hierarchical systems of leadership that decentered staff and community.[1]

Governance that centers wealth: The common wisdom for board recruitment is to bring in fundraisers with high-net-worth networks. But Julia Roig, founder and chief network weaver at Horizons Project, calls this a "perverse incentive" where executive directors become accountable to wealthy board members' perspectives rather than to the constituencies they're meant to serve. A national survey found that 49% of chief executives don't have the right board members to build trust with the communities they serve.[2]

Latonya Slack, principal and founder at Slack Global Consulting, sees this dynamic up close. She finds that new leaders, particularly women and people of color, step into executive roles with roughly three months of operating cash flow. Then the board steps back, having successfully recruited a woman of color to be the hero and face for their organization. But they all too often forget to follow up where support really matters, such as providing coaching budgets and conscious introductions to donors and their networks.

Ebony Twilley Martin lived through this reality. She spent 12 years at a large global environmental organization—rising from talent acquisition director to executive director. She stepped into this role during an existential moment, with major litigation threatening the organization's survival. In response, she built a measured strategy, consulting every former executive director.

But the board's capacity to support that strategy was limited. Most members only had experience leading small local nonprofits—not a $40 million global institution funded primarily through individual donors. The support they offered didn't match what the organization actually needed. When the legal crisis came to a head, the board overrode her strategy. The organization paid a significant price.

The experience reflects a pattern familiar to many Black women in social impact organization leadership: the conditions that recruit them rarely match the institutional competency required to sustain them. After years of all-encompassing work, Twilley Martin faced both professional loss and profound personal grief—the kind that never shows up in an annual report.

But that experience became a catalyst. She now understands that the work she built didn't disappear—it lives on through her experience and coaching. Twilley Martin is now the founder of the Regenerative Leadership Lab, helping leaders move from extraction cultures to regenerative ones: systems that keep leaders anchored in purpose under pressure, so the work outlasts any one person or moment.

Twilley Martin's story highlights an all-encompassing reality: 41% of BIPOC leaders who are planning to leave their nonprofit jobs report burnout as the top reason, compared with 31% of their white peers. These 10 percentage points are the tax levied on leaders of color who courageously navigate systems that have historically excluded them.[3]

The lone heroic leader, pressure to corporatize, and wealth-centered governance are not our only truths. We have the capacity to intentionally redesign all of them. Before we start, we should name a key advantage the sector holds.

The Advantage to Social Benefit Culture: Being "Purpose-Driven"

The narrative that nonprofits need to "professionalize" misses something important: nonprofits have an advantage over for-profit corporations that corporate best-practice cannot easily replicate. Importing culture from the private sector doesn't just fail to help—it can actively undermine the thing that makes nonprofits work in the first place.

For decades, for-profit corporations have been chasing the same question: How do we get employees to do more and make better decisions? In *Primed to Perform*, Neel Doshi and Lindsay McGregor synthesize the research and find the strongest drivers of performance are play, purpose, and potential—not pay, perks, or pressure. The "why" behind someone's work matters more than the rewards attached to it.

Purpose is exactly the thing public benefit organizations have in abundance, and it is what corporations struggle to manufacture.

Direct and Indirect Motivators for Performance[4]

Direct Motivators: Increase performance	**Play:** Your culture is creative and has an open space for learning and experimentation.	**Purpose:** Your organization drives toward a higher goal and positive impact on your community/world.	**Potential:** Your job helps you reach your personal or professional goals.
Indirect Motivators: Decrease performance over time	**Emotional Pressure:** Your work culture runs on shame, guilt, or not wanting to disappoint (your boss, funders, or community).	**Economic Pressure:** Employees work for the reward (salary/material benefits) or to avoid punishment.	**Inertia:** Your organization continues to run simply because employees were there working yesterday.

The scale of this advantage is clear. Jan Masaoka notes that the majority (about 70%) of U.S. nonprofits operate with a budget of less than $50,000—that's $10,000 less than the median annual salary in the United States. Thus, the majority of nonprofits are operating entirely with volunteers. These organizations catalyze millions of hours of unpaid labor every year to feed and clothe the under-resourced, advocate for civil rights, and protect the environment. Even organizations with paid employees sustain their impact with in-kind help from their communities.

For social movements, purpose-driven culture is our infrastructure—which is why we should be wary of culture-focused advice from the for-profit sector. Julia Roig puts the irony plainly: nonprofits "made a mistake by adopting for-profit business models that emphasized competitive advantage and ROI metrics." Kavita Ramdas distills the operating principle: "How we do our work is as important as what we do." Apply that not just to programs but to governance, hiring, and decision-making, and it becomes clear that we can't always bring corporate models into public benefit organizations. You cannot fight for equity through a structure built for extraction. You cannot advance community power through a system designed to concentrate it.

Emerging Leadership Structures

What organizational structures can we adopt that prioritize purpose and shared leadership? Across the sector, organizations are experimenting with new models that are transforming how they hire, govern, and make everyday decisions. These models cluster around four design questions: who leads, who governs, how infrastructure is shared, and what daily work feels like.

Who Leads?

Co-directorship

The simplest fix for the "lone hero" E.D. role: stop asking one person to do it alone. The E.D. role demands a range of skills, demands, and time that virtually no individual possesses. Co-directorship splits the executive function between two people, typically along complementary strengths.

Roselie Vasquez-Yetter, co-executive director for PartnersGlobal, came to the model during what she calls "the fourth rebirthing cycle of the organization." It was a transition period following the founder's passing and the departure of his handpicked successor. She and her co-director Kira divided responsibilities into roughly eight categories based on their background, skills, and interest: Kira, drawing on her legal training, leads on financial accountability, compliance, board interactions, and office operations. Roselie drives organizational strategy, strategic communications, network-based resilience, and brand identity. Externally, Kira represents the organization in U.S. government spaces; Roselie covers other relationships. Their funding portfolios are distinct.

The arrangement preserves something executive directors typically lose—the ability to stay close to the actual work. "Because there are two of us that are dividing those responsibilities, it allows us to continue to be active in our sort of professional, technical capacity," Roselie explains. "The work as a practitioner tends to go away" in a traditional E.D. role, consumed by board management, financial oversight, fundraising, and administrative demands.

Then there is the practical matter of covering for each other. The organization operates a global network—travel is constant, and the work doesn't pause when one leader is on the ground in another country. Roselie calls the ability to stand in for one another "a game changer." When they stepped into the co-directorship, the organization had roughly 30 staff and was growing toward 55. In a single-E.D. structure, an executive traveling for two weeks would have meant two weeks of deferred decisions.

Both co-directors work full-time and earn approximately two-thirds of a typical E.D. salary—a cost that puts each between standard director and executive director compensation. What stands out in Roselie's account is how clear the division feels—eight domains, distinct portfolios, coverage when needed. That clarity doesn't come by default: it requires intentional, consistent decision-making between the two co-directors.

Ashley Marshall, writing in the Nonprofit Quarterly, frames co-leadership as a continuous negotiation of power: "In co-leadership, power is a balancing dance. Power must be navigated explicitly and consciously, with a commitment to a mutual leadership relationship." Her research found that identity and intersectionality shape how authority flows between co-leaders.[5]

The model is more common than people assume. A Candid analysis found roughly 18% of public charities sharing demographic data list two leaders—more than 10,000 organizations that share data with Candid.[6]

A comparative study of eight co-led social impact organizations and three sole E.D. organizations found consistent success factors for the collaborative approach: shared vision, strong communication, clear decision processes, and mutual understanding of when to step in or back. The study found risks, too: symbolic equality that masks real power imbalance, staff confusion about who decides in a crisis, and inadequate communication or alignment.[7]

What makes co-directorship work in practice? The research and the practitioners converge on a short list:

- Divide responsibilities clearly from the start, in specific categories and based on complementary strengths, the way Roselie and Kira mapped eight distinct domains before they began.
- Invest in transparent and clear communication practices: regular check-ins on KPIs, successes, and challenges, shared planning, and systems that give visibility into each other's work.
- Offer to support each other, brainstorm solutions to challenges, and encourage play, rest, and learning.
- Educate the board early: if directors don't understand how to evaluate a leadership pair, they may default to treating one person as the "real" leader.
- Be explicit about how decisions get made when a question falls between your lanes or when you disagree—ambiguity in those moments is where symbolic equality breaks down into real power imbalance.
- Compensate consciously: co-directorship is an expansion of leadership capacity, not a cost-saving measure, and organizations that treat it as two half-roles will get half-commitment in return.

Pros	**Cons**
Eliminates the single-point-of-failure problem	Can fail if equality is symbolic, not operational
Built-in sustainability and mutual support	Possibility for slower decisions or lack of clear authority protocols

(continued)

(continued)

Pros	Cons
Complementary skill coverage	Boards and funders may need education
Leaders stay involved in programmatic work	Requires ongoing relationship maintenance
Can reduce burnout and improve organizational balance	Possibility for duplication of effort or tasks that slip through the cracks without clear organization

Distributed and Flat Leadership

Distributed leadership models challenge traditional hierarchies, sharing decision-making power across the organization.

This is NTEN's modus operandi. The CEO carries the organization's legal risk—Amy Sample Ward told us, "if anyone's going to jail, I'm making sure it's me"—but otherwise the role is built to facilitate rather than direct. Staff set the organization's direction, and the CEO clears the way. When someone leaves NTEN, they leave with project experience far beyond their job description. "People get to be whole humans," Ward says, "when you treat them like whole humans that have lots of skills and value."

The Leadership Learning Community pursues a similar model, organizing through four circles—strategy, liberatory operations, liberatory programs, and communications—with leads chosen by strengths and interest rather than rank.

At LLC, two design features make this work. First, radical transparency: all staff attend board meetings with full access to materials; budgets are shared organization-wide. Second, decision infrastructure matched with open communication. LLC has begun to use a Pilot/Co-pilot/Contributor framework for each project, assigning roles by "natural strengths, capacity, and interest," and directly communicating with each other when uncertainties arise. Without these practices, flat structures reproduce informal hierarchies, where the loudest voices are prioritized.

LLC names the unresolved tensions openly: What is the right balance between love and accountability? How do you share information when not everyone is in every meeting? Questions like these meet uncertainties with courage and transparency.

Pros	**Cons**
Activates talent across the organization.	Requires years of intentional culture change.
Richer staff experience and development.	Some staff need clearer hierarchy and will self-select out.
No single point of failure.	Requires strong facilitation and decision protocols.
Staff-led strategy is more innovative.	Can reproduce informal hierarchy without deliberate design.

Teal/Self-Management

The Teal model, from Frederic Laloux's *Reinventing Organizations*, replaces traditional, hierarchical management with self-organizing teams that operate with autonomy, transparency, and purpose. It rests on three pillars: **self-management** that distributes authority among the organization; **wholeness** that values the full person; and **evolutionary purpose**, which anchors the organization in meaning. Each of these pillars is married with coherent principles and practices, as detailed in Figure 7.1.

Laloux defines a "Teal" organization as a living organism: decentralized, with shared power. He maps Teal teams as the next stage of organizational evolution. For nonprofits already organized around purpose, Teal's aspirations feel natural. But what does it look like in practice—and how do Teal teams maintain a cohesive direction?

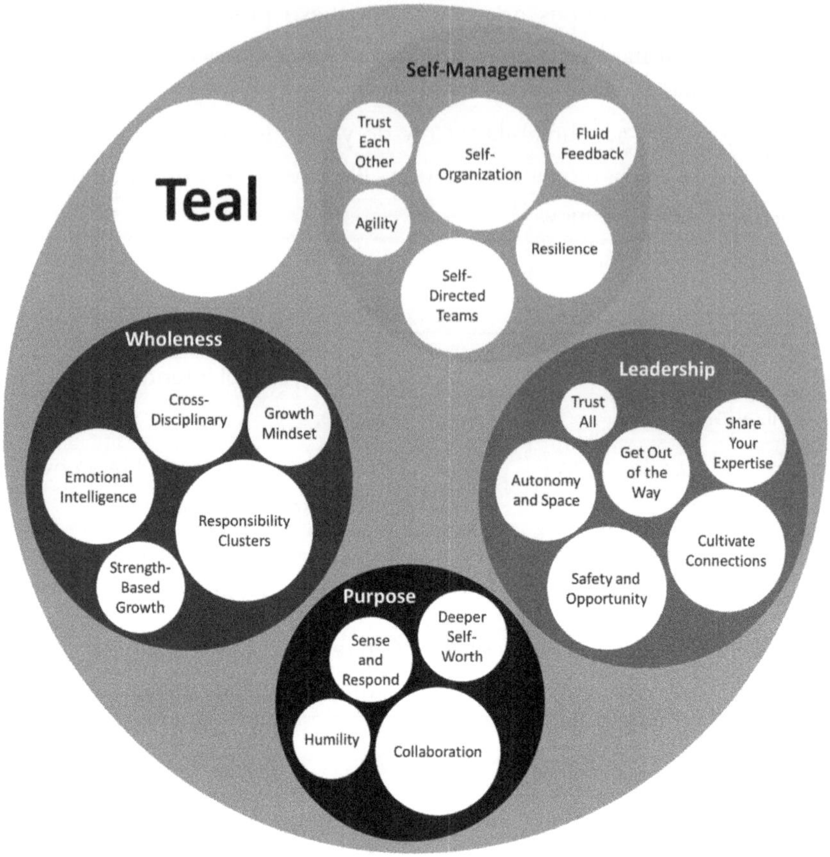

Figure 7.1 TEAL principles and practices

The answer is through conscious structure and care. Work is often organized through circles: self-directed teams with clear domains and explicit decision-making authority. Anyone can initiate a project, but consulting team members who have relevant experience and people who will be impacted is expected. Decision-making doesn't always require a consensus. Instead, it follows sociocratic principles—decisions advance unless someone raises a principled objection.

Matthew Spaur, co-author of the Teal Team's research report tracking more than 300 self-managed organizations, clarifies that the fully self-managed ideal is rare. What's far more common are organizations adopting Teal practices selectively: distributing decision authority in specific domains, building psychological safety, and creating space for people to bring their whole selves to work.

Teal can present specific challenges for nonprofits. Social benefit organizations that depend on volunteers or part-time staff may not have the sustained engagement in organizational culture that self-management requires. As Spaur puts it, some volunteers "just want to show up and feed the rescued squirrels and go home." Funding constraints can make achieving Teal difficult too: building the capacity for staff to take risks requires a level of stability.

An organization doesn't need to check every Teal box to benefit. But it can't skip the first step: the leader's own transition. As Spaur observes, "an organization really can't go past the consciousness of their main leader." If the executive director isn't ready, the rest is theoretical.

Pros	**Cons**
To achieve self-management, appropriate decision-making is distributed to each role.	Fragile without clear guardrails on what decisions are irreversible and need leader guidance.
Honors whole human identities.	Requires significant participation in the culture, as well as openness and flexibility of staffing if many workers are volunteers.
Eliminates hierarchical bottlenecks meaning more can be done by nonprofit team members.	Can reproduce informal hierarchy if not carefully designed.
Adaptive and responsive to the focus of the nonprofit.	Cultural change can be difficult for traditional organizations.

The E.D./COO Model

Not every organization is ready to take on fully distributed leadership. The E.D./COO model offers a targeted intervention: pair a vision-focused executive director with a chief operating officer who has elevated operational authority and veto power.

Mathis Wackernagel pointed to this exact model when asked how social impact organizations should restructure, describing it as one of the most clarifying frameworks he'd encountered across years of running organizations: "The idea is a core team: an executive director, in the end beholden to the board, with the vision. And then there is an operational person, typically called a COO, that runs things on their own, more inward-looking. One of the big breakthrough ideas for me is that both discuss things—and the last word is with the COO."

The key principle: the COO should have the final word on operational decisions. This is a structural check that prevents the E.D. from making demands that can't be executed. As Wackernagel put it, "The E.D. has to convince the world—but also has to convince the COO. And if they cannot be convinced, then it cannot be done, because the COO has to make it happen on the ground." The E.D. handles vision, fundraising, Board management, compliance, and external relationships. The COO handles programs, operations, finance, and HR.

This model addresses E.D. overload without needing to fully overhaul the system. It's a plausible on-ramp for organizations that recognize the single-leader model is unsustainable but aren't ready for fully distributed power.

Pros	Cons
Addresses E.D. overload without full redesign	Requires ongoing relationship and decision-making maintenance
Prevents vision-operations disconnect	Requires genuine willingness to cede authority
Accessible on-ramp for traditional orgs	More work needs to be done to redistribute power among other team members and constituents

Who Governs?

While leadership structures shape daily authority, governance sets organizational accountability. The following models ask a question that many boards rarely do: accountability to whom?

Community-Centered Boards

If boards aren't organized around influence and wealth, what should they be organized around? The most direct answer: the communities the organization serves.

Kavita Ramdas built governance around this principle at the Global Fund for Women in the late 1990s, placing activists from outside the United States—many of them grassroots leaders, many grant recipients—directly on the board as decision-makers. "The same people who received grants were making decisions," she recalls. "That was considered unheard of." Strong conflict of interest policies prevented self-dealing. With this initiative, 50% of the board were activists.

At the time, the broader sector treated this as radical. But in fact, there was federal precedent. Community health centers receiving federal support must have boards where at least 51% of members are patients served by the center. If governments can prioritize equity, so can we.

NTEN also offers a picture of what community-centered governance can look like. Board members come entirely from NTEN's community programs, emerging through staff nomination. The governance infrastructure is built around three equity committees: staff, board, and community. Each of these operates under a charter that allows any committee to send recommendations to the others. For instance, when the community committee raises questions about NTEN's bylaws, staff research the answer and relay the findings. The board committee can then change the bylaws based on community input. Governance authority flows through the organization's community, staff, and board, often resulting in shared evolution. Board members aren't expected to arrive with technical expertise, but they are expected to exercise duty of care.

Participatory grantmaking extends the same logic to funding. The West Marin Fund's Community Impact Partnership uses collaborative review meetings where local residents vote on letters of interest. The people affected by funding decisions participate in making them—this increases the equitability of funding.

Pros	Cons
Accountability flows to communities, not donors.	May require compensation/tech, travel, and childcare stipend infrastructure to ensure equitable access.
Lived experience enters strategic decisions.	Traditional board members and funders may resist.
Grant recipients become decision-makers.	May need other avenues to build buy-in with fundraisers.
A well-tested and proven model.	Requires conscious development of conflict of interest policies.

Representative Governance

In representative governance structures, boards act like small governments, with each seat accountable to a defined constituency. Jensine Larsen, founder of World Pulse and Unfurl Futures, built this model at World Pulse. Here, she designed governance around the global community of women activists the organization existed to serve. The aim was to create an autonomous structure that represented the global activist constituency.

The model demands more organizing infrastructure than an MVP board: representatives must be selected responsibly and must sustain connection with the constituencies they represent. But the payoff is highly democratic governance built for longevity. The organization doesn't lose its center of gravity even if an E.D. steps away, as it is propelled forward by dedicated community voices.

Pros	Cons
Communities have dedicated seats at the table.	Requires more management and organizing infrastructure.
Authority flows from constituencies, not personalities.	Selection and governance processes can be contested or slow.
Built for longevity beyond the founder.	Maintaining constituency contact takes sustained effort.
Board legitimacy is grounded in representation, not wealth or proximity.	May be premature for early-stage organizations.

Minimum Viable Boards

Some organizations, especially those that are in an earlier life cycle, would be better served by limiting the board to a smaller group of as little as three to seven members. Larsen framed this as a practical evolution away from outdated governance structures. Drawing on two decades of board experience, she observed that most leaders feel their traditional boards simply aren't working.

Her recommendation: "Becoming more agile and nimble with our boards and having nonprofit leaders create healthy minimal boards—MVP boards—just the very basics you need. But then making healthy use of advisory boards and angel investor circles, that directly map to the needs of the organization."

With a more intimate group, it takes less time to dive into deeper strategic questions, and it's possible to build more trust that leads to better alignment. So, smaller boards can be more equipped to develop a clear vision and differentiated strategy. Plus, they're often easier for an E.D. to manage, and this lessens the risk and momentum loss of having inactive board members.

Larsen offers one more principle that applies regardless of board size: the "service work journey." Before governing, board members undertake hands-on experience with the organization—instead of a PowerPoint orientation, cultivating actual contact with the work. Board members govern better when they've spent real time building relationships with the community it serves. Service work journeys are also far more feasible on a lean board; the larger the board, the harder it becomes to ask this of every member.

Pros	**Cons**
Higher individual board member engagement and alignment	Requires capacity to coordinate advisory structures
Right expertise at the right moments	With fewer board members, potential for less in-kind contributions or fundraising support
Less governance overhead, more strategy	Potential for less skill sets and/or collective wisdom

Compensated Boards

If board positions are uncompensated, only people who can afford to donate their labor will serve. As one advocate puts it, "Unpaid board positions inadvertently replicate existing power structures by favoring those with financial means, similar to how unpaid internships benefit those from wealthy backgrounds."

Compensated boards address this by paying members through minimal stipends, per-meeting payments, or annual retainers. The corporate sector has long considered board compensation standard.

Compensation introduces complications, adding costs to attend meetings. Not all nonprofits can afford this cost, and it can introduce less altruistic incentives. But the alternative—governance structurally available only to the wealthy—carries costs that fall disproportionately on the communities being served. Nonprofits may consider more limited compensation structures that specifically target equity: travel stipends, providing food, beverage, or childcare during meetings, and/or compensation only for an "advisory board" that represents the community's diversity.

Pros	Cons
Opens governance to those excluded by unpaid model	Additional cost for resource-constrained orgs
More representative boards, more grounded decisions	Requires stricter governance processes to prevent conflict of interest
Signals that governance labor has value	Cultural resistance remains significant

How Can We Share Infrastructure Across Social Benefit Organizations?

Redesigning who leads and who governs still keeps each organization in its own lane, carrying the full weight of its own operations. The following models distribute that weight across organizations, creating shared and networked infrastructure to reduce the burden on any single organization.

The Nonprofit Business Incubator

Thousands of small nonprofits each build their own accounting, legal, HR, and office infrastructure from scratch. Each reinvention consumes resources that could go to their missions.

Daphne Scott, community development leader, proposes an alternative: a shared hub where 20 to 25 small nonprofits access centralized services—attorneys, accountants, office space, coaching, HR—so they can "thrive rather than just survive." The model goes beyond co-working. Scott's vision includes cross-sector partnerships: for-profit companies coaching public benefit organizations on launching ventures. Some fiscal sponsors already operate this way, "pairing compliance and back-office infrastructure with capacity-building and launch support" and spinning incubated projects into independent nonprofits when they're ready.

For funders who care about ROI, incubators are particularly attractive: one investment in shared legal support serves twenty-five organizations instead of one.

Third Sector New England (TSNE) in Boston is a $60+ million organization that provides fiscal sponsorship and shared operational services, management consulting, and capacity-building support to other nonprofits. Crucially, it combines shared services with physical space: the NonProfit Center, owned and operated by TSNE, is home to more than 50 nonprofits and was the first mission-based, multitenant center for public benefit organizations in Massachusetts—nine floors of office space and meeting facilities available at below-market rates. Their shared services model provides essential administrative and operational support to small and midsized nonprofits, especially BIPOC-led and BIPOC-serving organizations, with services on a sliding scale based on organizational budget size. TSNE incubated and supported the development of *Nonprofit Quarterly* magazine from 1997 through 2006, when it spun off as an independent publication.[8,9]

Pros	**Cons**
Dramatically reduces per-organization overhead.	Requires significant startup investment.
Small organizations can access expertise they couldn't afford.	Organizations may resist sharing operational autonomy.
Cross-sector learning accelerates innovation.	Works best with co-located or regional clusters.

Fiscal Sponsorship

Not every social impact initiative needs its own 501(c)(3). The conventional path of nonprofit incorporation is expensive and time-consuming and can be a barrier to launching for many emerging and diverse grassroots leaders. Fiscal sponsorship offers an alternative: a project operates under an established nonprofit's legal and fiduciary umbrella, so the people doing the work can focus on mission while the sponsor handles tax-exempt status, financial reporting, and regulatory compliance.

Fiscal sponsorship arrangements vary. In some cases, the project has no separate legal existence—the sponsor employs its staff, holds its contracts, and treats it as an internal program. In others, the project is its own entity, and the sponsor re-grants funds under a formal agreement. Either way, fiscal sponsorship reduces operational overhead and accelerates the pathway to impact. When a community sees an urgent need, the answer doesn't have to be "spend 18 months forming a nonprofit." It can be "find the right sponsor and start working."

The fiscal sponsorship landscape is larger than most people realize. A 2023 field scan by Social Impact Commons and the National Network of Fiscal Sponsors—the first such study in 17 years—found that the 100 sponsors surveyed steward more than $2.6 billion in funding. The authors estimate that as many as 5,000 fiscal sponsors may be active across the United States, supporting upward of 50,000 projects.[10] Well-known sponsors like Earth Island Institute and Tides host dozens of projects each, providing back-office infrastructure—payroll, legal compliance, insurance, HR—so that project leaders can focus on mission. Many sponsors also offer training, capacity building, and shared fundraising opportunities. Sponsored projects typically operate without formal boards, sometimes relying on advisory committees that meet periodically. Without that governance architecture, projects have more flexibility, but they may find it harder to scale.

Fees for fiscal sponsorship typically range from about 5% to 15% of all revenue received, depending on the model and level of service. Those percentages add up, and they can be negotiated. If your project lands a large grant of $100,000 or $250,000, the sponsor's administrative burden on that transfer is far less than on the equivalent sum raised through hundreds of small donations, yet the fee is calculated the same way. A well-negotiated fiscal sponsor agreement should include provisions for adjusting the fee rate as revenue grows or as the composition of funding shifts.

Not having to manage payroll, tax filings, and legal oversight is a big plus—but the trade-off is autonomy. Project leaders cede some control to the sponsor, and outgrowing the arrangement can entail navigating a complex transition to independence.

Pros	**Cons**
Eliminates stand-alone nonprofit overhead.	Project leaders cede some operational autonomy.
Accelerates charitable capital deployment.	Fiscal sponsor quality and fit matter enormously.
Project spends less energy on compliance and more energy on mission.	Transition to independence can be complex.

Decentralized Network Hubs

Some organizations are better understood as networks—broad coalitions of regional actors connected by shared purpose, governed locally, supported by central facilitation that serves rather than directs.

An organization creating networked infrastructure is the Fito Network, a global network-of-networks supporting the leaders, funders, and consultants who work across social impact issue areas. Fito connects more than 4,000 network leaders across more than 100 countries and maintains two resources that shift the sector's center of gravity: a database of 500+ funders who support systemic change, and an atlas of 1,800+ networks to help organizations find collaborators or funding partners. The premise is straightforward—network leaders are often isolated in their roles, funders often lack models for resourcing relational work, and both groups benefit from a shared field of practice. Fito brings these pieces together so that they can be cultivated and supported.[11]

Pros	Cons
Adapts to local contexts, no one-size-fits-all.	Complex coordination across nodes.
Central facilitation amplifies local power.	Requires investment in connective infrastructure.
Deep collaboration across geographies.	Consistency may vary across hubs.

How Can We Cultivate Positive Culture Within These Structures?

Distributing authority is only half the redesign. The emerging models we've explored in this chapter can redistribute decision-making power yet still reproduce extractive or fear-based work cultures. Structure sets the foundation, but culture determines whether those conditions produce something transformative.

Psychological Safety in Leadership

Psychological safety is the shared sense that it's safe to speak up, disagree, or admit you were wrong in your team. The term comes from Harvard's Amy Edmondson, whose research found that the highest-performing teams weren't the ones that made the fewest errors but the ones that felt safe enough to report them. Google's Project Aristotle reached the same conclusion: of five team dynamics they identified (dependability, structure and clarity, meaning, impact, and psychological safety), psychological safety was the most important—the foundation the others rested on.[12]

Chris Heuer, organizational coach and managing director at the Team Flow Institute, believes that integrating psychological safety is an inside-out transformation—a process that begins with leaders doing the difficult internal work first. "You can't create psychological safety for a team," he notes, "if you haven't resolved your own traumas and learned how to be present." Presence is an energetic force: one that either expands to include others or contracts around ego and scarcity. This is where Heuer cites Dr. Jef van den Hout's team flow model. Flow begins with collective ambition: a shared values-mission-vision that connects individual purpose to something larger. From there, open communication becomes the mechanism that unlocks psychological safety.

The practices that sustain psychological safety aren't complicated, but they do take intention. Praise in public, criticize in private. Model vulnerability as a leader. Work from abundance rather than scarcity. Leaders who fail at psychological safety, Heuer argues, usually aren't malicious—they're just not present, carrying unresolved fears into every interaction and mistaking urgency for action.

The Liberatory Framework

The Leadership Learning Community's Liberatory Leadership Framework was published in 2025 after five years of iterative development with practitioners across the sector. It offers one of the most concrete sets of practices, strategies, and questions to bring to more conscious leadership.

Their 10 liberatory leadership strategies move from principle to practice:

- **Commit to learning and experimentation** by framing new initiatives as experiments with explicit learning questions.
- **Dedicate time and resources to unrestrained imagining,** carving out protected space to ask, "what would liberation actually look like?"
- **Commit to internal and external alignment of values and practices,** using LLC's test when shaping policy: "How will this allow us to do just work in just and joyous ways?"
- **Do the inner work** through coaching and somatic practices that confront internalized patterns of dominance, avoidance, or extraction.

- **Build, shift, and share power** by mapping how positional authority interacts with race, gender, and identity.
- **Invest in trust and relationship-building** by embedding collaboration into unexpected places—like sharing job postings with allied organizations and connecting unsuccessful candidates to opportunities across the ecosystem.
- **Embrace conflicting points of view,** treating "generative conflict" as an opportunity for learning and reconnection rather than a threat.
- **Focus on liberatory impact** by assessing external effects: How is the community more liberated, and how do our actions undermine racism, patriarchy, and oppression?
- **Incorporate play** as a productive practice that stimulates curiosity, fosters innovation, and reclaims joy from systems designed to steal it.
- **Adopt a culture of care** by operationalizing well-being through sabbaticals, modeling vulnerability, and actively countering grind culture.

Leaders cannot adopt these strategies through force of will alone. LLC argues that liberatory leaders can't be liberatory in a vacuum: they require relational work in communities that practice these principles. Other supports can help, such as coaching for all full-time employees, mentorship, and mental health resources.[13]

The social benefit sector's relationship to coaching has evolved over the years. A 2001 report from the Urban Institute's Center on Nonprofits and Philanthropy, *Building Capacity in Nonprofit Organizations*, found that many nonprofit managers and boards had limited experience using outside consultants. The concept of executive coaching, already gaining traction in the corporate sector, had barely entered the public benefit conversation.[14]

Since then, foundations have become far more open to funding coaching as a legitimate line item. The Coaching and Philanthropy Project—a partnership between CompassPoint Nonprofit Services, Grantmakers for

Effective Organizations, and Leadership that Works, funded by the W.K. Kellogg Foundation, the James Irvine Foundation, and others—produced some of the first systematic research on how philanthropy could support coaching in the nonprofit sector. Today, organizations like the Center for Nonprofit Professional Coaching offer structured programs starting as low as $300 for six sessions, and funders from the Allstate Foundation to the American Express Leadership Academy now subsidize coaching for nonprofit executives. But the practice is far from universal. Executive directors who want to build staff and board competencies through coaching still need to advocate for it.[15]

Movement Mindset

A final shift transcends any single organization. It is the move from survival mentality to network weaving and movement-building. The question becomes, how does my organization strengthen the larger ecosystem of change?

Network weaving offers a discipline for that connective work. June Holley, who originated the field and founded the Network Weaver platform now stewarded by the Leadership Learning Community, defines a network weaver simply: "someone who is aware of the networks around them and works to make them healthier." Network weaving draws on complexity science and the ecological insight that resilience lives in relationships, not in any single node. Holley adds critical framing: people in a network don't need to agree on much; they need a shared understanding of the system they're trying to shift, and many places to intervene at once. The Network Weaver community explicitly orients this work toward racial equity and collective liberation, treating interconnected networks as the architecture through which systemic change actually moves.[16]

The implications are: invest in network weavers, orchestrators, and movement builders—people who tend ecosystems rather than just running programs. Share annual workplans openly so priorities are co-created. Build narrative infrastructure that lets movements coalesce. Create incentives for collaboration over competition. Jensine Larsen advocates for "moving at the speed of care" in this work, building deep roots instead of sprinting. The most important work may be the work that connects organizations, not what any single organization does alone.

What the Transition Requires: Building the Pathway Toward More Equitable Leadership

All of these models take intentional effort and care to implement. They are built and refined through years of miscalculation, adjustment, failures and successes studied, retrial and redesign, and persistence.

NTEN's pathway is instructive. When Amy Sample Ward joined as membership director, the culture was siloed and cautious. Ward didn't announce a revolution. They started by sending out a PowerPoint template that team members could use to propose new ideas for the organization as a whole. This was a structured way for staff to contribute outside of their formal roles. Over several years, the template became unnecessary as staff gained confidence, forming project teams on Slack without waiting for approval. The critical move, Ward says, was creating "processes as bridges between traditional structures and fully collaborative environments"—transition tools that "unlocked so much authority for people to feel like they could move forward."

Beth Kanter, nonprofit strategist, offers useful language: give bad practices a "joyful funeral." Don't automate dysfunction or distribute a toxic culture. Name what isn't working, acknowledge what it once provided, consider alternatives and options in your teams, and let go of the old.

Counterarguments

There are places where emerging models of leadership and governance have their limits. Jan Masaoka, co-leader of the Philanthropy Project, offers a bracing observation: "Many calling for new structures simply want to avoid accountability through boards, preferring to maintain complete control." Some people who advocate for smaller or community-centered boards may not be interested in distributing power—they may be more interested in having less oversight. Masaoka suggests they "might be better suited to for-profit structures rather than nonprofits, which are movement-based."

We don't want to create environments where charisma substitutes for governance. Maurice Mitchell, activist and national director of the Working Families Party, notes: "Atomized individuals that loosely assemble cannot do this at the scale needed to take on entrenched power." The models in this chapter are not anti-institutional: they are institutional in a different way. Every one requires more intentionality and transparency than traditional structures, complete with clear protocols and explicit accountability.[17]

The size and stage of your organization also matter. A three-person startup and a 200-person institution face different design problems. A networked or representative architecture might not fit a local organization with a $50,000 budget. A liberatory framework with staff sabbaticals requires resources many organizations don't have. Organizations must decide which redesign fits where they are.

But Amy Sample Ward challenges the deference most organizations bring to their own structures. Most nonprofits, Ward points out, don't have in-house legal counsel, so fear fills the void, and leaders treat bylaws with "misplaced reverence." Amy advocates for destructing these mental barriers to change: "[They aren't] chiseled into stone. Change your bylaws! Change them as often as you like."

Funders' Role in Organizational Redesigns

Organizations that adopt healthier structures need funders who support transitions, not just outcomes. Chapter 6 made the case for funding infrastructure; this section narrows to a specific question: What funding practices make leadership redesign possible?

The NCRP's Power Moves framework names three dimensions. Funders who are committed to building and sharing power fund under-resourced communities for the long term. They invest in their grantees' personal and organizational success and solicit input from the communities they aim to benefit. They seek and share in-kind assets and connections to shift resources toward underinvested communities.[18]

Multiyear unrestricted funding lets nonprofits make strategic investments and build space for creative problem-solving rather than living grant cycle to grant cycle. Trust-based philanthropy pairs that funding with reduced compliance burdens.

Some funder practices can unintentionally restrain new nonprofit structures from developing. Requiring a single point of accountability reinforces the lone-leader model. Demanding low overhead ratios starves the infrastructure that makes healthy structures possible. Evaluating on annual outputs punishes the slow, deliberate redesign and partnership-building that this chapter describes.

Conclusion

Co-directorships operate across thousands of organizations, and community-centered boards govern health centers, activist funds, and technology social impact organizations. Networks connect regional hubs around the world, and fiscal sponsors promote the quick development of thousands of projects. Each model has trade-offs and prerequisites, and none is universal. But together they prove that we can choose to create more compassionate, equitable organizations and cultures.

We invite you to consider these models, try them, and design new ones. Share what you're learning at www.redesigningnonprofits.org—we'll continue to post examples from organizations doing this work.

Yet governance and culture can take us only so far when the legal architecture beneath the sector hasn't kept pace. The final chapter turns to reforms in tax policy, regulation, and federal infrastructure that can accelerate the redesigns described here.

Chapter 8

A Call to Action: Transforming the Nonprofit Sector

"Never depend upon institutions or government to solve any problem. All social movements are founded by, guided by, motivated and led by the passion of individuals."

—Attributed to Margaret Mead

Nonprofits are key to our democracy; they are essential components in promoting and sustaining equality and liberty and are powerful engines for moving the nation forward.

Yet almost nothing in America's national infrastructure exists to support the sector that does this work. Federal policy affecting social benefit organizations is scattered across half a dozen agencies with no coordination. Philanthropy warehouses wealth in donor-advised funds while community organizations scramble for one-year grants. The public sees individual organizations, not a civic sector—and certainly not one that deserves the same investment we make in roads, schools, and public health through federal funding or business contributions.

This chapter challenges that gap. It asks two questions: What would it take to treat the nonprofit sector as essential infrastructure for a healthy democracy? And how can we, as individuals and organizations, build toward this?

To answer these questions, we draw on what's been tried in the United States and abroad and on proposals from sector leaders for federal and state infrastructure, sector capacity building, philanthropic reform, and cross-sector partnership. Some ideas are complementary; others are in productive disagreement. They are not meant to be a finished set of recommendations—they are meant to spark the debate this sector deserves. We invite you, the reader, to decide which you will champion.

Since 2026 marked the 250th anniversary of our country, there is no better moment to reimagine the future of the sector that has always moved America forward.

Vision for the Future

Let's begin by looking ahead.

It is 2035, and in cities, towns, and rural communities across the United States, nonprofit organizations are thriving. Communities are stronger. The conditions that drive homelessness, food insecurity, and health inequity have begun to ease. Children have more opportunities for after-school programs. Communities prioritize racial justice in their work.

Public benefit organizations are no longer seen as peripheral actors. They are recognized as essential to community well-being, democracy, social trust, cultural expression, environmental stewardship, and human dignity. Together with government and business, funders, and volunteers, they form the operating system of a healthy democracy: government ensuring public accountability and shared goods, business driving innovation and economic vitality, and nonprofits anchoring the civic life that holds the whole thing together.

This recognition did not happen by accident. It came from intentional redesign and from a cultural shift that began years earlier.

The public narrative shifted first. Americans came to value social benefit organizations not as peripheral "charities" but as civic infrastructure that are just as vital to national well-being as roads, schools, and public utilities. Media coverage began highlighting nonprofit leaders and innovations. Civic service was celebrated. Citizens came to see participation in nonprofit organizations—as volunteers, funders, board members, coaches and advocates—as a natural expression of democratic responsibility. They are the connective tissue that allows democracy to function.

That cultural shift unlocked institutional change. Government began treating social impact organizations as strategic partners, not just grant recipients. A White House Office for Civic and Nonprofit Partnership, as previously conceived under the Obama administration, began coordinating federal policy and ensuring that communities informed national decision-making. Federal grant systems—once fragmented and unpredictable—were streamlined. Smaller and community-based organizations gained equitable access to funding and technical support.

Philanthropy evolved. Foundations, major donors, and donor-advised funds increasingly invested in nonprofit infrastructure, leadership, and long-term sustainability, recognizing that durable social change requires durable institutions. Multiyear, unrestricted funding allowed organizations to plan, innovate, and respond quickly when crises arise. Activist-informed grantmaking expanded, so communities received more dollars and capacity.

And investment in people transformed the sector from the ground up. Civic engagement and service learning became part of the K–12 curriculum. Colleges and universities began offering nonprofit leadership, social innovation, and philanthropy studies as widely respected academic pathways, and graduate programs in nonprofit management expanded dramatically across the country. Paid career pathways followed: fellowships, service years, apprenticeships, and early-career leadership roles that allowed young people to contribute their talent while earning a living wage. Young people now see nonprofit leadership as a respected career—not a sacrifice—and bring their full talent and ambition to solving society's most urgent problems.

Mid-career professionals and retirees transitioned from corporate and public-sector roles into nonprofit leadership, bringing expertise in technology, finance, logistics, and communications. Social benefit work came to be seen as not only a respected profession but also a vital form of public service, at any age of life, where innovation happens. By investing in their capacity, society's ability to solve problems has increased.

None of these pieces was a revolution in themselves. Instead, what happened was an evolution of the sector and our surrounding society. This is what happens when the sector responsible for so much of our collective care for each other is given the infrastructure, resources, and respect to match.

Foundations to Build On: Examples from the United States and Abroad

As we build toward this 2035 vision, the good news is that there have been serious efforts to support the public benefit sector on a national and regional basis, both in the United States and in other countries. Some didn't last, for a range of reasons. Some remain. But each offers lessons and potential pathways forward.

Corporation for National and Community Service

During President Obama's administration, the Corporation for National and Community Service (CNCS) played a pivotal role in coordinating nonprofit efforts and expanding national service opportunities. Originally established in 1993 under President Clinton, CNCS was significantly expanded under the Obama administration through the Edward M. Kennedy Serve America Act of 2009, when the administration's commitment to service was integral to addressing national priorities. Key initiatives included the American Recovery and Reinvestment Act, which provided $200 million to support AmeriCorps members serving in economically distressed communities.[1]

AmeriCorps placed people inside nonprofits, schools, and local agencies with defined roles, training, and outcomes, and helped normalize the idea that government can fund operational capacity for service. The administration set a goal of expanding AmeriCorps from 75,000 to 250,000 members. These efforts signaled that government can be a partner in scaling what works, not just a funder. The CNCS modeled public–philanthropic leverage—an important building block for civic infrastructure. It continued to operate throughout all eight years of the Obama administration, was renamed AmeriCorps in 2020, and continues to partially operate today.

Jason Franklin, a philanthropic advisor and entrepreneur, referenced the Obama-era Office of Social Innovation and Civic Partnership (led first by Sonal Shah and later by David Wilkinson) as a precedent for federal-level nonprofit sector engagement, though it lacked significant authority. He compared potential social impact sector support to the chief technology officer role created under Obama, which made significant technocratic improvements across the executive branch despite being a small office. He emphasized that any federal office focused on nonprofits should be charged with harnessing the federal government to build up the sector, rather than just leading volunteer programs or fundraising.

Yet these efforts were not enough to make them last. CNCS still sat primarily in the service lane and never became a whole-of-government nonprofit partnership platform with cross-agency authority. Innovation funding didn't automatically build the sector's baseline infrastructure—technology, reserves, and workforce pipelines across millions of organizations. The Office of Social Innovation, for all its promise, remained a small office without the institutional permanence or authority to reshape how the federal government related to the sector as a whole.

Global Lessons: How Other Democracies Structure Civic Partnerships

When we limit our imagination to U.S. models alone, it's easy to assume the current system is the only way. But other countries have drawn the boundaries differently, expanding the umbrella of public services or designing intentional incentives that encourage citizens to give back.

What can we learn from these models? None of them is a perfect system, and not all of them would easily translate to U.S. political contexts, but they offer proof that the relationship between government, philanthropy, and civil society can be structured in fundamentally different ways. The following examples illustrate what's possible when a nation decides that a thriving civic sector is worth designing for.

United Kingdom: Office for Civil Society

The United Kingdom created an Office for Civil Society in 2008 as a quasi-autonomous body to advise the government on the needs of social benefit and voluntary organizations. Reorganized and renamed in 2011 as the Civil Society and Youth Directorate, it is funded by the UK government and has consistently focused on strengthening public benefit organizations, volunteering, youth policy, and community engagement.[2]

What makes the UK model instructive is its scope. The office's work spans volunteering and social action, philanthropy and charitable giving, social investment and impact bonds, policy on community ownership and alternative business models, and youth programs. Its approach is less about delivering programs directly and more about shaping the ecosystem—through data, policy, funding frameworks, and public engagement. It treats the civic sector as infrastructure worth maintaining, not a collection of individual organizations to be managed.

Canada: Voluntary Sector Initiative

Canada's Voluntary Sector Initiative (2000–2005) was a five-year partnership between the federal government and the voluntary sector, backed by significant federal commitment. Its aim was straightforward: strengthen the relationship between the two sectors and enhance the capacity of voluntary organizations.

The accomplishments were concrete. In 2001, the Government of Canada and the voluntary sector signed a landmark accord establishing shared principles for how they would work together. Two codes of good practice followed in 2002—one on policy dialogue, the other on funding—providing guidelines for transparent, consistent engagement and funding relationships. The initiative produced new tools, information, and resources accessible to voluntary organizations, especially small and medium-sized ones. It also established a Human Resource Council and a Task Force on Community Investments focused on paid employment in the nonprofit sector.[3]

The VSI ended in 2005 with a change in governing party leadership and the election of a minority Conservative government. The new government did not continue the initiative, and the political momentum behind federal–voluntary sector collaboration dissipated. Canada's experience is a cautionary tale: even well-designed partnerships require institutional permanence and political independence to survive political transitions.

India: Mandated CSR Spending

India took a different approach entirely. The Companies Act of 2013 mandates that companies meeting certain financial thresholds—a net profit exceeding ₹5 crore (roughly $500,000), a turnover of ₹500 crore ($50 million), or a net worth of ₹1,000 crore ($100 million)—must spend at least 2% of their average net profits from the previous three years on corporate social responsibility (CSR) activities. The law requires the formation of a CSR committee to formulate policies, select projects, monitor implementation, and report annually. Noncompliance can result in penalties, including fines and imprisonment for defaulting officers.[4]

The model is blunt—and that is partly its strength. It doesn't rely on voluntary generosity or cultural norms of giving. It builds social investment into the legal architecture of corporate governance itself.

Hungary and Central Europe: Tax Designation for Civil Society

Hungary introduced its 1% Law in 1997, under which individuals can designate 1% of their personal income tax to a nonprofit beneficiary. The designated amount is declared and transferred by the tax authority. It is not technically a donation but a form of budgetary support, and it reaches roughly 25,000 organizations each year.

The mechanism has been continuously adapted to reflect changes in tax regulations, professional consultations, and feedback from experience. It has proven to be an efficient tool for promoting the culture of philanthropy and strengthening the civil society sector. Several other countries have adopted similar models: Poland introduced a 1% system in 2004, Slovakia adopted one in 2002 (later expanded to 2% for corporate donors), and Lithuania and Romania have implemented their own variations.[5]

The percentage designation model is provocative for U.S. audiences because it reframes the question. Instead of asking citizens to give *more*, it asks them to direct what they already owe. It turns every taxpayer into a micro-philanthropist—and it does so at virtually no administrative cost to the organizations that benefit.

The Gap That Remains

Effective systems share three traits: authority, permanence, and investment in sector-wide infrastructure. The UK's Office for Civil Society has all three. Canada's VSI had the first two but lost them to political transition. India's CSR mandate has permanence and authority but invests in individual projects rather than sector-wide capacity. Hungary's tax designation model has permanence and broad participation but limited authority over how the sector develops.

The United States has never combined all three.

This is not for lack of ideas. Dan Pallotta, entrepreneur and author, has proposed a "National Civil Rights Act for Charity and Social Enterprise"—comprehensive national legislation that would advance the sector the way civil rights legislation advanced equality through a visionary, well-funded legal framework. As Pallotta argues, the social benefit sector lacks the kind of sweeping legislative commitment that other movements have used to reshape public understanding and institutional behavior. The general lack of understanding among state and local representatives about the realities of the humanitarian sector's needs demands a strategic response at that scale.

Whether the answer is a Civil Rights Act, a permanent federal office, a tax designation system, or something not yet imagined, the precedents are clear: other democracies have decided that a thriving civic sector is worth designing for. The question is whether the United States is ready to do the same with the ability and passion to do it.

Questions for discussion: *What can the United States learn from these examples? Could India's mandated CSR spending or Hungary's tax designation model work in an American context? What organizations or coalitions might take on these ideas—and what would it take to give them the authority, permanence, and infrastructure investment that history suggests they need? Should we reconsider giving billionaires and many companies so many tax breaks while low income people and nonprofits rarely advance? What barriers do we face in the U.S. to real change for nonprofits, and how does our form of capitalism and taxation limit our progress?*

Building the Infrastructure: A Federal Agenda

Nonprofits carry an enormous share of the country's civic and service work, yet they are the only sector of this scale without coordinated federal architecture. Advocacy groups have periodically called for a White House Office on the Nonprofit Sector or a formal advisory role, but no administration has created one. And the idea carries a tension: greater government engagement could mean greater government control.

Many of the leaders we interviewed weren't deterred by that tension—they leaned into it. What follows are their proposals for how federal infrastructure could strengthen rather than constrain the civic sector. All of these ideas could lend authority, investment, and permanence to supporting the nonprofit sector. They are not meant as a finished set of recommendations—rather, they are meant to spark the debate this sector deserves. They all respond to an urgency to redesign a dysfunctional system that limits not only the sector but society as a whole. As you read, consider: Which of these could you champion, pressure-test, or build toward in your own community?

The Problem: A Sector Without a Home

Right now, U.S. federal policy affecting public benefit organizations is scattered across Treasury (tax policy), Labor (workforce rules), HHS (human services), FEMA (disaster response), AmeriCorps (service and volunteering), and OMB (grant rules). No single office coordinates across these agencies. No unified federal strategy exists for nonprofit economic data, volunteerism metrics, grantmaking transparency, or workforce trends. Nonprofits routinely face late payments, complex reporting, and inconsistent rules that vary from one agency to the next.

The result is a sector that is structurally underrepresented in government. The rules, institutions, and decision-making bodies that shape society are not designed to give nonprofits a meaningful seat at the table. Despite their essential contributions, nonprofits rarely have a coordinated voice in national policy discussions that directly affect their work.

A White House Office on the Social Benefit Sector

A number of our interviewees including Dan Pallotta proposed a federal office to coordinate national effort and data related to the nonprofit sector. As Dan explains, "There should be a White House Office of Philanthropy. It should be a cabinet level position and it should be coordinating all of this consolidated capital at large foundations and government money toward the specific goal of solving problems, such as homelessness. And we should be building NASA-like entities in each community—in Detroit, in Boston and elsewhere."

A White House office could standardize data collection, partner with the Census Bureau, and produce annual "State of the Nonprofit Sector" reports—addressing one of the biggest gaps in U.S. public benefit policy today. It could modernize federal grant systems, push for uniform standards across agencies, reduce administrative burden, and improve equity in federal funding access. It could facilitate structured dialogue between government and nonprofits, building long-term relationships and ensuring that public benefit organizations have a seat at the table on policy issues that affect the communities they serve. And it could coordinate national volunteer strategies, strengthen AmeriCorps partnerships, promote youth civic pathways, and support disaster-response volunteer networks—an area where the United States lags behind countries with national volunteer strategies.

The goal would not be to centralize control. It would be to deepen the partnership between the federal government and nonprofits, ensuring that the nonprofit sector and the communities it serves are stronger, more equitable, and continuously improving America's future. As the United Kingdom's Office for Civil Society and Canada's Voluntary Sector Initiative demonstrated, this is an area where intentional federal infrastructure—when designed with the sector, not imposed on it—can make real progress.

A National Interagency Council and Advisory Board

A complementary proposal is a National Interagency Council on Nonprofits—a formal table where federal agencies coordinate around the shared mission of improving how government and nonprofits work together. Such a council could provide specific recommendations to the president on how the social benefit sector can best leverage and accelerate federal investments to rebuild American communities and offer recommendations for strengthening the overall health of the sector.

An Interagency Council could align federal priorities, reduce contradictory rules, produce a unified national strategy for the sector, and ensure nonprofits are considered in major policy decisions. The concept is not unprecedented: the United States already has an Interagency Council on Homelessness, a congressionally established independent federal agency that works with 19 federal agencies, state and local governments, and nonprofits. This model has potential to be applied to the whole civic sector.

Several social impact leaders have also proposed a complementary nongovernmental body—a National Advisory Board for the Nonprofit Sector—that would bring together leading public benefit and philanthropic organizations that represent the interests of the broad sector. This board would comprise foundation staff, philanthropists, donor advisors, government representatives, academic partners, grassroots leaders, and community members to collectively guide the nonprofit ecosystem on strategy, problem-solving, and long-term vision. Representatives would reflect the wide range of issue focuses, as well as the racial, gender, ethnic, and geographic diversity of the sector.

The National Advisory Board would blend cross-sector insight to reduce barriers and open new doors for innovation. They could be available to many who sought their advice (i.e., presenting to state and congressional nonprofit offices who are establishing policy priorities). The Advisory Board would also advise the president and the Interagency Council on policy areas affecting issue focuses, civic participation, the nonprofit sector itself, and other related topics.

The Interagency Council and the National Advisory Board are not competing proposals. One works inside government; the other works alongside it. Together, they would create the structured, ongoing dialogue between the federal government and the civic sector that the United States needs now.

National Service as Civic Duty

Building infrastructure for nonprofits also means building its human capital pipeline and embedding civic responsibility deeper into our culture.

Gary Lucks, author and environmental attorney, proposes the creation of a mandatory national service program similar to the Peace Corps, VISTA, AmeriCorps, or Teach for America, where citizens would perform two years of service as part of their civic responsibility. The concept is not new, but Lucks' approach is pragmatic. He suggests starting with state-level legislation in California, arguing that as the fourth-largest economy in the world, California could effectively pilot such an initiative before expanding to other states.

The service program could specifically address critical state needs. California's foster care system alone serves up to 50,000 people yearly; Lucks argues that proactive service would be more cost-effective than reactive spending on prisons and other social services. The broader vision is that citizens should view service as an obligation similar to jury duty, with the understanding that "the cavalry is us" in preserving democratic rights.

Lucks also believes the model could be adapted for red and purple states, potentially with frameworks that align with faith communities' service values. The political appeal of national service has historically crossed partisan lines—what varies is the framing. In conservative communities, service can be positioned around patriotism, faith, and local self-reliance. In progressive ones, around equity, civic infrastructure, and democratic participation. The underlying commitment—that citizens owe something to their communities—is shared.

A new program offers one model for rekindling that ethic at scale. America Gives, launched in January 2026 by America250—the nonpartisan body Congress charged with leading the nation's 250th-anniversary commemoration—aims to make the year the largest period of volunteer service in U.S. history, challenging businesses, nonprofits, schools, and faith communities to expand and measure their service.

Building Political Will: From Caucuses to Champions

Federal infrastructure proposals are only as strong as the political will behind them. How can we advocate for this will, especially in an era when the current government is working to restrict the work of the sector?

The most promising model may already be emerging at the state level, where dozens of legislatures have begun formalizing the nonprofit sector's role in policymaking.[6] The bipartisan National Nonprofit Caucus of State Legislators—supported by the National Council of Nonprofits—encourages lawmakers across the country to establish nonprofit caucuses in their own statehouses.[7] At the federal level, the bipartisan Congressional Philanthropy Caucus serves as a forum for educating members of Congress about the role of philanthropy and nonprofits in strengthening local communities, suggesting that this framing already resonates on Capitol Hill.[8]

The path forward starts with these steps:

1. Leading on district and state relevance—educating lawmakers on the numbers and significance of local nonprofit jobs, payroll, volunteers, and government contracts
2. Asking lawmakers to join or create caucuses, which are easier to launch than formal committees and have a proven track record at the state level
3. Giving legislators a short, bipartisan menu of nonprofit policy issues: grant simplification, advance payments, bridge loans, prompt payment parity, charitable giving incentives, and regulatory reform
4. Organizing district-based briefings for lawmakers and staff
5. Recruiting a few bipartisan champions who have either nonprofit backgrounds or strong local sector ties: leaders who can carry our message

State and Local Momentum

Caucuses are one piece of the picture. Dedicated offices and advisory bodies are another, and in several states they are already taking shape.

Select committees on the nonprofit sector now operate in both chambers of the California legislature, reflecting growing recognition of nonprofits' role in community well-being and the state economy. California's proposed SB 1240 would go further, creating an Office of Nonprofit Empowerment—a dedicated hub in Sacramento to streamline and strengthen how public benefit organizations and state government work together. Just as California businesses can turn to Go-Biz and the Office of the Small Business Advocate, nonprofits would have a liaison office to help them navigate the complexities of state government, strengthen compliance, and provide a channel for their input on state priorities.[9]

New York City launched a Nonprofit Advisory Council in 2024 to advise the Mayor's Office of Nonprofit Services. At the national level, the FASB Not-for-Profit Advisory Committee, established in 2009, advises the Financial Accounting Standards Board on accounting and reporting standards—a narrower mandate than policy but an important step toward treating the sector's institutional needs as worthy of dedicated attention. Organizations like the National Council of Nonprofits and Independent Sector regularly advise policymakers, functioning as de facto advisors even without formal government standing.

Every state that creates a nonprofit liaison office, every city that launches an advisory council, every legislature that forms a nonprofit caucus adds to the proof of concept—and makes the case for federal infrastructure harder to ignore.

Questions for discussion: *There are real pros and cons to developing a federal office—particularly when the current government is working to restrict the sector's work rather than expand it. But might this be the right idea for a future administration? What state or local infrastructure, or independent nonprofit office, could you help build now? And which of these proposals could you advocate for in your own community?*

Building the Sector's Backbone: Capacity, Knowledge, and Public Narrative

Federal infrastructure and policy reform matter, but they are not enough on their own. The social benefit sector also needs to build its own internal capacity, knowledge systems, and public narrative. Some of these knowledge systems already exist (see Figure 8.1), but there is significant room to grow. The proposals in this section are about what the sector can do for itself, and what it needs from philanthropy and the public to do it. Together, they describe a sector that is not just better funded but better equipped, better understood, and better able to learn from its own experience.

Figure 8.1 Nonprofit and philanthropy news and analysis. Publications compiled by authors' analysis; not intended to be a complete list

The Information Commons

Sara Hudson, CEO and editor-in-chief of Nonprofit Quarterly, argues that the nonprofit sector's persistent struggles are not always a funding problem—they can also be a design problem. Specifically, she says, the sector lacks the shared information commons that every other major profession takes for granted. This hurts a nonprofit leader's decision-making process and can thus slow progress.

"Other industries have built the knowledge infrastructure their practitioners depend on," Hudson said. "Medicine has JAMA and PubMed. Law has Westlaw and case law. Finance has Bloomberg. We have newsletters—and we keep relearning the same lessons at enormous cost." In many ways this knowledge asymmetry is a democratic failure.

The consequences are concrete. A physician in Tulsa can learn from a clinical trial conducted in Boston within months, through peer-review systems that systematically disseminate knowledge across the field. A public benefit executive director in Tulsa has no equivalent. Every new E.D. essentially reinvents board governance, fundraising strategy, and crisis communications from scratch—because there is no living, searchable body of practice they are expected to know.

Hudson proposed a structural solution: a PubMed-style platform for the nonprofit sector—a publicly accessible, collectively maintained, field-wide body of knowledge serving as the sector's shared repository of practice. The platform could document outcome data, program evaluations, leadership transition learnings, governance failures, and other critical institutional intelligence in a searchable, open-access database.

The economics are not prohibitive. Twenty major foundations contributing $1 million each annually would generate $20 million per year—less than 0.02% of total U.S. foundation grantmaking and a fraction of what the sector loses each year by requiring every organization to learn from its own mistakes rather than from each other's.[10] The model has a real-world precedent: Candid, the merger of GuideStar and Foundation

Center, operates on roughly $40 million annually to maintain financial and organizational data on 1.9 million nonprofits.[11,12] Its 2019 merger alone required $27 million in startup capital, anchored by a four-year, $16 million grant from the Bill & Melinda Gates Foundation with additional support from Mott, Hewlett, Lodestar, and Fidelity Charitable, just to integrate two existing systems.[13] What Hudson is proposing goes further—adding outcome tracking, peer-reviewed program evaluation, governance failure documentation, and a sector-wide leadership pipeline index.

"The barrier isn't money," Hudson said. "It's that foundations have historically preferred to fund individual or proprietary knowledge products, often branded to their own institutional strategy. Building this requires foundations to subordinate their individual brand to collective field intelligence—and that's a culture change."

The $20 million figure, she acknowledges, reflects a Phase 1 build; sustained infrastructure of this kind requires the kind of 10-to-20-year funding commitment that foundations routinely make to endowments but rarely extend to collective field-building.

Hudson draws an explicit parallel to aviation safety, where near-miss reporting transformed flight outcomes not by punishing failure but by making it systematically visible. "Grantees rationally hide failure because honesty risks the next grant renewal," she said. "That incentive structure is entirely funder-created—which means funders can fix it." A mandatory failure-documentation requirement, tied to grants above a certain threshold and feeding into a shared commons, would accelerate the sector's collective learning by a generation.

"Every fix I've described already exists in another sector," she said. "We're not being asked to invent anything. We're being asked to decide that this work is important enough to deserve the same infrastructure that medicine, law, and finance take for granted. The real question isn't whether we can build it. It's whether we're committed enough to this sector to invest in its bones—not just its programs."

Governance Standards

Hudson also proposed a nonprofit governance standards board, addressing a structural weakness that undermines even the best-funded organizations. Nonprofit leaders are held to CEO-level accountability, she noted, yet they are governed by what amounts to "PTA-style volunteer boards" without standardized practices.

"Board governance is the load-bearing wall of nonprofit sustainability, but it's built on individual volunteers without standard policies on issues like board terms—some rotate every two years, others stay 20 years," she explained. "When governance fails, it actively destroys credibility, momentum, brand, and trust that organizations may have spent years or decades building, yet the sector dramatically underinvests in governance infrastructure."

Her proposal: state-level board governance associations, similar to bar associations for lawyers, that would set minimum standards, create public accountability, and provide training for board members to understand effective governance practices. Just as the information commons would give the sector a shared body of knowledge, governance standards would give it a shared floor of institutional practice—ensuring that the organizations entrusted with public benefit are held to standards commensurate with that responsibility.

Telling the Nonprofit Story

The sector's internal capacity matters—but so does how the public understands its role. Right now, most Americans see individual charities, not a civic sector. They see organizations asking for donations, not institutions defending democracy. Changing that perception is not a communications project. It is a structural challenge that requires the same intentionality as building a knowledge commons or reforming governance.

Roselie Vasquez-Yetter, co-executive director of Partners Global, has proposed developing partnerships with journalists and independent media to create a cohesive understanding and narrative for civil society. The goal is to tell real stories about the function and role of civil society beyond individual organizations—to establish a collective identity for the sector. As Vasquez-Yetter put it, it's important for social benefit leaders to feed information to journalists to build that identity. Without it, creating a unified understanding of civil society's purpose will remain elusive.

The Independent Sector for a decade had a campaign called GIVE FIVE (5% per year of income or assets, and five hours a week of volunteer time). This mobilized the nonprofit community with stories of engaged donors and volunteers who were doing their part and upping their commitments.

Dan Pallotta has proposed something complementary: a "Got Milk"–style campaign for nonprofits—a sector-wide communications effort to highlight the benefits of the sector and respond to the negative unpaid media it often receives. The original "Got Milk" campaign, one of the most memorable advertising efforts of the 1990s, succeeded because it marketed an entire category, not a single brand. The sector needs marketable storytelling—a narrative that elevates the whole, not just its most visible parts.

These two proposals work at different scales—Vasquez-Yetter's through sustained journalism partnerships, Pallotta's through a mass-market campaign—but they share a premise: the sector will remain undervalued until it takes responsibility for its own public narrative. Individual organizations telling their own stories, no matter how compelling, cannot substitute for a sector-wide effort to change how Americans understand the civic infrastructure they depend on.

We, The Civic, is an example of what this narrative-building looks like in practice. This initiative, led by Nonprofit Quarterly, is a national narrative effort timed to the 250th anniversary of the United States in 2026. It is putting multiracial nonprofit and civil society voices at the center of how America tells its 250-year story. It is a celebration of nonprofit and civic workers, voices, and journalism doing the daily work to advance a thriving, inclusive democracy. The series focuses on people of color and women who represent the largest percentage of the field. Public benefit organizations advancing the promises of a multiracial democracy are telling these stories, and holding the door open for every community that has historically been written out of them. The initiative matters not just for what it produces but for what it models: a sector telling its own story on its own terms, grounded in the actual diversity of the people who do the work.

The Expanding Civic Sector

Finally, building the sector's backbone may require rethinking what "the sector" means in the first place. Figure 8.2 maps the sector as it exists today. It is a substantial ecosystem. But as the rest of this chapter shows, it is also a fragmented one, operating without the federal coordination, knowledge systems, public narrative, or cross-sector partnerships that would let it function as the pillar of democracy it could be.

Julia Roig, founder of Horizons, has predicted that the evolution of the civic sector will include a diversity of organizational structures beyond traditional nonprofits—the emergence of a broader "civic sector" incorporating various legal forms. She points to the increasing use of alternative organizational structures: membership-based organizations, for-profits with social missions, and B-corps as part of a changing landscape. As Roig suggests, making positive social change doesn't necessarily require starting a nonprofit.

Jensine Larsen agrees, noting the need to evolve from organization-level thinking to ecosystem-level design thinking. The current approach has caused fragmentation and duplication that persistently drags down the sector. She suggests that organizations consider replacing traditional partnership directors with ecosystem coordinators or network coordinators who think beyond single-organization boundaries. Shared infrastructure based on common topics or missions can benefit multiple organizations simultaneously.

Questions for discussion: *Which of these proposals could your organization or community champion? What would it take to fund a shared information commons for the sector? How might national service be designed to work across the political spectrum? And what does it mean for the sector's identity if "civic" becomes a bigger tent than "nonprofit"?*

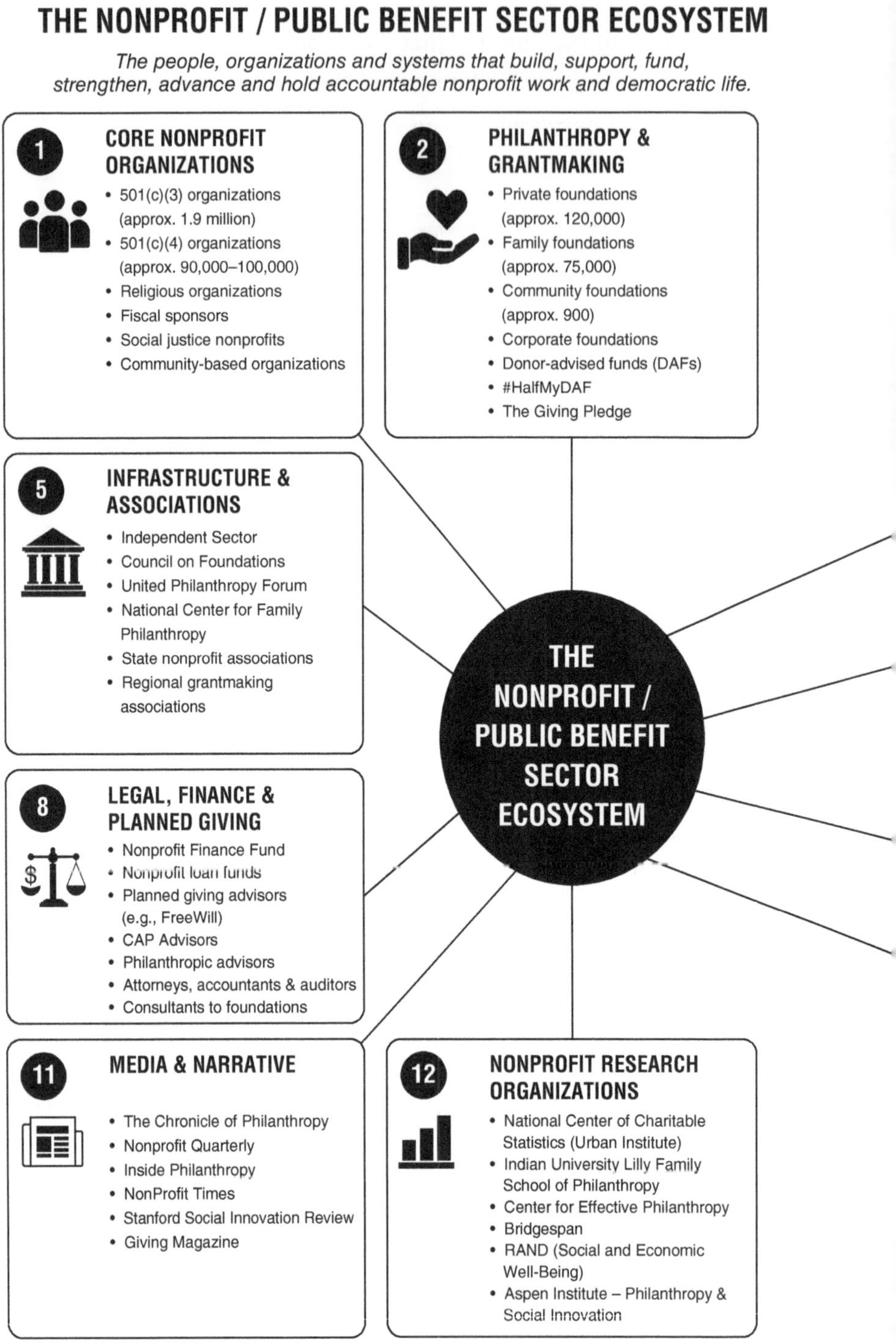

Figure 8.2 The nonprofit/public benefit sector ecosystem. Compiled by authors' analysis; not intended to be a complete list. To view this and other figures fully, or to download in pdf, please go to www.redesigningnonprofits.org

3 DONOR & ACTIVIST NETWORKS

- Solidaire
- Women Donors Network
- Resource Generation
- OutGiving
- Women Moving Millions
- Skoll World Forum

4 GRANTMAKING AFFINITY GROUPS

- Neighborhood Funders Group
- Association of Black Funders (ABFE)
- Hispanics in Philanthropy
- Asian Americans / Pacific Islanders in Philanthropy
- Native Americans in Philanthropy
- Funders for LGBTQ Issues
- Grantmakers Without Borders

**there are 40 affinity groups at the Council of Foundations*

6 ADVOCACY & ACCOUNTABILITY

- NCRP
- Inequality.org
- The Philanthropy Project
- Alliance for Justice
- Philanthropy Roundtable

7 RESEARCH, DATA & KNOWLEDGE

- Candid / GuideStar
- Urban Institute / NCCS
- Giving USA Foundation
- Indiana University Lilly Family School of Philanthropy
- Women's Philanthropy Institute
- Nonprofit degree programs (approx. 250–350)

9 TRAINING, TECHNICAL ASSISTANCE & CAPACITY BUILDING

- TechSoup (technology support)
- DEI trainers & consultants
- Fundraising schools (including Women's Philanthropy Institute)
- Strategic & fundraising coaches
- Board development & governance trainers
- Nonprofit consultants & capacity builders
- National Nonprofit Academic Centers

10 YOUTH & NEXT-GEN PHILANTHROPY

- Youth in philanthropy programs
- Next-gen donor networks
- Family foundation youth boards
- Student philanthropy programs (campus & community)
- Youth-led z programs
- National Center for Family Philanthropy

13 ADDITIONAL SUPPORT SYSTEMS

- Government grants (federal, state, local)
- Business sponsorships
- Corporate volunteer & engagement programs
- Community partnerships & collaboratives
- Nonprofit rating systems (Charity Navigator, GreatNonprofits, GiveWell)

Philanthropy and Policy Reform

The redesign described in this chapter cannot happen without a parallel redesign of how charitable capital reaches the sector. Chapter 6 takes up that argument in full—the cultural, behavioral, and policy shifts required to move dormant capital, grow new pathways to giving, and ground funding decisions closer to the communities affected. This section is a reminder that funders, donors, and advisors are essential partners in the transformation this chapter calls for and that funding infrastructure belongs in any serious conversation about civic infrastructure. What is most important is to emphasize the need for generosity across all levels.

Three commitments deserve to sit alongside the federal, sector, and partnership proposals described earlier.

Move what is parked. By 2026, donor-advised funds held roughly $328 billion across 3.6 million accounts, and most foundation endowments treat the 5% payout floor as a ceiling. Reform—through a donor-advised fund (DAF) payout requirements, higher foundation distribution rates during sustained crises, transparency requirements for DAFs and foundations, and closing loopholes that convert charitable vehicles into tax shelters—would release capital that has already received public tax subsidy but is not yet reaching working organizations. Voluntary commitments like #HalfMyDAF and MacArthur's "Set it at Six" show the field can move ahead of legislation. Even modest shifts matter at this scale: moving just 5–10% of DAF assets into active deployment would unlock tens of billions of dollars for working organizations.

Grow the base of giving. Restoring and expanding the universal charitable deduction would broaden participation across income levels, alongside state-level tax incentives for charitable giving and government-nonprofit funding partnerships that create more stable, equitable relationships between the public sector and the field. Donor learning communities, women-led giving networks, giving circles, and the next generation of inheritors entering philanthropy through the largest intergenerational wealth transfer in American history all expand the pool of civic generosity—if the sector and its advisors are equipped to invite them in. Bringing inheritors and next-generation families to the table not just as donors but as leaders of philanthropic change is essential to sustaining momentum. Community-centered models of philanthropy are shifting power from elite donors to collective decision-making. These models deserve investment and institutional support, not as alternatives to large-scale philanthropy but as a necessary counterweight to it. Additionally, support fiscal sponsorship agents and their projects with capacity-building dollars.

Ground capital in community. Trust-based and participatory grantmaking, multiyear unrestricted support, and resourcing of BIPOC-led, women-led, disability-led, and LGBTQ+-led funds direct capital toward the people closest to the need. These practices are no longer experimental. They are documented, replicable, and ready for adoption at scale. The National Committee for Responsive Philanthropy (NCRP) recommends that at least 50% of grant dollars go to marginalized communities. The current figure is far below that. Field organizing—nonprofits and philanthropy leaders building a shared platform, aligning messaging, and educating donors and advisors—is what turns these documented practices into sector-wide norms.

Crucially, philanthropy cannot substitute for a fair tax system—it must complement one. The deepest reforms will address not only how charitable dollars are distributed but the economic structures that determine how much wealth is available for the public good in the first place.

NCRP also recommends that at least 25% of philanthropic funding support advocacy, organizing, and civic engagement. Nonprofits are not just service providers—they are democracy builders. But the funding system overwhelmingly rewards direct service while starving the advocacy and organizing work that addresses root causes.

Funders are not auxiliary to the transformation this chapter envisions. They are inside it. None of the reforms mentioned in this chapter will function without a philanthropic system willing to fund civic infrastructure as infrastructure: durably, flexibly, and at the scale of the moment.

Questions for discussion: *What would it take to make DAF payout reform a political reality? How can the sector hold foundations accountable to equity and payout benchmarks without regulatory mandates? What role should next-generation donors and inheritors play in reshaping philanthropic norms? To strengthen corporate partnerships, what policy changes should be implemented (i.e., limiting corporations from buying their own stock)?*

The Three-Sector Partnership

Social benefit organizations often carry the weight of solving problems that neither markets nor governments fully address. But they can't do it alone. The most effective social-impact efforts happen when government, business, and nonprofits work together, each contributing what it does best: government sets policy and provides scale, business brings innovation and resources, nonprofits bring community insight and trust.

Kimberlee Riley of Purposeful Philanthropy Advisors, who has worked across all three sectors, puts it simply: the challenge is not convincing anyone that collaboration is a good idea. It is making collaboration routine and embedded into our structures.

What does that look like in practice? It could look like any of the following:

- Government inviting social benefit organizations to co-design affordable housing policy, not just deliver services after the policy is set.
- A corporation embedding its data scientists inside a workforce development nonprofit for six months, not just writing a year-end check.

- A city creating a shared data hub that nonprofits, businesses, and public agencies can all plug into—so that a homeless services provider, a hospital, and a job training program are working from the same information about the same community.
- Multiyear government contracts with inflation-adjusted funding and timely reimbursements so that a small community-based organization isn't crippled by a late payment cycle.
- Corporate employees doing 3- to 12-month rotations inside nonprofits, and nonprofit leaders sitting on government task forces as community experts.

Right now, too little of this is happening—and even where the will for reform exists, progress can stall when it becomes a bargaining chip in partisan fights. Government contracts with public benefit organizations to deliver services but rarely includes them in policy development. Businesses donate money but don't offer the pro bono consulting, technology support, or leadership development that would build lasting capacity. Nonprofits are expected to prove impact without being given the evaluation tools to do so. The relationship between the sectors remains largely transactional instead of truly collaborative.

Each sector can learn from each other. Melanie Greenberg highlighted the importance of business and management skills for nonprofit leaders who often enter the sector with passion but lack training in legal issues, financial management, and other operational aspects. Businesses can incorporate the social benefit sector's emphasis on purpose, mission, and values. And government can expand its reach and offer more services in partnership with nonprofits.

The sector itself also has work to do. Dan Pallotta's proposal for a national leadership movement speaks to entrenched social problems, trains media and regulatory agencies, responds to inaccurate coverage, and aggregates the sector's collective voice. The social benefit sector cannot wait to be invited to the table. It must build the table.

A detailed menu of actions that government and business can take—from grant simplification to skills-based volunteering to shared infrastructure—is included in the chapter appendix.

Conclusion: A Call to Build

Nonprofits are a pillar of democracy. But they have been designed, funded, and governed as if they are not. Our chapters have traced what that mismatch costs us: leaders burning out under structures built for a smaller era, funding models that reward incrementalism over impact, collaboration missing from the infrastructure.

We can draw powerful lessons from leaders who elevated public service, volunteerism, conservation, and partnerships between government and nonprofits over the past 250 years. Franklin D. Roosevelt set the stage with the New Deal, mobilizing the nation through bold public works and civic action. John F. Kennedy's call to service inspired the creation of the Peace Corps, while Lyndon B. Johnson expanded national commitment through the War on Poverty and the Great Society. The life and legacy of Martin Luther King Jr. shaped the National Day of Service and the Corporation for National and Community Service. Jimmy Carter carried the torch through decades of hands-on humanitarian work with Habitat for Humanity and the founding of the Carter Center. George H. W. Bush championed a "thousand points of light," celebrating the power of volunteers in every community. Bill Clinton strengthened this tradition by helping create AmeriCorps; Hillary Clinton championed NGOs working on human trafficking, global health, and girls', education; and Barack Obama deepened partnerships with nonprofits to broaden the reach of national service.

These leaders' efforts form a rich legacy of civic responsibility that continues to guide and inspire us today. Each existed in their own time, imaginatively pushing the boundaries society had set on the social sector. They teach us that it is always a small group of changemakers who catalyze a shift in the full landscape. May our next generation rise to the moment.

Caring for ourselves matters, but so does caring for the commons—the well-being of the whole. The future of American democracy will be shaped not by one sector alone, but by the strength of collaboration among all three.

None of this gets redesigned by waiting. And it will not get redesigned only by the largest organizations and the largest funders. If you lead a small or midsize social benefit organization, you may wonder where you fit in a chapter about national advocacy and philanthropy reform. You fit everywhere. The redesign is happening in your bylaws when you rewrite a board term limit, in your funder conversations when you push back on a one-year grant, in the regional information commons that does not yet exist because no one has convened it, in the merger you have been quietly considering. Two million nonprofits will redesign this sector together, or no one will.

So step into a larger role. Champion an idea or structure in this book that fits your community, mission, or moment—whether that is updated governance standards, DAF reform, a state nonprofit caucus, or the cross-sector partnership your community needs and does not have. Join a local or national coalition. Tell your funders what one-year restricted grants actually cost you. Share a leadership role you have been holding alone. Mentor someone coming up, and let them mentor you back. Tell the sector's story—share what your work makes possible, on social media and in traditional outlets, so philanthropy and impact stay visible.

The sector's deepest contributions are not just the services nonprofits provide. They are the values that sustain democracy itself: equity, accountability, voice, community, and the belief that every person's well-being is a shared responsibility. Those values do not maintain themselves. They require institutions strong enough to defend them, infrastructure built to support them, and a public that understands why they matter.

This is not merely an organizational challenge. It is a democratic opportunity, and it is ours.

Start where you are. Start now.

Please join this initiative with us at www.redesigningnonprofits.org.

Appendix for Chapter 8

A. How Government Can Step Up: An Action Agenda

1. **Simplify funding and reporting** by streamlining grant applications so social benefit organizations spend less time on paperwork and more on mission, standardizing reporting requirements across agencies, and offering multiyear grants instead of one-year cycles to reduce instability.
2. **Shift from transactional to strategic partnerships** by co-designing programs with nonprofits rather than dictating terms and involving nonprofits early in policy development, especially those closest to affected communities.
3. **Invest in capacity, not just programs,** by allowing grant dollars to cover overhead, technology, staff development, and evaluation, and funding infrastructure like data systems, not just direct services.
4. **Pay on time.** Late reimbursements can cripple small nonprofits. Faster payment cycles make a huge difference.
5. **Use government data to empower nonprofits** by sharing anonymized datasets that help nonprofits target services, measure impact, and understand community needs.

B. How Businesses Can Support Nonprofits

1. **Move beyond check-writing** by providing skills-based volunteering (e.g., marketing, legal, engineering, data analysis) and offering pro bono consulting or technology support.
2. **Build long-term relationships** through multiyear commitments that help nonprofits plan and grow, and co-create initiatives that align with both the company's expertise and the nonprofit's mission.
3. **Support nonprofit capacity** by sponsoring leadership development, digital transformation, or operational upgrades, and donating software, workspace, or equipment.

4. **Use corporate influence for good** by advocating for policies that strengthen the nonprofit sector and amplifying nonprofit stories through corporate channels.
5. **Integrate nonprofits into business strategy** by partnering with nonprofits as part of ESG, DEI, or community investment strategies, and treating nonprofits as thought partners, not beneficiaries.
6. **Create and expand loan funds** so that those needing to scale or waiting for grants that are delayed can thrive.
7. **Lend more employees to nonprofits.** It's a win-win as employees love to serve and return invigorated as service representatives of the corporation.

C. Tri-Sector Collaboration: From Charity to Ecosystem Mindset

The following actions describe what genuine tri-sector collaboration looks like in practice—when government, business, and public benefit organizations treat each other as essential, permanent partners.

1. **Support innovation, not just maintenance.** Many nonprofits are stuck in survival mode. Governments and businesses can help them experiment, iterate, and scale what works through innovation grants for pilot programs, access to corporate R&D teams or data scientists, and government "regulatory sandboxes" that allow nonprofits to test new models safely.
2. **Create shared infrastructure.** Instead of every nonprofit building its own systems, shared platforms can dramatically reduce costs and increase impact. Examples include shared accounting, HR, or IT services funded by government or corporate partners; community data hubs that nonprofits can plug into; and shared physical spaces—hubs, incubators, and co-working spaces for mission-driven organizations.

3. **Invest in measurement and learning.** Nonprofits are often asked to "prove impact" without being given the tools to do so. Partners can help by funding evaluation frameworks and data systems, providing pro bono analytics or research support, and creating shared metrics across sectors so nonprofits don't have to reinvent the wheel.
4. **Strengthen social impact leadership pipelines.** Leadership burnout is one of the biggest threats to the sector. Support includes fellowships, coaching, and leadership academies funded by business or government; succession planning support for small and midsize nonprofits; and mental health and wellness resources for nonprofit staff.
5. **Make funding more equitable.** Many nonprofits serving marginalized communities are underfunded despite being closest to the issues. Government can prioritize funding for community-based organizations with lived-experience leadership. Business can diversify corporate philanthropy beyond the "usual suspects." Both can simplify access for small, grassroots groups.
6. **Encourage cross-sector talent flow.** Talent exchange can be transformative. Examples: corporate employees embedded in nonprofits for 3–12 months; nonprofit leaders serving on government task forces; government staff doing short-term rotations in community organizations.
7. **Stabilize the financial foundation of nonprofits.** Nonprofits need predictable revenue, not just sporadic grants. Government can offer multiyear contracts, inflation-adjusted funding, and timely reimbursements. Business can provide recurring corporate sponsorships or subscription-style giving. Joint pooled funds can reduce competition and increase stability.
8. **Partner on systemic change, not just programs.** Nonprofits often see root causes up close. Government and business can help

address them by collaborating on policy reforms informed by nonprofit insights, using corporate influence to push for structural improvements (e.g., housing policy, workforce standards), and funding advocacy and community organizing—not just direct services.

9. **Support technology modernization.** Many nonprofits are running on outdated tools. Partners can donate or subsidize modern software, provide cybersecurity support, and offer training on AI, data management, and digital transformation.

Glossary of Key Nonprofit and Philanthropy Terms

990 An annual informational return filed with the Internal Revenue Service (IRS) by tax-exempt organizations such as charities and nonprofits. They are online (through Guidestar/Candid) and available to the public for review.

501(c)(3) A U.S. tax-exempt nonprofit eligible to receive tax-deductible charitable contributions.

501(c)(4) A social welfare organization that can engage in advocacy; contributions are not tax-deductible.

B-corps For-profit companies verified by B-Lab to meet the highest standard of social and environmental performance, accountability, and transparency. There are more than 10,000 certified B-corps across 100 countries; they dedicate a portion of their profits, time, or partnerships to nonprofits and NGOs.

Bequest A gift left to a nonprofit through a donor's will or estate plan.

BIPOC Black, Indigenous, and People of Color; a term recognizing shared and distinct experiences of racial inequity.

Collective impact Coordinated, cross-sector efforts using shared goals and metrics to address complex social issues.

Donor-advised fund (DAF) A charitable account where donors receive a tax deduction and recommend grants over time.

Donor intent The original purpose or restrictions a donor sets for how a gift should be used.

Donor stewardship Ongoing relationship-building with donors through communication, recognition, and impact reporting.

Endowment Invested funds that generate long-term income while preserving the principal.

Equity-centered philanthropy Grantmaking that prioritizes fairness and addresses systemic social and economic inequities.

Fiscal sponsorship An arrangement where an established nonprofit provides legal and financial oversight to a project.

Flow funding Moving resources quickly to communities, often shifting decision-making power to those closest to the work.

General operating support (GOS) Unrestricted funding that allows nonprofits to allocate resources where most needed.

Giving and legacy plans A detailed annual or lifetime plan, often done with a financial plan, and a financial or philanthropic advisor. It includes donor or family goals, intentions with priority categories, and percentages and amounts that will be given and volunteer hours.

Giving circle A group that pools funds and makes collective decisions about where to give.

Impact investing Investments that seek measurable social or environmental impact alongside financial returns.

Intersectionality A framework recognizing that people experience overlapping forms of discrimination and privilege shaped by race, gender, class, sexuality, disability, and other identities.

Major gifts Large donations cultivated through personalized engagement and long-term relationships.

NAACP National Association for the Advancement of Colored People.

Participatory grantmaking A model where community members directly help decide how funds are distributed.

Payout rate The percentage of private foundation assets distributed annually; U.S. minimum is about 5%.

Planned giving Donations arranged in advance, often through wills, trusts, or other financial plans.

Program-related investment (PRI) Foundation investments made primarily to advance charitable purposes rather than maximize profit.

Public/social benefit sector A term reframing nonprofits as a core sector advancing the common good alongside government and business.

Restricted funds Donations designated by the donor for a specific purpose or time period.

Theory of change A framework explaining how an organization's activities lead to desired outcomes and impact.

Trust-based philanthropy An approach emphasizing multiyear, unrestricted funding and streamlined, trust-centered practices.

Unrestricted funds Flexible donations that can be used at the organization's discretion for mission and operations.

Selected Resources for Redesigning Nonprofits

This resource list is a starting place for readers, not a comprehensive or endorsed directory. Links and organizations may change over time; readers are encouraged to verify current information and select resources that fit their own goals, communities, and values. Please add resources to and watch for updates on this book's website: redesigningnonprofits.org.

AI, Technology, and Innovation

- AI for Nonprofits—ai4np.org
- Anthropic—anthropic.com
- Change Agent—thechange.ai
- NTEN—nten.org
- OpenAI—openai.com
- Stanford Institute for Human-Centered AI—hai.stanford.edu
- TechSoup—techsoup.org

Boards, Governance, and Leadership

- BoardSource—boardsource.org
- Blue Avocado—blueavocado.org
- CompassPoint—compasspoint.org
- Nonprofit Academic Centers Council [NACC]—nonprofit-academic-centers-council.org/accreditation/nacc-accredited-programs/
- Leadership Learning Community—leadershiplearning.org

- Liberatory Leadership Partnership—liberatoryleadership.org
- Nonprofit Quarterly—nonprofitquarterly.org
- Rockwood Leadership Institute—rockwoodleadership.org
- Klein and Roth Consulting—kleinandroth.com

Donor Communities

- EDGE Funders Alliance/Engaged Donors for Global Equity—edge funders.org
- Exponent Philanthropy—exponentphilanthropy.org
- Gill Foundation OutGiving Conference—gillfoundation.org/outgiving
- Good Ancestor Movement—goodancestormovement.com
- The Giving Pledge—givingpledge.org
- Kindle Project—kindleproject.org
- Millionaires for Humanity—millionairesforhumanity.org
- Organize the Rich, Michael Gast—organizetherich.com
- Patriotic Millionaires—patrioticmillionaires.org
- Resource Generation—resourcegeneration.org
- Solidaire Network—solidairenetwork.org
- Threshold Foundation—thresholdfoundation.org
- United Philanthropy Forum—unitedphilforum.org
- Women Donors Network—womendonorsnetwork.org
- Women Moving Millions—womenmovingmillions.org

Donor-Advised Funds, Giving, and Legacy Planning

- American Endowment Foundation—aefonline.org
- Chartered Advisors in Philanthropy (CAP designation)—theamerican college.edu

- Fidelity Charitable—fidelitycharitable.org
- FreeWill—freewill.com
- Half My DAF—halfmydaf.com
- Inspired Philanthropy; giving and legacy plan worksheets—inspiredphilanthropy.org/resources.htm
- Jewish Communal Fund—jcfny.org
- National Philanthropic Trust—nptrust.org
- Schwab Charitable—schwabcharitable.org
- The American College CAP Program—theamericancollege.edu
- Vanguard Charitable—vanguardcharitable.org

Equity, Democracy, and Movement Building

- AAPIP—aapip.org
- ABFE—abfe.org
- Bioneers—bioneers.org
- Change Philanthropy—changephilanthropy.org
- Donors of Color Network—donorsofcolor.org
- EDGE Funders Alliance—edgefunders.org
- Equity in the Center—equityinthecenter.org
- Frameworks Institute—frameworksinstitute.org
- Funders for LGBTQ Issues—lgbtfunders.org
- Hispanics in Philanthropy—hipfunds.org
- Impact Collective—impactcollect.org
- Native Americans in Philanthropy—nativephilanthropy.org
- Neighborhood Funders Group—nfg.org
- Race Forward—raceforward.org

Family Philanthropy and Intergenerational Giving

- Family Circle Advisors, Lisa Parker—familycircleadvisors.com
- National Center for Family Philanthropy—ncfp.org
- National Network of Consultants to Grantmakers—nncg.org

Fiscal Sponsorship and Fiscal Agents

- Community Partners—communitypartners.org
- Earth Island Institute—earthisland.org
- National Network of Fiscal Sponsors—fiscalsponsors.org
- Social Good Fund—socialgoodfund.org
- Social Impact Commons—socialimpactcommons.org
- Tides—tides.org
- TSNE—tsne.org

Foundations and Philanthropic Infrastructure

- Center for Effective Philanthropy—cep.org
- Community Foundation Atlas—communityfoundationatlas.org
- Council on Foundations—cof.org
- Council on Foundations Community Foundation Locator—cof.org/page/community-foundation-locator
- Emerging Practitioners in Philanthropy—epip.org
- Grantmakers for Effective Organizations—geo.org
- Independent Sector—independentsector.org
- Lilly Family School of Philanthropy—philanthropy.iupui.edu

- National Council of Nonprofits—councilofnonprofits.org
- The Philanthropic Initiative—tpi.org
- Philanthropic Roundtable—philanthropicroundtable.org
- Power Moves—ncrp.org/power-moves
- Trust-based Philanthropy Project—trustbasedphilanthropy.org
- United Philanthropy Forum—unitedphilforum.org/our-work

Fundraising and Development

- Association of Fundraising Professionals—afpglobal.org
- Bloomerang—bloomerang.com
- Candid—candid.org
- Donor Organizer Hub—donororganizerhub.org
- GivingTuesday—givingtuesday.org
- "Corporate Sponsorships: Complete Guide" by OneCause—onecause.com
- Joan Garry Consulting—joangarry.com
- Klein and Roth Consulting—kleinandroth.com

Media and Publications

- Chronicle of Philanthropy—philanthropy.com
- Giving Magazine—philanthropy.org/giving-magazine
- Inside Philanthropy—insidephilanthropy.com
- Nonprofit Quarterly—nonprofitquarterly.org and its initiative #WeTheCivic
- Stanford Social Innovation Review—ssir.org
- The NonProfit Times—thenonprofittimes.com

Nonprofit Mergers and Strategic Alliances

- La Piana Consulting—lapiana.org
- MAP for Nonprofits—mapfornonprofits.org
- Mission + Strategy Consulting—missionandstrategy.com
- SeaChange Capital Partners—seachangecap.org

Research, Data, and Sector Infrastructure

- Aspen Institute, Philanthropy and Social Innovation—aspeninstitute.org/programs/philanthropy-and-social-innovation
- Candid/Foundation Center—candid.org
- Giving USA—givingusa.org
- Inequality.org, led by Chuck Collins and team—https://ips-dc.org/project/inequality-org/
- Institute for Policy Studies—https://ips-dc.org/
- Urban Institute—urban.org

Social Investing and Impact Investing

- Calvert Impact—calvertimpact.org
- Criterion Institute—criterioninstitute.org
- ImpactAssets—impactassets.org
- Just Economy Institute—justeconomyinstitute.org
- Ktisis Capital (Jason Franklin and team)—http://ktisiscapital.com/
- RSF Social Finance—rsfsocialfinance.org
- The Transformative 25—transformative25.org

Women's Philanthropy and Giving Circles

- Giving Circle Network—philanthropytogether.org/networks
- Grapevine Giving Circle Directory—grapevine.org/giving-circle-directory

- Ms. Foundation For Women—forwomen.org
- Prospera—prospera-inwf.org
- Women's Funding Network—womensfundingnetwork.org
- Women Moving Millions—womenmovingmillions.org
- Women's Philanthropy Institute—philanthropy.iupui.edu/wpi

Youth Giving and Youth Philanthropy

- Michigan Youth Education Fund—sharedetroit.org/nonprofit/michigan-youth-education-fund
- Youth Advisory Councils—Community Foundation for Northeast Michigan—cfnem.org/youth-advisory-councils
- Youth Giving Circles, Redesigning Nonprofits —redesigningnonprofits.org

Selected Exemplary Books

- *The Accidental Fundraiser* by Haley Bash and Stephanie Roth
- *AI for Nonprofits* by Darian Rodriguez Heyman and Cheryl Contee
- *Burned by Billionaires: How Concentrated Wealth and Power Are Ruining Our Lives and Planet* by Chuck Collins
- *Charity Case; Uncharitable; The Everyday Philanthropist;* and *The Flat Org Chart* by Dan Pallotta
- *Co-Intelligence: Living and Working with AI* by Ethan Mollick
- *Creating a Women's Giving Circle* by Sondra Shaw-Hardy
- *Decolonizing Wealth: Indigenous Wisdom to Heal Divides and Restore Balance* by Edgar Villanueva
- *Free the People to Free the Money to Free the People* by Michael Gast, Marian Moore, and Alex T. Tom
- *Fundraising for Social Change* by Kim Klein and Stan Yogi

- *Governance as Leadership: Reframing the Work of Nonprofit Boards* by Richard P. Chait, William P. Ryan, and Barbara E. Taylor
- *Imagination: A Manifesto* by Ruha Benjamin
- *Inspired Philanthropy: Your Step-by-Step Guide to Creating a Giving Plan and Leaving a* Legacy by Tracy Gary with Nancy Adess
- *Joan Garry's Guide to Nonprofit Leadership* by Joan Garry
- *Leading with Joy: Practices for Uncertain Times* by Akaya Windwood and Rajasvini Bhansali
- *National Directory of Corporate Giving*, compiled by the Foundation Center; by Suzanne W. Haile
- *A New Era of Philanthropy* by Dimple Abichandani
- *Nonprofit Management 101* by Darian Rodriguez Heyman and Laila Brenner
- *Nonprofit Mergers and Alliances* by Thomas A. McLaughlin
- *Primed to Perform* by Neel Doshi and Lindsay McGregor
- *Raise More Money: The Best of the Grassroots Fundraising Journal* by Kim Klein
- *Redesigning Nonprofits: Catalysts for a Stronger Democracy* by Tracy Gary, Kimberly Weichel, and Shannon Kollasch
- *Reimagining Nonprofits and Philanthropy* by Vu Le
- *Reinventing Organizations* by Frédéric Laloux
- *The Happy, Healthy Nonprofit; Measuring the Networked Nonprofit; The Networked Nonprofit;* and *The Smart Nonprofit* by Beth Kanter, with coauthors Aliza Sherman, Katie Delahaye Paine, and Allison H. Fine
- *The Soul of Money: Transforming Your Relationship with Money and Life* by Lynne Twist
- *The Uprising of Women in Philanthropy* by Ndana Bofu-Tawamba, Ruby Bright, Stephanie Clohesy, Christine Grumm, Musimbi Kanyoro, Helen LaKelly Hunt, Ana Oliveira, Laura Risimini, Jane Sloane, and Jessica Tomlin

- *Transformative Donor Organizing* by Isaac Lev Szmonko/Solidaire Network
- *Unrig the Game* by Vanessa Priya Daniel
- *We Gave Away a Fortune* by Christopher Ellinger and Anne Ellinger
- *Women and Philanthropy* by Sondra Shaw-Hardy, Martha A. Taylor, and Buffy Beaudoin-Schwartz
- *What It Takes to Heal: How Transforming Ourselves Can Change the World* by Prentis Hemphill

Additional Book and Website Resources

- *Redesigning Nonprofits* book website—redesigningnonprofits.org
- Inspired Philanthropy giving and legacy plan worksheets, podcasts, exercises, appendixes, and links—inspiredphilanthropy.org/resources.htm

Acknowledgments

It takes a village to create a book like this. We are profoundly grateful to all the individuals who participated in this book and shared their wisdom that helped make the book what it is.

We begin by giving thanks to our Advisory Council, who guided us on our journey with their wisdom: Deborah Heiser, Dennis Robinson, Rebecca Young, Sreya Panuganti, Tezikiah Gabriel, Darian Rodriguez Heyman, and Phil Cubeta.

We are ever so grateful to our peer reviewers who took the time to read our chapters and offered invaluable advice and suggestions: Amy Sample Ward, Beth Kanter, Dennis Robinson, Jeff C. Jensen, Jensine Larsen, Julie Motz, Matthew Spaur, Mike Gast, Rebecca Young, Sreya Panuganti, Tezikiah Gabriel, Sara Hudson, and Phil Cubeta.

We especially thank Sara Hudson who authored the foreword, for her vision, insight, and years of work to improve the nonprofit sector.

We interviewed over 40 leaders whose voices and perspectives are woven throughout this book—their full bios appear at the back of this book. We are grateful to each of them. We also thank the 30 friends and colleagues who filled out our survey with their experiences and recommendations for the sector, and Cristina Logg, who distilled insights from the survey. We acknowledge Rosina Wilson for her editing assistance.

Alongside our Advisory Council, reviewers, and interviewees, we honor just a sampling of the many other leaders whose vision for nonprofits inspires us—including Frances Hesselbein, Pablo Eisenberg, Marie C. Wilson, Virginia Hodgkinson, Greta Thunberg, Peter Drucker, Kim Klein, Dolores Huerta, Dan Pallotta, Jan Masaoka, Van Jones, Clara Miller, Vu Le,

Akaya Windwood, Darren Walker, Melinda French Gates, Michael Bloomberg, Oprah Winfrey, MacKenzie Scott, Kitty Tilsch, Wendy Kopp, Oseola McCarty, and Marion Weber.

We also honor leading women of color whose leadership has helped reshape and make more responsive the nonprofit and philanthropic sectors in the United States: Claire Babineaux-Fontenot, La June Montgomery Tabron, Tonya Allen, Cecilia Conrad, Carmen Rojas, Ai-jen Poo, Angelique Albert, Pia Infante, Vanessa Priya Daniel, Ebony Twilley Martin, Rajasvini Bhansali, Ann Mei Chang, and Peggy Saika.

We thank our publishing team at Wiley, including Brian Neill, Michael Joseph Das, Pinky Mancuso, Julie Kerr, Kim Wimpsett, and others who helped us bring this book to fruition. We acknowledge Irene Young for her photographic professionalism, and Julian Weichel for helping create our website.

Finally, to the partners, friends, and supporters who held us up along the way—thank you. Special thanks to Tracy's housemate Daphne, Shannon's partner Jeff, and Kim's husband Carl: your love, patience, and steady belief in this work carried us through. We are so grateful.

About the Authors

Tracy Gary has been a donor activist, fundraiser, and philanthropic advisor for more than 53 years. She's co-founded more than 20 nonprofits, including the Women's Foundation of California, Changemakers, the Women's Funding Network, Outgiving, the Women Donors Network, Inspired Legacies, and the Women's Building. Matching donors' interests with nonprofits with strategic solutions is her passion. She's been on 26 boards as a feminist philanthropist. She gave 100% of her inheritance to grantees by age 35 ($7 million in today's dollars) and then an additional $1 million (giving 20% of her income annually).

She is the author of *Inspired Philanthropy: Creating a Giving and Legacy Plan* and has been to 50 states and 20 countries promoting giving and leadership. She grew up in multiple cities, receiving guidance from her parents about service and generosity. She is regarded as an inspiration for all generations for the gifts received through giving with heart for the good of the whole. See www.unleashinggenerosity.org.

Kimberly Weichel is a global leadership expert, author, and cross-cultural strategist with more than three decades of experience advancing women's leadership and international cooperation. She has directed major nonprofit initiatives, led peacebuilding and development projects worldwide, and worked closely with UN-related agencies, including UN Women. Kim teaches at the Lifelong Learning Institute at American University in Washington, DC; mentors emerging women leaders; and advises organizations committed to social impact. Her publications include *Inside Crossroads* (1979), *The Future of the Pacific Rim* (1994), *Healing the Heart of the World*

(2005), *Beyond Borders* (2016), *Our Voices Matter* (2019), and *Uncovering New Possibilities* (2021). A Rotary Peace Fellow and recipient of multiple leadership awards, Kim is recognized for her lifelong commitment to building a more just and peaceful world. See www.kimweichel.com.

Shannon Kollasch lives at the intersection of nonprofits, arts, and technology. As program director at Amplifi Napa Valley, she is growing a sustainable arts ecosystem in California's North Bay, discovering and developing emerging musicians from underrepresented communities. She has advised Fortune 500 companies on strategy and leads strategic planning for nonprofits in the arts, health, and education. Previously she founded Lumi Tutors, which connects underserved Chicago high schoolers with college mentors. She holds BS and MS degrees in materials science and engineering from Northwestern University, where she was a researcher in clean energy. She lives in Berkeley / Oakland, California, and enjoys live music, cooking, and jumping out of planes.

About the Advisory Council and Interviewees

Advisory Council

Darian Rodriguez Heyman

Darian is the author of the bestselling *AI for Nonprofits* (Wiley, 2025) and founder of AI4NP.org, an NTEN-sponsored initiative building a Learning Hub and national Learning Lab series to advance responsible AI adoption across the sector. A nonprofit strategist and keynote speaker with 20+ years of experience, he launched Craigslist Foundation's Nonprofit Boot Camp as ED, helped shape the UN's SDGs on climate and gender, co-founded 2XGlobal to direct $33B+ to women-led businesses, and helped channel more than $200M to Black-led nonprofits. He's also the author of the bestselling *Nonprofit Management 101* and *Nonprofit Fundraising 101*. Through his consultancy Helping People Help, he provides executive coaching and advisory services in AI implementation, fundraising, board development, and strategic planning. See https://helpingpeoplehelp.com.

Deborah Heiser, PhD

Deborah Heiser, PhD, is a psychologist and researcher whose work focuses on mental health, mentorship, and purpose across the lifespan. She is the founder of Mental Mapping and My Legacy Tree, digital platforms that translate evidence-based psychological frameworks into accessible tools for assessment, reflection, and well-being. Dr. Heiser also founded and served as CEO of The Mentor Project, a global nonprofit dedicated to advancing mentorship and intergenerational learning. Her scholarship and applied work emphasize the role of mentorship and meaning in promoting psychological resilience and long-term mental health outcomes, and contribute to public discourse through writing and speaking that bridge science and practice.

Dennis M. Robinson

Dennis M. Robinson brings 35 years of philanthropy and nonprofit experience, specializing in strategies for high-net-worth donors, family foundations, governments, universities, and hospitals, with prior roles at Silicon Valley Community Foundation, the Southern Poverty Law Center, and MedShare International. He has raised more than $1 million for major disaster response efforts, including the invasion of Ukraine, India's COVID surge, Hurricane Maria in Puerto Rico, and the 2010 Haiti earthquake. Dennis holds a BA in communications and speech from Fisk University and a graduate certification from the Middlebury Institute of International Studies at Monterey. He serves on the global board of trustees of the Charter for Compassion.

Phil Cubeta

Phil Cubeta founded Philanthropy Offerings in 2022 to help former students and friends bring philanthropy home to the communities in which they are personally engaged. He served for 12 years as the Wallace Chair in Philanthropy at the American College of Financial Services, where he was responsible for the Chartered Advisors in Philanthropy (CAP®) designation. During his tenure, more than 2,000 advisors and nonprofit gift planners received this designation. Previously, Phil served as chief of staff for the Nautilus Group, a service of New York Life Insurance Company providing estate, business, and philanthropic strategies to affluent clients through 200 of the company's top agents.

Rebecca Young

Rebecca Young is the cofounder of Human First Works, where she advises businesses and nonprofits, with a particular focus on guiding companies through the transition to worker cooperatives. Over a career spanning more than two decades in corporate leadership—including building a half-billion-dollar credit card portfolio, co-founding and exiting a 100-person technology company, and serving as COO of a genomics firm—she has held senior roles across financial services, technology, biotech, and clean energy. Today she focuses on advising women-founded businesses, nonprofits, and purpose-driven companies, bringing hard-won operational expertise to organizations who are redesigning how power, ownership, and leadership are shared.

Sreya Panuganti

Sreya Panuganti leads external engagement across McKinsey & Company's global philanthropy portfolio, working with senior leaders on partnership strategy and program design. Her work focuses on building and activating cross-sector partnerships that translate complex social challenges into structured, actionable pathways. She brings particular expertise in convening leaders and shaping collaborative platforms that strengthen how the social impact sector works together.

Tezikiah Gabriel

Tezikiah Gabriel is the executive director of Pathways To Peace (PTP), a UN Peace Messenger Organization, in consultation with ECOSOC and DGC. As the owner and senior consultant for Gabriel Associates for more than 33 years, Tezikiah has worked with mission-based organizations and initiatives to create mission impact, relevant, and sustainable environments that affect real and positive change in our world. Tezikiah is also an ordained minister who conducts interfaith and intercultural ceremonies and works with individuals and groups to "Empower the Divine Within Each of Us."

Interviewees

Aaron Dorfman

Aaron Dorfman is president and CEO of the National Committee for Responsive Philanthropy (NCRP), a research and advocacy organization that works to ensure America's grantmakers and wealthy donors are responsive to the needs of those with the least wealth, opportunity, and power. Before joining NCRP in 2007, Dorfman served for 15 years as a community organizer with two national organizing networks, spearheading grassroots campaigns on a variety of issues. He holds a bachelor's degree in political science from Carleton College and a master's degree in philanthropic studies from the Lilly Family School of Philanthropy at Indiana University and serves on the boards of three national justice-focused nonprofits. See https://ncrp.org.

Amy Sample Ward

Amy Sample Ward (they/them) is the CEO of NTEN, a nonprofit working to make missions and movements more successful through the skillful and equitable use of technology. They believe technology should be accessible and accountable to everyone, especially communities historically excluded from the digital world. Amy currently serves as a visiting scholar on AI at Independent Sector and as a board member and advisor to several organizations. Their latest book, *The Tech That Comes Next*, co-authored with Afua Bruce, charts how changemakers, technologists, philanthropists, and policymakers can build an equitable world with technology.

Ann Mei Chang

Ann Mei Chang is the CEO of Candid, a nonprofit that provides the most comprehensive data about the social sector—where money comes from, where it goes, and why it matters. She is also the author of *Lean Impact: How to Innovate for Radically Greater Social Good*. A leading expert on social innovation, Ann Mei previously served as the chief innovation officer at the U.S. Agency for International Development, Mercy Corps, and Pete for America. As the first E.D. of the U.S. Global Development Lab, she harnessed best practices for innovation to accelerate the impact and scale of solutions to the world's most intractable challenges. See www.annmei.com.

Beth Kanter

Beth Kanter is an internationally recognized thought leader and trainer in AI skilling and well-being in the nonprofit workplace. She is the co-author of four award-winning books, her most recent on workplace well-being and artificial intelligence. Named one of the most influential women in technology by *Fast Company* and recipient of the NTEN Lifetime Achievement Award, she has more than three decades of experience in designing and delivering training programs for nonprofits and foundations. As a sought-after keynote speaker and workshop leader, she has presented at nonprofit conferences around the world. See www.bethkanter.org.

Cheryl Contee

Cheryl Contee is the chief innovation officer at BrightWorksAI.com. She is a pioneering technology entrepreneur and digital transformation expert. Cheryl is renowned as a trailblazing startup founder, a trusted advisor on innovation and impact, and a leading voice on inclusive entrepreneurship and social enterprise. She has co-authored a bestselling new book called *AI for Nonprofits: Putting Artificial Intelligence to Work for Your Cause* with Darian Rodriguez Heyman sharing insights from more than 50 AI experts intended to help nonprofit leaders embrace new tech. She is also a senior advisor for PosterChild.AI and cofounder of Change Agent AI, mission-driven and game-changing AI-powered startups. See https://BrightWorksAI.com.

Chris Heuer

Chris Heuer is an entrepreneur, community builder, and human-centered AI advocate with 30 years of experience empowering leaders and their organizations to put people first. As founder of the H Corp Foundation and managing director of the Team Flow Institute, he transforms organizations by augmenting human capabilities with better systems and technologies. He is passionate about mentoring startup founders and social impact leaders to think more holistically in serving their markets. His work spans startup ecosystem design, engagement strategy, and the belief that organizations choosing human-first approaches to AI will compound returns that pure efficiency-driven models cannot match. See linkedin.com/in/chrisheuer.

Chuck Collins

Chuck Collins is a campaigner and storyteller who has worked for decades on environmental and economic justice campaigns. He is the director of the Program on Inequality and the Common Good at the Institute for Policy Studies where he co-edits Inequality.org and founded the Charity Reform Initiative at IPS (https://ips-dc.org). His new book is *Burned by Billionaires: How Concentrated Wealth and Power are Ruining Our Lives and Planet* (New Press, 2025). See www.chuckcollinswrites.com.

Dan Pallotta

Dan Pallotta is a pioneer in the global effort to transform the way our culture evaluates the character and impact of nonprofit organizations. His iconic TED Talk on philanthropy has been viewed more than 5.7 million times. He is the author of *Uncharitable: How Restraints on Nonprofits Undermine Their Potential*, which was turned into an award-winning film. He also authored *Charity Case: How the Nonprofit Community Can Stand Up for Itself and Really Change the World* and, more recently, *The Everyday Philanthropist: A Better Way to Make a Better World*.

Daphne R. Scott

Daphne R. Scott has worked for 30 years in community development, nonprofit leadership, and philanthropy. She founded two nonprofit organizations: Revitalizing and Empowering Through Architecture for Community Health, and Arkansas Association of Community Development Corporations. She also founded a consulting enterprise—Period.9. She worked as the vice president of Community Impact for United Way of Sonoma, Mendocino and Lake, as program officer for the Women's Foundation of California, and as program manager for the Arkansas Single Parent Scholarship Fund.

Darian Rodriguez Heyman

Darian is the author of the bestselling *AI for Nonprofits* (Wiley, 2025) and founder of AI4NP.org, an NTEN-sponsored initiative building a Learning Hub and national Learning Lab series to advance responsible AI adoption across the sector. A nonprofit strategist and keynote speaker with 20+ years of experience, he launched Craigslist Foundation's Nonprofit Boot Camp as ED, helped shape the UN's SDGs on climate and gender, co-founded 2XGlobal to direct $33B+ to women-led businesses, and helped channel more than $200M to Black-led nonprofits. He's also the author of the bestselling *Nonprofit Management 101* and *Nonprofit Fundraising 101*. Through his consultancy Helping People Help, he provides executive coaching and advisory services in AI implementation, fundraising, board development, and strategic planning. See https://helpingpeoplehelp.com.

Dennis M. Robinson

Dennis M. Robinson brings 35 years of philanthropy and nonprofit experience, specializing in strategies for high-net-worth donors, family foundations, governments, universities, and hospitals, with prior roles at Silicon Valley Community Foundation, the Southern Poverty Law Center, and MedShare International. He has raised more than $1 million for major disaster response efforts, including the invasion of Ukraine, India's COVID surge, Hurricane Maria in Puerto Rico, and the 2010 Haiti earthquake. Dennis holds a BA in Communications and Speech from Fisk University and a graduate certification from the Middlebury Institute of International Studies at Monterey. He serves on the Global Board of Trustees of the Charter for Compassion.

Duane Elgin

Duane Elgin is a scholar and author of five books exploring a holistic vision of the planetary future and the paradigm shift. His work reflects deep concern for the long-range future of A1, Earth, and the renewal of democracy, free speech, and cooperation. He champions dimensional evolution, the unity of the cosmos as a co-arising system, and compassionate regard for the well-being of all life. See https://duaneelgin.com and https://ChoosingEarth.org.

Ebony Twilley Martin

Ebony Twilley Martin is the principal of the Regenerative Leadership Lab. As a regenerative leadership strategist and organizational advisor, she helps purpose-driven leaders build what endures—organizations with roots deep enough to weather storms and structures strong enough to grow. Her approach combines real-world executive experience with a deep understanding of how systems, people, and leadership intersect to either strengthen or strain an organization's mission. She is the former executive director of Greenpeace, U.S.A. See https://www.ebonytwilleymartin.org.

Eric Solomon, PhD

Eric Solomon, PhD, is a cognitive psychologist and founder of the Human Operating System, where he helps leaders and teams navigate a world moving faster than they can make meaning. He served as CMO at Bonobos and

Instagram Business, head of Brand Strategy at Spotify, and cofounder of YouTube's creative agency. Today, Eric advises companies and executives on strategic storytelling and how to lead through AI without losing what makes them human. He teaches at Fordham's Gabelli School of Business, writes for *Harvard Business Review* and *Psychology Today*, and is writing his first book—about losing authorship over the lives we're living and how to reclaim it. See www.TheHumanOS.co.

Gary Lucks

Gary Lucks, JD, CPEA, is a progressive author, activist, and environmental attorney. He has spent four decades at the intersection of law, policy, and sustainability, advising leaders, training future changemakers, and contributing to landmark legislation. He is also the founder of Progressive Action East Bay and Resistance Action East Bay Indivisible. He is the author of three books: *You are Not Alone: A Roadmap to Effective Political Action*, *We Are the Power: To Win the Future*, and an environmental law textbook, *California Environmental Law and Policy*. See www.garylucks.com.

Jan Masaoka

Jan Masaoka is currently co-chair of the Philanthropy Project, a national effort for regulatory and tax law changes to ensure that charitable funds benefit the public. She is former CEO of the California Association of Nonprofits (CalNonprofits) and wrote Blue Avocado for its first 15 years; her books include *Nonprofit HR* (Nolo Legal Press) and *Nonprofit Sustainability: Making Strategic Decisions for Financial Viability* (Wiley). See www.philanthropyproject.net.

Jason Franklin

Dr. Jason Franklin is a leading expert on social justice philanthropy, donor organizing, and collective giving who is deeply involved in efforts to strengthen U.S. democracy and advance climate and economic justice. His team at Ktisis Capital has directly advised and stewarded more than $700 million to the field since its founding in 2015. Additionally, he is deeply involved in political, media, and housing efforts including serving as general partner of the Michigan Independent Media Group, founder of the Fairhaven

Alliance organizing landlords as allies to housing justice, and board member of the Michigan Donor Alliance (chair), Democracy Alliance, and Democracy Fund. See www.ktisiscapital.com.

Jensine Larsen

Jensine Larsen is an award-winning digital impact entrepreneur, international journalist, and gender justice advocate with 20+ years of experience. She founded World Pulse, a social impact network connecting grassroots women leaders from 200+ countries who've collectively improved more than 25 million lives. A fellow of the Academy for Systems Change and recipient of the UN Social Impact Media award and 2022 UNESCO Prize in Gender, Wellbeing, and Cultures of Peace, she now leads Unfurl Futures and its flagship Connected Power initiative—creating ecosystem blueprints to ensure AI and digital technology amplify rather than silence the voices that can solve humanity's greatest challenges.

Joshua Korn

Originally from the United States, Joshua grew up in West Africa (Togo and Côte d'Ivoire) and Israel. He currently serves as chief development officer at ReSurge International and has worked in international nonprofit leadership for nearly 20 years, including with Musalaha and CURE International, where he served in various roles including the country director in Niger and the head of partnerships and impact. Joshua holds degrees from Gordon College, Ben-Gurion University of the Negev, and Baylor University.

Julia Roig

Julia Roig has more than 30 years of experience working for democratic change and conflict transformation around the world. After serving for almost 14 years as the president and CEO of PartnersGlobal, a preeminent international democracy and peacebuilding organization, Julia launched the Horizons Project in 2022 to focus on the intersection of peacebuilding, social justice, and democracy in the United States. Julia brings to Horizons her many years of diverse international experience and practical field work in more than 50 countries. She is a renowned public speaker, facilitator, and trainer and is the main architect of ground-breaking new research and approaches for more effective Narratives for Peace.

Kavita N. Ramdas

Kavita N. Ramdas is a globally recognized feminist activist, philanthropic leader and advisor, and independent consultant. As a senior advisor to the International Planned Parenthood Federation, she provides advice on philanthropic partnerships. She is the former president and CEO of the Global Fund for Women and serves on the boards of the Global Greengrants Fund, Grist.org, Visualizing Palestine, and the International Civil Society Action Network (ICAN).

Kim Klein

Kim Klein is an internationally known speaker and author. She was an adjunct faculty member at the School of Social Welfare at UC Berkeley and has worked in all aspects of fundraising: as staff, volunteer, and board member. Kim is the author of five books, including the McAdam Book Award winner, *Reliable Fundraising in Unreliable Times*, and her classic text, *Fundraising for Social Change*, now in its eighth edition, which is widely used in the field and in university programs. She co-founded the *Grassroots Fundraising Journal* in 1981 and was the publisher for 25 years. She is retired but still serves on boards and is active in neighborhood organizing. See www.kleinandroth.com.

Kimberlee Riley

Kimberlee Riley, CAP®, brings more than 30 years of experience across the independent, public, and private sectors, offering a distinctive three-sector perspective and a record of measurable impact. A servant leader and social entrepreneur, she specializes in growing revenue to address community needs through funding diversification, strong governance, and high-performing organizations and intentional donors. She applies Fortune 500–level strategies to help nonprofits scale through innovative partnerships, investment approaches, and program development and also supports donors in achieving their philanthropic aspirations. Kimberlee advances purposeful philanthropy for donors and sustainable outcomes for organizations and the communities they serve. See https://www.linkedin.com/in/kimberleeriley.

Latonya Slack

Latonya Slack looks for ways to weave spirit, energy, and intuition with social justice, nonprofit management, philanthropy, and law. As a facilitator and coach, she uncovers the inner workings and strengths behind the veil of nonprofit social justice leadership as affirmed by women of color founders and directors. Her work celebrates and affirms the stories and lived experiences that make the way we lead, not only necessary but different. Grounded firmly in an intersectional perspective centering race and gender, her work uplifts and affirms BIPOC nonprofit leadership through storytelling and a coaching approach. See https://behindtheveilbtv.org/about-us.

Mathis Wackernagel, PhD

If you have heard of "footprint," as in carbon or ecological footprint, you already met Mathis Wackernagel. He created this metric with his PhD advisor 30 years ago and co-founded Global Footprint Network, a sustainability think-tank, known for its resource accounts, showing that humanity is now using 1.7 Earths. He has been recognized by many honorary degrees and international awards. See https://www.wackernagel.info.

Matthew Spaur

Matthew is a marketing and strategic communications professional with more than 20 years of experience spanning many industries including enterprise software, education, HR, energy, and publishing. Matthew is the founder of the advisory firm Marketing the Social Good. He earned an MBA from the University of Nevada – Reno as well as an MFA in Writing from Eastern Washington University. He is a member of the Teal Team, helps lead the Teal Landscape Report research project, and is an editor of the Teal Team newsletter.

Megan Hyman

Megan Hyman, CAP, serves the Dallas Jewish Community Foundation (DJCF) and its related organization, the Southwest Community Foundation (SWCF), as president and CEO. She leads a team focused on advising families and community agencies, helping them achieve their philanthropic goals and increase support for the nonprofit community in Dallas and around the world. Megan brought to the CEO position more than 15 years of experience with J.P. Morgan, including service as both a private and commercial banker and advising individuals, families and foundations across the full spectrum of wealth management services, such as legacy and estate planning, governance and strategic philanthropy. See https://djcf.org.

Melanie Greenberg

Melanie Greenberg has spent her career in support of the field of peacebuilding, from the perspectives of philanthropy, practice, and academia. Melanie is currently managing director for Programs at Humanity United. She previously served as CEO of the Alliance for Peacebuilding and as associate director of the Stanford Center for International Security and Cooperation. Melanie has helped design and facilitate public peace processes in the Middle East, Northern Ireland, and the Caucasus, and she enjoys writing and teaching in international law, security, and peacebuilding. Melanie lives in McLean, Virginia, with her husband, yellow Lab, and frequent sightings of her adult children.

Michael Gast

Michael Gast is the director of a multimedia project, Organize the Rich, documenting the stories and lessons from the last 50+ years of efforts to organize the wealthy as part of grassroots movements for the common good. He has been organizing the rich for more than 20 years and now works as a strategist at Solidaire Network. Read more on the Organize the Rich Substack: https://organizetherich.substack.com. See also https://solidairenetwork.org.

Dr. Michael Ziccardi

Dr. Ziccardi directs the Karen C. Drayer Wildlife Health Center and the California Veterinary Emergency Team at UC Davis, where he also serves as associate director of Global Programs for the Oiled Wildlife Care Network and Health Science Clinical Professor at the School of Veterinary Medicine.

He holds a DVM, MPVM, and PhD in epidemiology from UC Davis, with a focus on free-ranging wildlife health and petroleum exposure. Since 1996, he has responded to more than 90 oil spills in the United States and abroad, including as marine mammal/sea turtle lead for NOAA during the Deepwater Horizon incident in 2010. His prior roles include executive director of the One Health Institute, chair of the Global Oiled Wildlife Response System project, and chair of NOAA's Working Group on Marine Mammal Unusual Mortality Events.

Nikki Dinh

Nikki Dinh is a field builder committed to liberatory leadership and centering historically excluded communities. With a background spanning law, philanthropy, consulting, and nonprofit leadership, she amplifies the people, practices, and possibilities that just and joyous social change requires.

Olivia E. Dodd

Olivia E. Dodd is a nonprofit executive and filmmaker. Since 2010 she has specialized in founding and redesigning community-centered arts organizations, emphasizing meaningful impact and sustainability. She is currently CEO of Amplifi Napa Valley, which discovers and develops emerging musicians.

Phil Cubeta

Phil Cubeta founded Philanthropy Offerings in 2022 to help former students and friends bring philanthropy home to the communities in which they are personally engaged. He served for 12 years as the Wallace Chair in Philanthropy at the American College of Financial Services, where he was responsible for the Chartered Advisors in Philanthropy (CAP®) designation. During his tenure, more than 2,000 advisors and nonprofit gift planners received this designation. Previously, Phil served as chief of staff for the Nautilus Group, a service of New York Life Insurance Company providing estate, business, and philanthropic strategies to affluent clients through 200 of the company's top agents.

Rajasvini Bhansali

Rajasvini Bhansali is the executive director of Solidaire Network. She is a passionate advocate for participatory grassroots-led power building and a lifelong student of social movements. In a wide-ranging career devoted to racial, economic, and climate justice, she has previously led an international public foundation funding grassroots organizing in Asia, Africa, and Latin America; grown a national youth development social enterprise; and managed a public telecommunications infrastructure fund addressing the digital divide in the southern United States. Born and raised in India, Rajasvini now lives in California and co-authored *Leading with Joy: Practices for Uncertain Times*. See https://solidairenetwork.org.

Roselie Vasquez-Yetter

Roselie Vasquez-Yetter is co-executive director of PartnersGlobal and an international leader in organizational resilience, with more than 25 years of experience guiding institutions through democratic backsliding, civic space restrictions, and political volatility. A social entrepreneur and co-author of the Resiliency+ Framework, she has led programs in highly restrictive environments—including Russia, Turkmenistan, and Saudi Arabia—helping organizations adapt strategically when disruption is constant and rules are rewritten. Her work offers practical leadership lessons on foresight, resilience, and ethical decision-making, shaped by frontline experience and a renewed commitment to human dignity. See https://www.partnersglobal.org.

Sara Hudson

Dr. Sara Hudson is a writer, researcher, and senior strategist advising philanthropic and civil organizations to solve complex civic challenges faced by communities historically ignored, overlooked, or made invisible. Her work elevates individual lives and opportunities while addressing systemic breakdowns. She has a PhD in American Studies from Yale University. She is the interim CEO and editor-in-chief at *Nonprofit Quarterly*. See https://nonprofitquarterly.org.

Sarah Hobson

Sarah Hobson is a social justice practitioner partnering with local leaders and community-based organizations to strengthen rural communities focusing on healthy food systems, rural women's rights and resources, and collaborative solutions. As Executive Director of International Development Exchange (now Thousand Currents), New Field Foundation and West Marin Fund, she channeled more than $50 million to grassroots organizations to support their vision and priorities, advocated successfully for changes in relevant policy and practice, and developed new models of philanthropic partnerships. She is currently director at Open Channels (www.openchannels.net). Connect at https://www.linkedin.com/in/sarahhobsonca.

Stephanie Roth

Stephanie Roth is a principal of Klein & Roth Consulting and has been a trainer, writer, consultant, and coach on fundraising, and organizational and board development from a social and racial justice perspective for more than 30 years. She co-founded Grassroots Institute for Fundraising Training (GIFT), was the editor of the *Grassroots Fundraising Journal*, and is the co-author (with Haley Bash) of *The Accidental Fundraiser: A Step-by-Step Guide to Raising Money for Your Cause, 2nd Edition*. Stephanie has been an active member of Jewish Voice for Peace for more than 25 years. She lives in Berkeley, California. See www.kleinandroth.com.

Susan Tenby

Susan Tenby is a veteran community builder and nonprofit technology leader with nearly 30 years of experience in online community management. She started her community journey in 1997, creating a community for young women with cancer (and she was one of them); she joined TechSoup in 2000 and has led its community efforts in roles ranging from community manager to director of Global Community and director of Community Partnerships. Susan has built, grown, and sustained global nonprofit and civic-tech communities through events, meetups, consulting, partnerships, and platforms, and speaks often on community, public-good technology, and distributed engagement. See SusanTenby.com.

Tezikiah Gabriel

Tezikiah Gabriel is the executive director of Pathways To Peace (PTP), a UN Peace Messenger Organization, in consultation with ECOSOC and DGC. As the owner and senior consultant for Gabriel Associates for more than 33 years, Tezikiah has worked with mission-based organizations and initiatives to create mission impact, relevant, and sustainable environments that affect real and positive change in our world. Tezikiah is also an ordained minister who conducts interfaith and intercultural ceremonies and works with individuals and groups to "Empower the Divine Within Each of Us." See www.gabriel-consult.com.

Vanessa Priya Daniel

Vanessa Priya Daniel is an author, organizer, and award-winning leader for racial and gender justice. The heart of her work is supporting movements and philanthropy to build grassroots power. Her book, *Unrig the Game: What Women of Color Can Teach Everyone About Winning*, was published by Random House in 2025. See www.vanessapriyadaniel.com.

Zafra Lerman, PhD

Zafra Lerman is a chemist, educator, and humanitarian who uses science as a bridge to peace. She is president of the Malta Conferences Foundation, which brings together scientists from across the Middle East, including Nobel Laureates, to collaborate despite political conflict. She has also championed human rights worldwide, helping free imprisoned scientists and dissidents in multiple countries. Lerman has received more than 40 international honors, including the Bill Clinton Presidential Award for Excellence in STEM Mentoring, the American Association for the Advancement of Science Award for Science Diplomacy, the American Physical Society Andrei Sakharov Prize for Human Rights, and the 2025 International Advocate for Peace Award. See www.maltaconferencesfoundation.org.

A Note on AI

We wrote this book during a moment when nonprofits are working out our relationship with generative artificial intelligence (GenAI). The "how" of that relationship matters just as much as the "whether," and we believe it should be a collective conversation. So, we're opening with ours: we used AI in our writing process, and here is what that looked like.

A few values guided us:

- **Humans stay at the center.** At its core, this book was written by three coauthors reflecting together on the wisdom of the over 40 leaders we interviewed: their voices, our voices, and the generative experience of writing in community with each other. AI research also helped us access collective wisdom in the field.
- **Our voices are the first and final say.** We made the creative decisions: what to explore, what belonged in this book, and what didn't, especially at the beginning and ending of each process. AI was a partner in the middle for developmental editing, drafting, research synthesis, interview summaries, and communications.
- **Partnership over automation.** As we discuss in Chapter 6, these tools project patterns from their training data; they do not think consciously, and they do not tell us how they arrived at what they produce. We collaborated with AI from a posture of learning, using it to sharpen our judgment, not replace it.

In practice, that meant bookending our use of AI with dedicated human focus time, printing drafts on paper to create distance from the tools, and talking openly with each other about when and how we were using them. The tools themselves varied (Claude Opus 4.7 and Sonnet, ChatGPT o3, 4, 5, and Deep Research, NotebookLM, Fellow, GitHub Copilot, and Gemini, across different tasks). We name these for transparency, not as a recommendation.

We believe the nonprofit sector has a real chance to shape how AI shows up in mission-driven work. Our own thinking will evolve, and we've committed to checking in with each other as it does. We encourage nonprofits to undertake this journey together, doing the deliberate work of naming how AI is used in your organization and what values it shouldn't replace. Those answers will look different everywhere. The true innovation lies in asking the questions together.

Notes

Introduction

1. Bennington-Castro, J. (2020) How AIDS remained an unspoken—but deadly—epidemic for years. *History*. https://www.history.com/articles/aids-epidemic-ronald-reagan (accessed 23 May 2026).
2. AIDS Project of Los Angeles (1986) *Fight the Fear with the Facts* [poster]. Visual Culture and Health Posters, Profiles in Science. Bethesda, MD: National Library of Medicine. https://profiles.nlm.nih.gov/101584655X105 (accessed 23 May 2026). Reproduced with permission of the AIDS Project of Los Angeles.
3. Crimp, D. (2011) Before Occupy: how AIDS activists seized control of the FDA in 1988. *The Atlantic* (6 December). https://www.theatlantic.com/health/archive/2011/12/before-occupy-how-aids-activists-seized-control-of-the-fda-in-1988/249302/ (accessed 23 May 2026).
4. De Tocqueville, A. (2003) *Democracy in America* (trans. G. Bevan). London: Penguin.
5. AmeriCorps (2024) *Volunteering and Civic Life in America*. Washington, DC: AmeriCorps. Available at: https://www.americorps.gov/about/our-impact/volunteering-civic-life (accessed 27 May 2026).
6. Independent Sector and Do Good Institute (2026) *Value of Volunteer Time*. Washington, DC: Independent Sector. Available at: https://independentsector.org/research/value-of-volunteer-time/ (accessed 27 May 2026).
7. U.S. Bureau of Labor Statistics (2024) *Nonprofits accounted for 12.8 million jobs, 9.9 percent of private-sector employment, in 2022*. Washington, DC: U.S. Department of Labor. Available at: https://www.bls.gov/opub/ted/2024/nonprofits-accounted-for-12-8-million-jobs-9-9-percent-of-private-sector-employment-in-2022.htm (accessed 25 May 2026).

8. U.S. Bureau of Economic Analysis (2023) *Gross Domestic Product, Fourth Quarter and Year 2022*. Washington, DC: U.S. Department of Commerce. Available at: https://www.bea.gov (accessed 25 May 2026).
9. Federal Reserve Bank of Richmond (2025) *How big is the nonprofit sector?* Richmond, VA: Federal Reserve Bank of Richmond. Available at: https://www.richmondfed.org/research/national_economy/macro_minute/2025/how_big_is_the_nonprofit_sector (accessed 25 May 2026).
10. The BLS publishes "healthcare and social assistance" as a single combined NAICS sector accounting for 66.3% of nonprofit employment. To split these per the request, I disaggregated using the longer-run CPS-based industry shares reported in BLS's 2024 *Monthly Labor Review* analysis, which yields approximately 53.9% healthcare and 12.4% social assistance—proportions consistent with the GMU Nonprofit Employment Data Project's separate reporting of these two fields. Because the two source datasets (QCEW versus CPS) use slightly different methodologies, these split values should be read as best-available estimates rather than exact figures published jointly by BLS.
11. U.S. Bureau of Labor Statistics (2024) *Nonprofit sector research data: 2022 nonprofit data file*. Washington, DC: U.S. Department of Labor. Available at: https://www.bls.gov/bdm/nonprofits/nonprofits.htm (accessed 25 May 2026).
12. Casebook PBC (2024) New Casebook study finds majority of nonprofits struggling with staffing in 2024. Press release (15 October). https://www.prweb.com/releases/new-casebook-study-finds-majority-of-nonprofits-struggling-with-staffing-in-2024-302276059.html (accessed 23 May 2026).
13. Schlachter, L.H. and Marshall, T. (2024). U.S. volunteerism rebounding after COVID-19 pandemic. *America Counts: Stories* (19 November). U.S. Census Bureau. https://www.census.gov/library/stories/2024/11/civic-engagement-and-volunteerism.html (accessed 23 May 2026).
14. FrameWorks Institute (2024) *Why Most Americans Think the System Is Rigged*. Washington, DC: FrameWorks Institute. https://www.frameworksinstitute.org/app/uploads/2024/12/FWI-System-Is-Rigged-V4-12.6.24.pdf (accessed 23 May 2026).

Chapter 1

1. Nonprofit Finance Fund (2025) 2025 State of the Nonprofit Sector Survey. Available at: https://nff.org/state-of-the-nonprofit-sector-survey/2025-state-of-the-survey-nonprofit-sector-survey/ (accessed 28 May 2026).
2. The NonProfit Times (2025) NPO jobs, wages jumped between 2017–2022, 7 July. Available at: https://thenonprofittimes.com/npt_articles/npo-jobs-wages-jumped-between-2017-2022/ (accessed 28 May 2026).
3. Buchanan, P., Broder, L. and Im, C. (2023) *State of Nonprofits 2023: What Funders Need to Know*. Cambridge, MA: Center for Effective Philanthropy. Available at: https://cep.org/state-of-nonprofits-2023-report/ (accessed 28 May 2026).
4. Pettijohn, Sarah L., and Elizabeth T. Boris. 2013. *Nonprofit-Government Contracts and Grants: Findings from the 2013 National Survey*. Washington, DC: Urban Institute.
5. Salesforce.org (n.d.) Nonprofit Trends Report. Available at: https://www.salesforce.org/nonprofit/nonprofit-trends/ (accessed 28 May 2026).
6. Deloitte (n.d.) Gen Z and Millennial Survey. Available at: https://www2.deloitte.com/global/en/pages/about-deloitte/articles/genzmillennialsurvey.html (accessed 28 May 2026).
7. CNBC (2017) Technology killing off corporate America: Average life span of companies under 20 years, 24 August. Available at: https://www.cnbc.com/2017/08/24/technology-killing-off-corporations-average-lifespan-of-company-under-20-years.html (accessed 28 May 2026).
8. Konczal, E. (2021) What is unrestricted funding? Two philanthropy experts explain. The Conversation, 23 August. Available at: https://theconversation.com/what-is-unrestricted-funding-two-philanthropy-experts-explain-164589 (accessed 28 May 2026).
9. Miller, E., Talansky, J. and Deshmukh, A. (2025) 2025 State of the Nonprofit Sector Survey: National Findings. Nonprofit Finance Fund. Available at: https://nff.org/wp-content/uploads/NFF-2025-Survey-Report.pdf (accessed 28 May 2026).
10. Miller, E., Talansky, J. and Deshmukh, A. (2025) 2025 State of the Nonprofit Sector Survey: National Findings. Nonprofit Finance Fund. Available at: https://nff.org/wp-content/uploads/NFF-2025-Survey-Report.pdf (accessed 28 May 2026).

11. Tierney, T.J. (2006) *The Nonprofit Sector's Leadership Deficit*. Boston, MA: The Bridgespan Group. Available at: https://www.bridgespan.org/getmedia/0f11d280-6ff9-4e4a-9f4d-5be7742cdfe6/leadership-deficit-white-paper-pdf.pdf (accessed 28 May 2026).
12. Landles-Cobb, L., Kramer, K. and Smith Milway, K. (2015) 'The Nonprofit Leadership Development Deficit'. Stanford Social Innovation Review, 22 October. Available at: https://ssir.org/articles/entry/the_nonprofit_leadership_development_deficit (accessed 28 May 2026).
13. Building Movement Project (2019) Race to Lead: Women of Color in the Nonprofit Sector (CEO/Executive Director report). Available at: https://racetolead.org/ceo-2019/ (accessed 28 May 2026).
14. Gregory, A.G. and Howard, D. (2009) 'The Nonprofit Starvation Cycle', *Stanford Social Innovation Review*, 7(4), pp. 49–53. Available at: https://ssir.org/articles/entry/the_nonprofit_starvation_cycle (accessed 28 May 2026).
15. BoardSource (n.d.) Leading with Intent: National Index of Nonprofit Board Practices. Available at: https://leadingwithintent.org/ (accessed 28 May 2026).
16. Dorsey, C., Bradach, J. and Kim, P. (2020) *Racial Equity and Philanthropy: Disparities in Funding for Leaders of Color Leave Impact on the Table*. Echoing Green and The Bridgespan Group.
17. Independent Sector (n.d.) Recruit new donors to turn the tide for nonprofits. Available at: https://independentsector.org/blog/recruit-new-donors-to-turn-the-tide-for-nonprofits/ (accessed 28 May 2026).
18. Chang, A.M. (2018) *Lean Impact: How to Innovate for Radically Greater Social Good*. Hoboken, NJ: Wiley.
19. charity: water (n.d.) *About*. Available at: https://www.charitywater.org/about (accessed 28 May 2026).
20. van der Tang, F. (2024) Clean drinking water update: 696 million people still lack access. Made Blue Foundation. Available at: https://madeblue.org/en/clean-water-update-771-million-people/ (accessed 24 June 2026).
21. Wei-Skillern, J. and Marciano, S. (2008) 'The Networked Nonprofit', *Stanford Social Innovation Review*, 6(2), pp. 38–43. Available at: https://ssir.org/articles/entry/the_networked_nonprofit (accessed 27 May 2026).
22. CNBC (2025) *The most surprising benefits of a 4-day workweek, from the researcher who's studied thousands of cases*, 24 July. Available at: https://www.cnbc.com/2025/07/24/the-most-surprising-benefits-of-a-4-day-workweek-from-researcher-whos-studied-thousands-of-cases.html (accessed 28 May 2026).

23. PsyPost (n.d.) *Large-scale trial finds four-day workweek improves employee well-being and physical health.* Available at: https://www.psypost.org/large-scale-trial-finds-four-day-workweek-improves-employee-well-being-and-physical-health/ (accessed 28 May 2026).
24. Fidelity Charitable (n.d.) *Approaches to High-Impact Grantmaking: Strengthening Nonprofit Capacity.* Available at: https://www.fidelitycharitable.org/content/dam/fc-public/docs/3rd-party/approaches-to-high-impact-grantmaking-strengthening-nonprofit-capacity.pdf (accessed 28 May 2026).
25. Rockwood Leadership Institute (n.d.) *The nonprofit four-day workweek: Take care of yourself and still change the world.* Available at: https://rockwoodleadership.org/nonprofit-four-day-workweek-can-take-care-still-change-world/ (accessed 28 May 2026).
26. Brooklyn Org (n.d.) *Three lessons learned from a holistic shift to participatory grantmaking.* Available at: https://brooklyn.org/article/three-lessons-learned-from-a-holistic-shift-to-participatory-grantmaking/ (accessed 28 May 2026).
27. Building Movement Project (n.d.) *Race to Lead.* Available at: https://racetolead.org/ (accessed 28 May 2026).
28. Nonprofit Quarterly (n.d.) *Coverage of distributed leadership trends.* Available at: https://nonprofitquarterly.org/ (accessed 28 May 2026).
29. Philanthropy.org (n.d.) *The future of philanthropy is unrestricted: MacKenzie Scott showed what's possible, JobsFirstNYC and others are proving it every day.* Available at: https://philanthropy.org/the-future-of-philanthropy-is-unrestricted-mackenzie-scott-showed-whats-possible-jobsfirstnyc-and-others-are-proving-it-every-day/ (accessed 28 May 2026).

Chapter 2

1. Benjamin, R. (2024) *Imagination: A Manifesto.* New York: W.W. Norton.
2. Benjamin, R. (2019) *Race After Technology: Abolitionist Tools for the New Jim Code.* Cambridge: Polity Press.
3. Eisler, R. (1987) *The Chalice and the Blade: Our History, Our Future.* San Francisco: Harper & Row; see also Eisler, R. (2007). *The Real Wealth of Nations: Creating a Caring Economics.* San Francisco: Berrett-Koehler.
4. Butler, O.E. (1993) *Parable of the Sower.* New York: Four Walls Eight Windows.
5. National Council of Nonprofits (n.d.) Myths about nonprofits. https://www.councilofnonprofits.org/about-americas-nonprofits/myths-about-nonprofits (accessed 23 May 2026).

6. Propel Nonprofits (2024) Operating reserves with nonprofit policy examples. https://propelnonprofits.org/resources/operating-reserves-with-nonprofit-policy-examples/ (accessed 23 May 2026).
7. BBB Wise Giving Alliance (n.d.) Accreditation process. https://give.org/accreditation-process (accessed 23 May 2026).
8. Gregory, A.G. and Howard, D. (2009) 'The nonprofit starvation cycle', *Stanford Social Innovation Review*, Fall. Available at: https://ssir.org/articles/entry/the_nonprofit_starvation_cycle
9. Dorsey, C., Bradach, J., and Kim, P. (2020) *Racial Equity and Philanthropy: Disparities in Funding for Leaders of Color Leave Impact on the Table*. Boston: The Bridgespan Group and Echoing Green. https://www.bridgespan.org/insights/disparities-nonprofit-funding-for-leaders-of-color (accessed 23 May 2026).
10. Gregory, A.G. and Howard, D. (2009) The nonprofit starvation cycle. *Stanford Social Innovation Review* 7 (4): 49–53. https://doi.org/10.48558/6K3V-0Q70.
11. Eckhart Queenan, J., Etzel, M., and Prasad, S. (2016) *Pay-what-it-takes Philanthropy*. Boston: The Bridgespan Group (originally published in *Stanford Social Innovation Review*, Summer 2016). https://www.bridgespan.org/insights/pay-what-it-takes-philanthropy (accessed 23 May 2026).
12. National Council of Nonprofits (n.d.) The nonprofit workforce shortage crisis. https://www.councilofnonprofits.org/nonprofit-workforce-shortage-crisis (accessed 23 May 2026).
13. Bahn, K. and Sanchez Cumming, C. (2020) Improving U.S. Labor Standards and the Quality of Jobs to Reduce the Costs of Employee Turnover to U.S. Companies (December). Washington, DC: Washington Center for Equitable Growth. https://equitablegrowth.org/wp-content/uploads/2020/12/122120-turnover-costs-ib.pdf (accessed 23 May 2026).
14. Independent Sector (2026) Value of volunteer time. Washington, DC: Independent Sector and the Do Good Institute, University of Maryland (21 April). https://independentsector.org/research/value-of-volunteer-time/ (accessed 23 May 2026).
15. Eckhart Queenan, J., Etzel, M., and Prasad, S. (2016) *Pay-what-it-takes Philanthropy*. Boston: The Bridgespan Group (originally published in *Stanford Social Innovation Review*, Summer 2016). https://www.bridgespan.org/insights/pay-what-it-takes-philanthropy (accessed 23 May 2026).
16. Waldron, L., Nayak, P., Lanre-Amos, T. et al. (2023) How nonprofits and NGOs can get real value from strategic planning. Boston: The Bridgespan Group

(1 June). https://www.bridgespan.org/insights/nonprofit-strategy/strategic-planning-for-nonprofits-and-ngos (accessed 23 May 2026).

17. NonProfit PRO (2022) New data quantifies impact of visual branding for nonprofits. *NonProfit PRO* (28 July). https://www.nonprofitpro.com/article/new-data-quantifies-impact-of-visual-branding-for-nonprofits/ (accessed 23 May 2026).
18. National Council of Nonprofits (2019) *Nonprofit Impact Matters: How America's Charitable Nonprofits Strengthen Communities and Improve Lives*. Washington, DC: National Council of Nonprofits. https://www.nonprofitimpactmatters.org/data/downloadable-charts/ (accessed 23 May 2026).
19. Hemphill, P. (2024) *What It Takes to Heal: How Transforming Ourselves Can Change the World*. New York: Random House.
20. Mitchell, M. (2022) Building resilient organizations: toward joy and durable power in a time of crisis. *The Forge* (29 November). https://forgeorganizing.org/article/building-resilient-organizations/ (accessed 23 May 2026).

Chapter 3

1. Cocco, F. and Najmabadi, S. (2026) 'As the cost of aging soars, families' wealth is evaporating', The Washington Post, 23 July. Available at: https://www.washingtonpost.com/business/2026/07/22/elder-care-costs-are-rising-depriving-families-their-inheritance/
2. BoardSource (2021) *Leading with Intent: BoardSource Index of Nonprofit Board Practices*. Washington, DC: BoardSource. Available at: https://leadingwithintent.org/wp-content/uploads/2021/06/2021-Leading-with-Intent-Report.pdf (accessed 24 May 2026).
3. U.S. Census Bureau (2024) *QuickFacts: United States*. Washington, DC: U.S. Census Bureau. Available at: https://www.census.gov/quickfacts/fact/table/US/PST045224 (accessed 24 May 2026).
4. Wikipedia contributors (2026) Youth On Board. Wikipedia, The Free Encyclopedia. Available at: https://en.wikipedia.org/wiki/Youth_On_Board (accessed 24 May 2026).
5. City of Saint Paul (n.d.) *Youth on Boards*. Saint Paul Parks and Recreation. Available at: https://www.stpaul.gov/departments/parks-and-recreation/sprockets/resources-just-teens/youth-boards (accessed 24 May 2026).
6. Board of Governors of the Federal Reserve System (2023) *Survey of Consumer Finances 2022*. Washington, DC: Federal Reserve. Available at: https://www.federalreserve.gov/econres/scfindex.htm (accessed 24 May 2026).

7. Board of Governors of the Federal Reserve System (2023) 'Changes in U.S. Family Finances from 2019 to 2022: Evidence from the Survey of Consumer Finances', *Federal Reserve Bulletin*, October 2023. Available at: https://www.federalreserve.gov/publications/october-2023-changes-in-us-family-finances-from-2019-to-2022.htm (accessed 24 May 2026).
8. For example, Flow Funding (a process for redistributing wealth designed by a female member of the Rockefeller family; see www.flowfunding.org), or donor networks that give together (The Women Donors Network, Solidaire Network, Resource Generation).
9. Board of Governors of the Federal Reserve System (2023) *Survey of Consumer Finances, 2022*. Washington, DC: Federal Reserve. Available at: https://www.federalreserve.gov/econres/scfindex.htm (accessed 24 May 2026).
10. Gast, M. (2023) '5 things I want you to know about wealthy people', Organize the Rich. Available at: https://organizetherich.substack.com/p/5-things-i-want-you-to-know-about-wealthy-people.
11. Learning to Give (n.d.) *Learning to Give*. Grand Rapids, MI: Council of Michigan Foundations. Available at: https://www.learningtogive.org (accessed 24 May 2026).
12. Maryland State Department of Education (n.d.) *Service-Learning Graduation Requirement*. Available at: https://marylandpublicschools.org/programs/Pages/Service-Learning/Graduation-Requirement.aspx (accessed 24 May 2026).
13. Arkansas Department of Education (n.d.) *Community Service Learning*. Available at: https://dese.ade.arkansas.gov/Offices/learning-services/curriculum-support/community-service-learning (accessed 24 May 2026).
14. Encampment for Citizenship (n.d.) *About Encampment for Citizenship*. Available at: https://encampmentforcitizenship.org/about/ (accessed 24 May 2026).
15. Patriotic Millionaires (n.d.) *About Patriotic Millionaires*. Available at: https://patrioticmillionaires.org/about/ (accessed 24 May 2026).
16. Institute for Policy Studies (n.d.) Our People. Inequality.org. Available at: https://inequality.org/about/our-people/ (accessed 24 May 2026).

Chapter 4

1. Park, E. (2025) *42% of social media users say the sites are important for them getting involved with political, social issues*. Pew Research Center. Available at: https://www.pewresearch.org/short-reads/2025/09/16/42-of-social-media-users-say-the-sites-are-important-for-them-getting-involved-with-political-social-issues/ (accessed 28 May 2026).

2. One caveat: this book is written for a primarily U.S. audience, and the data reflects that. Much of the world's social impact work happens in contexts where digital infrastructure is unreliable and data surveillance is a real threat. Additionally, different countries and cultures use different social media networks. The lessons that follow will land differently in those contexts and may require intentional adaptation.
3. Simon, H.A. (1971) 'Designing organizations for an information-rich world', in Greenberger, M. (ed.) *Computers, Communications, and the Public Interest.* Baltimore, MD: The Johns Hopkins Press, pp. 37–72.
4. Workday (n.d.) *Why human connection is an AI-era advantage.* Available at: https://www.workday.com/en-us/perspectives/hr/why-human-connection-is-ai-era-advantage.html (accessed 28 May 2026).
5. Elon University (2025) *Survey: 52% of U.S. adults now use AI large language models like ChatGPT.* Available at: https://www.elon.edu/u/news/2025/03/12/survey-52-of-u-s-adults-now-use-ai-large-language-models-like-chatgpt/ (accessed 28 May 2026).
6. Menlo Ventures (2025) *2025: The state of consumer AI.* Available at: https://menlovc.com/perspective/2025-the-state-of-consumer-ai/ (accessed 28 May 2026).
7. Altman, S. (2025) Quoted in Nolan, B. *Wall Street isn't worried about an AI bubble. Sam Altman is. Fortune*, 19 August. Available at: https://www.fortune.com/2025/08/19/wall-street-ai-bubble-sam-altman (accessed 28 May 2026).
8. Kanter, B. and Fine, A. (2022) *The Smart Nonprofit: Staying Human-Centered in an Automated World.* Hoboken, NJ: Wiley.
9. Association of Fundraising Professionals (n.d.) *Fundraising Effectiveness Project: Giving increases significantly in 2020, even as donor retention rates lag.* Available at: https://afpglobal.org/fundraising-effectiveness-project-giving-increases-significantly-2020-even-donor-retention-rates (accessed 28 May 2026).
10. Tufekci, Z. (n.d.) *Online social change: easy to organize, hard to win* [Video]. TED. Available at: https://www.ted.com/talks/zeynep_tufekci_online_social_change_easy_to_organize_hard_to_win (accessed 28 May 2026).
11. Free Minds Book Club & Writing Workshop (2025) *2024 Impact Report.* Available at: https://freemindsbookclub.org/wp-content/uploads/2025/04/Impact_Report_033125_2_nobleed.pdf (accessed 28 May 2026).

12. CEPR (n.d.) *Comparing online and in-person meetings*. VoxEU. Available at: https://cepr.org/voxeu/columns/comparing-online-person-meetings (accessed 28 May 2026).
13. Evidence Based Mentoring (n.d.) *What is your evidence-based mentoring IQ?* Available at: https://www.evidencebasedmentoring.org/what-is-your-evidence-based-mentoring-iq-2/ (accessed 28 May 2026).
14. U.S. Census Bureau (2024) *Civic engagement and volunteerism*. Available at: https://www.census.gov/library/stories/2024/11/civic-engagement-and-volunteerism.html (accessed 28 May 2026).
15. New_ Public (n.d.) *New_ Public*. Available at: http://newpublic.org (accessed 28 May 2026).
16. GivingTuesday (2023) *$3.1 billion in giving: millions united around generosity to celebrate GivingTuesday 2023*. Available at: https://www.givingtuesday.org/blog/3-1-billion-in-giving-millions-united-around-generosity-to-celebrate-givingtuesday-2023/ (accessed 28 May 2026).
17. Center for Effective Philanthropy (n.d.) *AI with purpose: how foundations and nonprofits are thinking about and using artificial intelligence*. Available at: https://cep.org/report-backpacks/ai-with-purpose-how-foundations-and-nonprofits-are-thinking-about-and-using-artificial-intelligence/ (accessed 28 May 2026).
18. Stanford Institute for Human-Centered Artificial Intelligence (n.d.) *Inspiring action: identifying the social sector AI opportunity gap*. Available at: https://hai.stanford.edu/policy/inspiring-action-identifying-the-social-sector-ai-opportunity-gap (accessed 28 May 2026).
19. Candid (n.d.) *How to use AI and human experts to surface nonprofit insights and community needs*. Available at: https://candid.org/blogs/how-to-use-ai-and-human-experts-surface-nonprofit-insights-community-needs/ (accessed 28 May 2026).
20. Shen, J.H. and Tamkin, A. (2026) How AI impacts skill formation. arXiv: 2601.20245. Available at: https://doi.org/10.48550/arXiv.2601.20245 (accessed 27 June 2026).
21. Shen, K. (2026) 'AI can't solve public benefits access, but it can help', *Link Health*, 18 February. Available at: https://link-health.org/2026/02/18/ai-cant-solve-public-benefits-access-but-it-can-help/ (accessed 28 May 2026).
22. NTEN (2024) *2024 Nonprofit Digital Investments Report*. Available at: https://www.nten.org/posts/publication/2024-nonprofit-digital-investments-report (accessed 28 May 2026).

23. *Nonprofit Quarterly* (n.d.) *How nonprofits can create ethical AI policies.* Available at: https://nonprofitquarterly.org/how-nonprofits-can-create-ethical-ai-policies/ (accessed 28 May 2026).

Chapter 5

1. Chang, A.M. (2018) *Lean Impact: How to Innovate for Radically Greater Social Good.* Hoboken, NJ: Wiley.
2. Ehrlichman, D. (2021) *Impact Networks: Create Connection, Spark Collaboration, and Catalyze Systemic Change.* Oakland, CA: Berrett-Koehler Publishers.
3. Agroecology Fund (n.d.) *Home.* Available at: https://agroecologyfund.org/ (accessed 24 May 2026).
4. U.S. Census Bureau (2015) *Projections of the size and composition of the U.S. population: 2014 to 2060.* Current Population Reports, P25–1143. Washington, DC: U.S. Government Publishing Office. Available at: https://www.census.gov/content/dam/Census/library/publications/2015/demo/p25-1143.pdf (accessed 28 May 2026).
5. Candid (2024) *The state of diversity in the U.S. nonprofit sector.* New York: Candid. Available at: https://candid.org/explore-issues/diversity-equity-inclusion (accessed 25 May 2026).
6. Nonprofit Quarterly (2025) Are there too many nonprofits? Or too few bridges between them?, *Nonprofit Quarterly*, 12 November. Available at: https://nonprofitquarterly.org/are-there-too-many-nonprofits-or-too-few-bridges-between-them/ (accessed 28 May 2026).
7. Candid (2024) *Organizations in the U.S. social sector.* New York, NY: Candid. Available at: https://candid.org/impact-insights/us-social-sector/organizations/ (accessed 28 May 2026).

Chapter 6

1. Indiana University Lilly Family School of Philanthropy (2025) *Giving USA 2025: Charitable Giving Reaches New Highs.* Indianapolis, IN: Indiana University Lilly Family School of Philanthropy. Available at: https://philanthropy.indianapolis.iu.edu/news-events/news/_news/2025/giving-usa-2025.html (accessed 24 May 2026).

2. Indiana University Lilly Family School of Philanthropy (2025) *Giving USA 2025: Charitable Giving Reaches New Highs*. Indianapolis, IN: Indiana University Lilly Family School of Philanthropy. Available at: https://philanthropy.indianapolis.iu.edu/news-events/news/_news/2025/giving-usa-2025.html (accessed 24 May 2026).
3. DAF Research Collaborative (2025) *Annual DAF Report 2025*. Available at: https://www.dafresearchcollaborative.org/annual-daf-report/2025 (accessed 24 May 2026).
4. Pollard, J. (2026) 'Marguerite Casey Foundation plans to give at least $50M annually, a rare increase at a time of need', Associated Press, 9 June. Available at: https://apnews.com/article/marguerite-casey-foundation-endowment-trump-nonprofits-305497c5a1a280e03cecfda439cd5a9a (accessed 26 June 2026).
5. MacArthur Foundation (2025) *Supporting Civil Society in Need with Increased Giving*. Available at: https://www.macfound.org/press/perspectives/supporting-civil-society-in-need-with-increased-giving (accessed 24 May 2026).
6. Indiana University Lilly Family School of Philanthropy (2025) *Giving USA 2025: Charitable Giving Reaches New Highs*. Indianapolis, IN: Indiana University Lilly Family School of Philanthropy. Available at: https://philanthropy.indianapolis.iu.edu/news-events/news/_news/2025/giving-usa-2025.html (accessed 24 May 2026).
7. Indiana University Lilly Family School of Philanthropy (2025) *Giving USA 2025: Charitable Giving Reaches New Highs*. Indianapolis, IN: Indiana University Lilly Family School of Philanthropy. Available at: https://philanthropy.indianapolis.iu.edu/news-events/news/_news/2025/giving-usa-2025.html (accessed 24 May 2026).
8. Bank of America Institute (2024) *Women and the Bigger Picture: Increasing Wealth, Influence and Impact*. Charlotte, NC: Bank of America Institute. Available at: https://institute.bankofamerica.com (accessed 25 May 2026).
9. McKinsey & Company, 2024. *The new face of wealth: The rise of the female investor*. New York: McKinsey & Company. Available at: https://www.mckinsey.com/industries/financial-services/our-insights/the-new-face-of-wealth-the-rise-of-the-female-investor (accessed 25 May 2026).
10. McKinsey & Company (2024) *The new face of wealth: women as the next wave of growth in U.S. wealth management*. Reported in Halftown, A. and Hyde, A. (2024) 'Women will control $30 trillion by 2030 in massive shift for wealth management', *Bloomberg*, 9 December. Available at: https://www.bloomberg

.com/news/articles/2024-12-09/women-will-control-30-trillion-by-2030-in-massive-shift-for-wealth-management (accessed: 25 May 2026).

11. Loson-Ceballos, A. and Layton, M.D. (2024) *In Abundance: An Analysis of the Thriving Landscape of Collective Giving in the U.S.* Philanthropy Together, Dorothy A. Johnson Center for Philanthropy, and Colmena Consulting. Available at: https://www.nonprofitpro.com/article/new-research-shows-multi-billion-dollar-growth-in-collective-giving/ (accessed 24 May 2026).
12. GoFundMe (n.d.) *About Us.* Available at: https://www.gofundme.com/about-us (accessed 24 May 2026).
13. Independent Sector (2024) *Health of the U.S. Nonprofit Sector.* Available at: https://independentsector.org/resource/health-of-the-us-nonprofit-sector/ (accessed 24 May 2026).
14. Institute for Policy Studies (2024) Inequality.org: *billionaire wealth tracking.* Washington, DC: Institute for Policy Studies. Available at: https://inequality.org/facts/wealth-inequality/ (accessed 25 May 2026).
15. Giving USA Foundation and Indiana University Lilly Family School of Philanthropy (2025) *Giving USA 2025: the annual report on philanthropy for the year 2024.* Chicago, IL: Giving USA Foundation.
16. Independent Sector, 2023. *The Retreat of Influence: Exploring the Decline of Nonprofit Advocacy and Public Engagement.* Washington, DC: Independent Sector. Available at: https://independentsector.org/resource/the-retreat-of-influence/ (accessed 25 May 2026).

Chapter 7

1. Stewart, A.J. (2014) *Understanding Nonprofit Professionalization: Common Concepts and New Directions for Research.* Philadelphia, PA: School of Social Policy and Practice, University of Pennsylvania. Available at: https://sp2.upenn.edu/wp-content/uploads/2014/08/Amanda-Stewart.pdf (accessed 28 May 2026).
2. BoardSource (n.d.) *Nonprofit Sector Research.* Available at: https://boardsource.org/nonprofit-sector-research/ (accessed 28 May 2026).
3. Thomas-Breitfeld, S. and Kunreuther, F. (2024) 'Why is leadership aspiration down among BIPOC nonprofit staff?', *Candid insights,* 6 March. Available at: https://blog.candid.org/post/why-bipoc-nonprofit-staff-leadership-aspirations-are-down/ (accessed 28 May 2026).

4. McGregor, L. and Doshi, N. (2015) *Primed to Perform: How to Build the Highest Performing Cultures Through the Science of Total Motivation*. New York: HarperBusiness.
5. Domínguez, A. (2024) 'Coleading as an Act of Rebellion', *Nonprofit Quarterly*, 25 July. Available at: https://nonprofitquarterly.org/coleading-as-an-act-of-rebellion/ (accessed 28 May 2026).
6. Clerkin, C. (2024) 'Co-leadership: A path to more diverse, sustainable nonprofits?', *Candid insights*, 17 April. Available at: https://candid.org/blogs/nonprofit-co-leadership-a-path-to-more-diverse-sustainable-sector/ (accessed 28 May 2026).
7. Cervas, S. (2021) *Nonprofit Leadership Models*. Asian Pacific Environmental Network (APEN).
8. Community Spaces (n.d.) *Member Highlight: TSNE*. Available at: https://communityspaces.org/member-highlight-tsne/ (accessed 28 May 2026).
9. TSNE (n.d.) *TSNE*. Available at: https://tsne.org/ (accessed 28 May 2026).
10. Social Impact Commons and National Network of Fiscal Sponsors (2023) *Fiscal Sponsor Field Scan 2023 Survey Report*. Available at: https://www.fiscalsponsors.org/blog/field-scan-2023-report (accessed 25 May 2026).
11. Fiscal Sponsorship Toolkit & Innovation Network (FITO) (n.d.) *FITO Network*. Available at: https://www.fito.network/ (accessed 28 May 2026).
12. Google re:Work (2017) *Guide: Understand team effectiveness*. Available at: https://rework.withgoogle.com/guides/understanding-team-effectiveness/ (accessed 28 May 2026).
13. Leadership Learning Community (n.d.) *Liberatory Leadership Framework*. Available at: https://leadershiplearning.org/publications/liberatory-leadership-framework/ (accessed 28 May 2026).
14. Urban Institute (n.d.) *Building the Capacity of Nonprofit Organizations*. Washington, DC: Urban Institute. Available at: https://www.urban.org/research/publication/building-capacity-nonprofit-organizations (accessed 28 May 2026).
15. CompassPoint Nonprofit Services, BTW informing change and Grantmakers for Effective Organizations (2010) *Coaching and Philanthropy: An Action Guide for Nonprofits*. San Francisco, CA: CompassPoint Nonprofit Services. Available at: https://www.compasspoint.org/sites/default/files/documents/1012_coachingandphilanthropyan.pdf (accessed 28 May 2026).
16. Network Weaver (n.d.) *Network Weaver*. Available at: https://networkweaver.com/ (accessed 28 May 2026).

17. Mitchell, M. (2022) 'Building Resilient Organizations: Toward Joy and Durable Power in a Time of Crisis', *The Forge*, 29 November. Available at: https://forgeorganizing.org/article/building-resilient-organizations/ (accessed 28 May 2026).
18. National Committee for Responsive Philanthropy (n.d.) *Power Moves: Your Essential Philanthropy Assessment Guide for Equity and Justice*. Washington, DC: NCRP. Available at: https://ncrp.org/power-moves/ (accessed 28 May 2026).

Chapter 8

1. Corporation for National and Community Service (2009) *American Recovery and Reinvestment Act: National Service Investments*. Washington, DC: Corporation for National and Community Service.
2. Cabinet Office (UK) (n.d.) *Office of the Third Sector/Office for Civil Society: Annual Reports and Structural Reform Plans*. London: HM Government.
3. Government of Canada (2005) *Voluntary Sector Initiative (2000–2005)*. Ottawa: Government of Canada.
4. Ministry of Corporate Affairs, Government of India (2013) *Companies Act, 2013: Section 135*. New Delhi: Government of India. Available at: https://www.mca.gov.in/content/mca/global/en/acts-rules/ebooks/companies-act-2013.html (accessed 24 May 2026).
5. European Center for Not-for-Profit Law (2012) *The 1% Mechanism: Comparative Overview*. Budapest: European Center for Not-for-Profit Law.
6. California Association of Nonprofits (CalNonprofits) (n.d.) Select Committees on the Nonprofit Sector. Available at: CalNonprofits—Select Committees on the Nonprofit Sector (accessed 24 May 2026).
7. National Council of Nonprofits (n.d.) National Nonprofit Caucus of State Legislators. Available at: National Council of Nonprofits—National Nonprofit Caucus of State Legislators (accessed 24 May 2026).
8. Association of Fundraising Professionals (AFP) (n.d.) Congressional Philanthropy Caucus. Available at: AFP—Congressional Philanthropy Caucus (accessed 24 May 2026).
9. California State Senate (2024) *SB 1240 (2023–2024 Session)*. Sacramento, CA: California Legislature.
10. Giving USA Foundation and Indiana University Lilly Family School of Philanthropy (2025) *Giving USA 2025: the annual report on philanthropy for the year 2024*. Chicago, IL: Giving USA Foundation.

11. Candid (2024) *Form 990: Candid, EIN 13-1837418, fiscal year ending December 2024*. Available at: https://projects.propublica.org/nonprofits/organizations/131837418 (accessed 28 May 2026).
12. Candid (2026) *Research Nonprofits, Funders, and Grants*. New York, NY: Candid. Available at: https://candid.org/ (accessed 28 May 2026).
13. Theis, M. (2019) 'Two information giants, Foundation Center and GuideStar, to join forces', *Chronicle of Philanthropy*, 5 February. Available at: https://www.philanthropy.com/news/2-information-giants-foundation-center-and-guidestar-to-join-forces/ (accessed 28 May 2026).

Index

O

P